FORDE ABBEY

FRONTISPIECE
Forde Abbey from the south, drawn by Sandra Oakins.

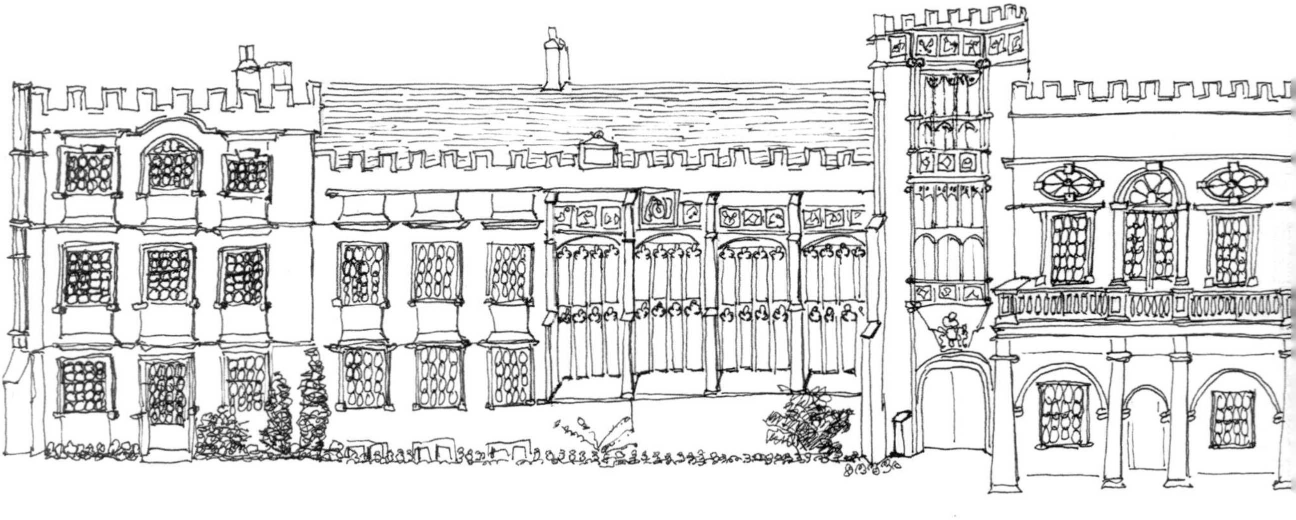

THE DOVECOTE PRESS

FORDE ABBEY

The Story Behind the Stones

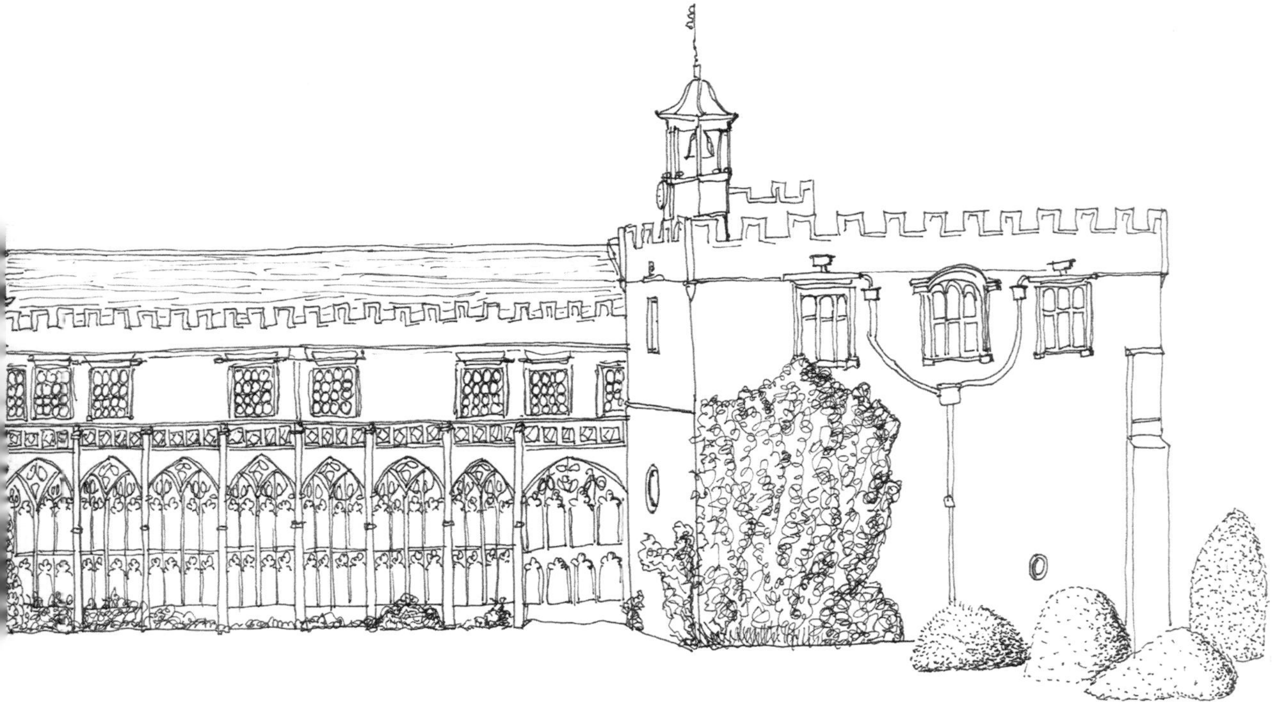

CHRISTIAN TYLER

First published in 2017 by The Dovecote Press Ltd
Stanbridge, Wimborne Minster, Dorset BH21 4JD

ISBN 978-0-9955462-2-6

Typeset in Sabon and designed by The Dovecote Press Ltd

Printed and bound in Spain by GraphyCems, Navarra

All papers used by The Dovecote Press are natural, recyclable products
made from wood grown in sustainable, well-managed forests.

A CIP catalogue record for this book is available from the British Library

1 3 5 7 9 8 6 4 2

Contents

Acknowledgements

The past is never quite over. There will always be more to say, new interpretations, gaps in the story to be filled. This history of Forde Abbey, therefore, can be only provisional.

But for helping me thus far I want to thank, first of all, the Roper family: Mark and Lisa for their generosity with private records, recollections and hospitality; Christopher Roper for notes and assistance with photographs and drawings; Charlotte Roper for the loan of family portraits; Alice and Julian Kennard for giving me free access to the abbey, its archives and photograph collections, and Carolyn Clay for help in the office.

I owe a particular debt of gratitude to Professor James Clark, a specialist in late mediaeval England at the University of Exeter, for his guidance on monastic history and for reading Chapter One. If mistakes remain, here or elsewhere in the book, they are mine alone.

For other notes, recollections, documents and references, I am grateful to John Allen, Susanna Austin, Catherine Boyd, Andrew and Penny Bullivant, Michael Fitzgerald, Christopher Gray, Michael and Jean Frampton, Emma Kirkby, Lucy Lomas, Miles Maskell, John Mingay, Douglas and Miranda Paterson, Martin Roundell Greene, Claude Rutter, John Simpson, Priscilla Smith, Fiona Laidlaw Smith, Jill Mowlem and Lionel Vale.

Thanks also to Maisie Hill for her excellent photographs and Sandra Oakins for her very fine drawings. David Risk Kennard contributed a splendid watercolour painting of the Tower. I would also like to thank Ildi Clarke for providing the index and Peter Lightfoot for the two estate maps on page 51, both of which are based on maps appearing in *The Cartulary of Forde Abbey*, published by the Somerset Record Society (1998).

A posthumous thank you is due to my late father, Richard Tyler, for many years consultant architect to the abbey. On my first visit to the Forde archive I found the papers carefully sorted and each file labelled with his distinctive italic handwriting. It was as if he had had a premonition I would write this book.

It is not just a convention for authors to thank their spouses. Ciaran, my wife, knows that writing is hard work – and not only for the writer. I owe her more than I can say for her constant love, support, forbearance and good judgement.

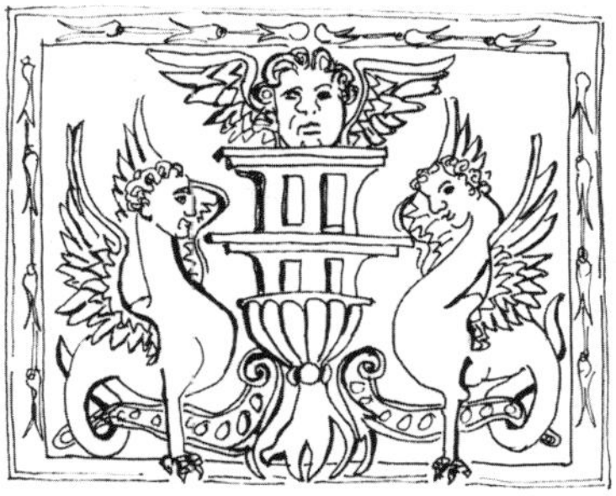

ONE

Between Heaven and Earth

Of all the beautiful houses in England, Forde Abbey is perhaps the most eccentric. It is not a typical country mansion, built to order with a grand symmetrical front looking proudly down from an eminence over park and gardens, but a former monastery founded nearly 900 years ago at a crossing on the River Axe where Devon, Dorset and Somerset meet. Imaginatively extended and converted during the first five centuries of its existence, its long, irregular but elegant face, lovingly retouched, looks modestly upwards from a site on the floor of the valley.

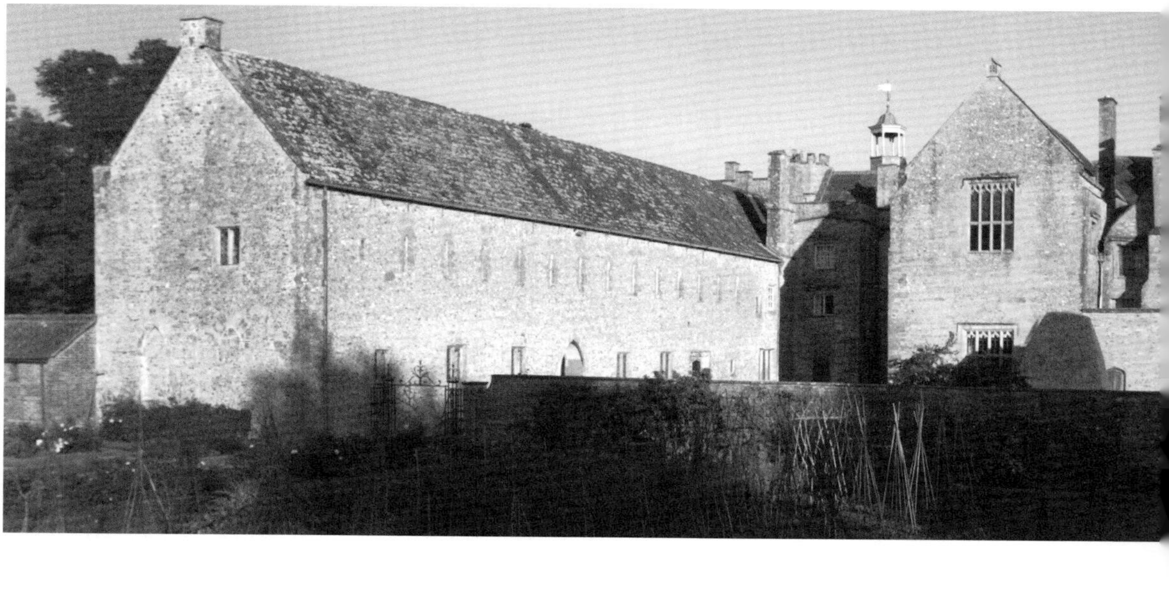

How low the house lies, how vulnerable it is to rolling frosts and floods, can be seen by taking the road which crosses the estate to the south. Close to, its venerable age is confirmed by the visitor's first sight: the massive mediaeval wall of the monks' dormitory running north towards the river. From the back, the house presents a picturesque – and at first incomprehensible – jumble of masonry of many periods. The front is a stunning contrast: a 250-foot array of warm yellow stone ranging from early Gothic to Perpendicular, Tudor to English Renaissance, with no attempt at symmetry but for the uniting element of a crenellated parapet along the length of the roof. The family quarters at the west end provide a sort of balance to the chapel at the east. But the centre has two features contesting for supremacy, the decorated tower built by the last abbot in the 1520s, and the seventeenth-century saloon with its balcony over a portico.

There is more to this place, however, than the sublime jumble of architecture which has earned it a place in the record books.[1] Every piece of the building has a tale to tell. Every room holds the memory of some notable who once occupied it. Forde Abbey may today occupy a quiet rustic corner of England but in its time it has witnessed great events, and on its very doorstep.

* * *

Opposite page: The line drawings at the start of every chapter are by Sandra Oakins and show details from the carved stonework on the south facade.

Below: 'A picturesque jumble of masonry,' the visitor's first close-up view of the Abbey.

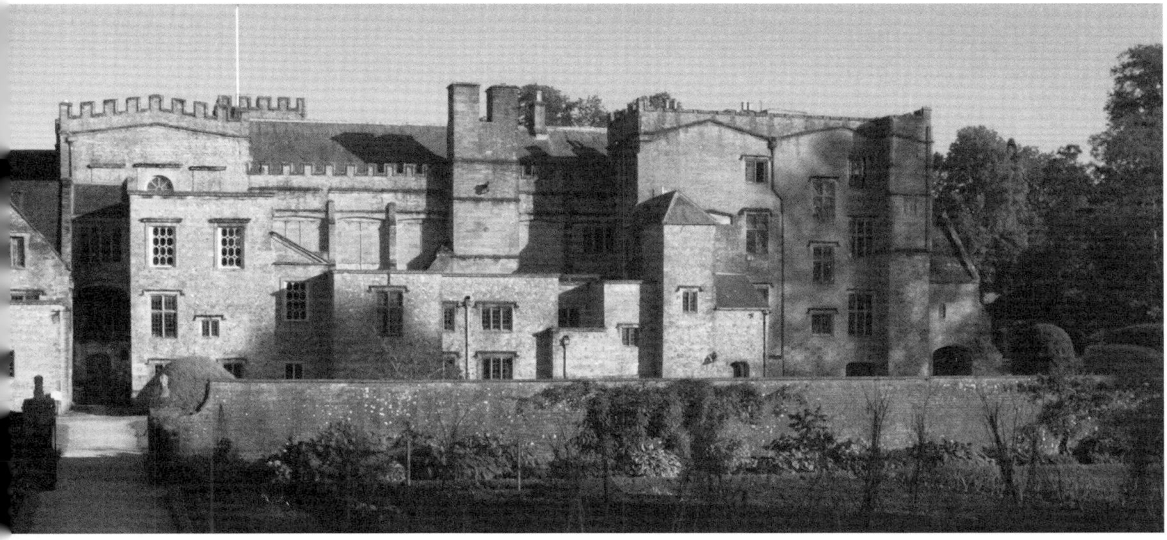

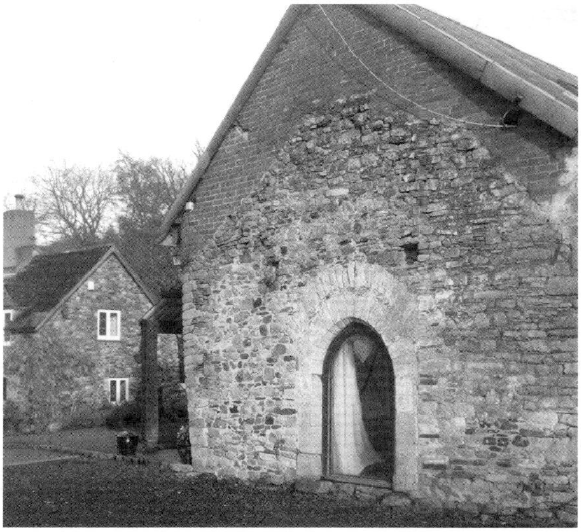

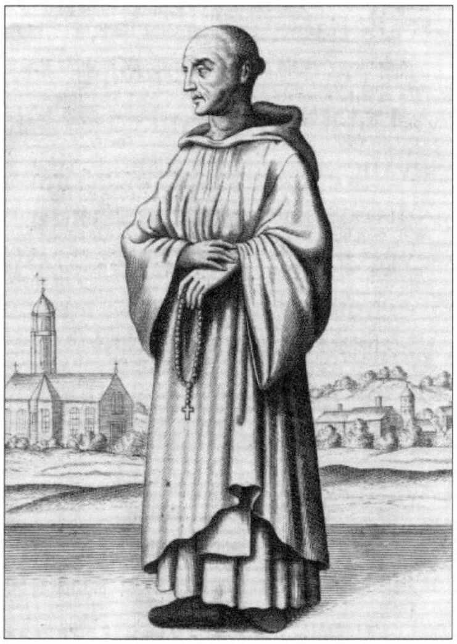

Above left: Brightley farm, near Okehampton, today. The converted barn with arched doorway may have been the chapel of the abandoned twelfth century priory.

Above right: A Cistercian monk (from Dugdale's *Monasticon*).

The earliest character to come into focus is the monastery's founder, a Norman noblewoman called Adelicia de Brionne who lived on her estate at Thorncombe – then, like Forde, in the county of Devon.[2] Adelicia's father Baldwin was one of William the Conqueror's knights, had married a niece of William's and had been made Sheriff of Devon and Baron of Okehampton. Adelicia and her brother Richard were thus beneficiaries of a conquest which has been described as the biggest land-grab in English history.

It was by chance, however, that in 1141 Adelicia became the founder of a monastery on her land. She did not ask for monks: they came to her as refugees from a failed priory which her brother Richard had established eight years earlier on his estate at Brightley, outside Okehampton.

In the heyday of monastic building such false starts were not unusual. Richard had invited the abbot of Waverley in Surrey, founded in 1128 as the first Cistercian monastery in England, to supply him with 12 monks and an abbot (the traditional nucleus, representing Christ and his 12 apostles). The monks arrived in 1133 and were settled at Brightley, on the river two miles north of Richard's castle at Okehampton. But they found the moorland soil poor ('only wild thyme and nightshade'). After a short time their abbot Richard died, followed by their patron Richard in 1137, and five years later they decided to give up. Led by Robert de Penington, the new abbot, they set off on the 150-mile walk back to Waverley, marching two by two and carrying a large wooden cross.

They left behind what is today an attractive farm with converted outbuildings. Set in a valley flanked by conifers, it does not look like the wilderness described in the old texts. The land is good but shallow, with river sand not far below the surface. Beyond the handsome farmhouse, one building in particular draws the eye: an old stone barn, now adapted for living, with a suggestive archway in its western wall. It looks as if it could easily have been the chapel of the twelfth century priory.

By accident or design, the monks' route took them through the estates of Adelicia who had inherited all her brother's lands on his death. The only report we have of the encounter comes from an anonymous monk of Forde writing in Latin several centuries later. His account of Adelicia's speech to the small party of monks is certainly invented, and rather underplays the loss of face the family would have suffered if she had not helped them. As the sister and sole heir of her brother Richard, she said, she could not bear the disgrace of failing to complete the work that he had begun 'for the glory of God and the salvation of all our souls.' She continued:

> Here where we stand is my manor, fertile enough, well-wooded and abounding with the fruits of the earth, which, with our entire domain and dwelling we will give you in perpetuity in exchange for the sterile earth of Brightley. Stay here until a more suitable monastery can be provided somewhere else on the property. We will not let you down, but give you every help with the building.

While building got under way, the monks lived at Adelicia's manor house in an attractive spot close to the river and about two miles downstream of the site chosen for the monastery. It was the manor, not the monastery, that originally bore the name 'Ford' and the house is usually identified as the farmhouse known today as West Ford or Westford Park. Though much modified, it contains some ancient features such as a little twisted staircase leading to a studded door. Old maps show the place as a deer park.[3]

The site chosen for the abbey was sometimes called 'Hartsbath' presumably because the deer were accustomed to drink there. It had the disadvantage of being in a populous – at least by the standards of the day – area which Cistercian monks preferred to avoid. Their rule of austere self-sufficiency sent them to places well away from the everyday world of peasant farmers and feudal lords. (Rievaulx, a sister house built on the North York moors a year before Brightley, was a typical Cistercian location). Although there is nothing to suggest the monks were not wanted by the Axe valley locals, their proximity was bound to complicate relations with neighbouring farmers and serfs. Abbey records confirm that there were many disputes over the succeeding 400 years.

The next problem was the ground plan. Like everybody in the Middle Ages, monks had to live near water. Their domestic buildings – kitchen, refectory and dormitory – were built on the bank of a stream or river, close to the water supply. The abbey church and cloister were constructed on the firmest ground, and usually to the north of the domestic buildings. The Hartsbath site, however, did not allow this. To achieve the typical lay-out the monks would have had to put their monastery on the north side of the River Axe. Either that bank was not level or broad enough, or it was not available to them. It was the south bank that was chosen. As a result, the monastery's ground plan is a mirror image of the usual one. Forde's vanished abbey church – dismantled at the Dissolution – was to the south of the monks' quarters, on what is now the front lawn of the house.

Adelicia's monks came well-prepared for their task. Because of their commitment to self-sufficiency and their experience of living in the wild, Cistercians had become the most expert farmers and engineers in Europe. In France, for example, they were said to be able to choose the best terrain for vines simply by chewing a lump of earth. True or not, historians agree that the Cistercians revolutionized mediaeval agriculture.

One of the first acts of the little community would have been to recruit local labour, in the form of lay brothers or *conversi*. Lay brothers were usually local men, often illiterate, who wanted the security and heavenly reward of monastic life but whose low social status and poor education prevented them being ordained priests. They were given a simpler schedule of worship along with a few prayers to memorize: the *Pater Noster*, the Creed and *Miserere*.

The monks needed water to power their mills for grinding corn and 'fulling' (scouring and cleaning) woollen cloth. Experts in hydropower, they channelled water from a stream on the hill two miles away to the south by means of a leat which emptied into the Great Pond at the top of the garden. A sluice at the exit controlled the flow down to the mills in the farmyard below. Today the chute is below ground; it runs via the Mermaid Pond to the Long Pond and thence under the present garden wall down to the River Axe. To the east, the monks made a dam in the river to divert water into their fishponds and drainage reservoir.

Once established in temporary buildings on site, the monks collected local flint and greensand to make a dormitory. Stone for the principal buildings came from a nearby quarry (re-opened in modern times for the railway). From the fourteenth century onwards, limestone was brought from Ham Hill. The abbey church would have been started at the same time, and took 50 years or more to finish. It may have been still incomplete when it was formally dedicated to the

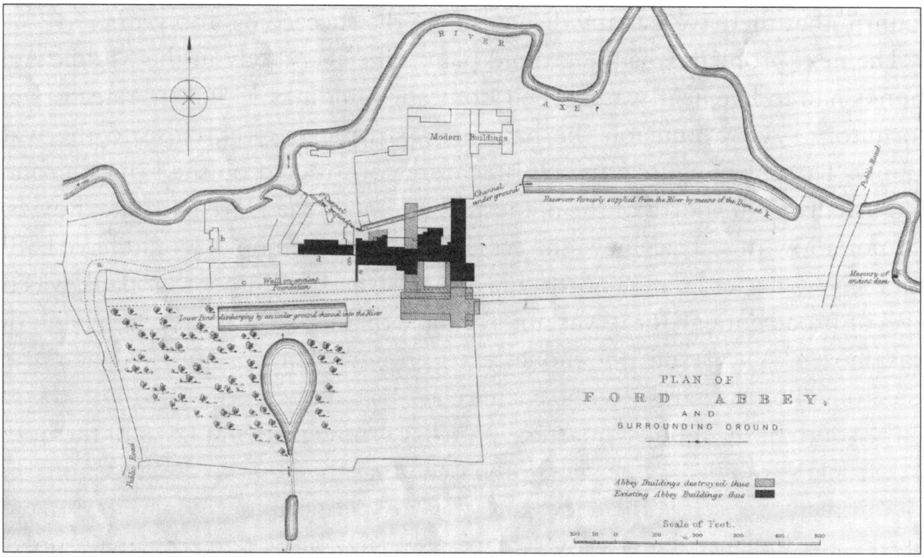

Plan of the abbey, showing the monks' hydro-engineering. The buildings in black are those still standing today, with the exception of the barn projecting from the west end (G. Hills, *Collectanea Archaeologica* vol. 2, 1871).

Blessed Virgin Mary, as all Cistercian churches were. Adelicia did not live to see the monastery. She died a year after her gift to the monks.

The monastery and church were built on a scale that demands explanation. Big as it was, the work would have been carried out almost entirely by the monks and lay brothers. There is a modern-day example which shows this is not as improbable as it sounds. Between 1906 and 1938 the abbey church of Buckfast in Devon was resurrected on its ancient foundations by a team of no more than four to six French Cistercian monks, of whom only one had any experience of building. They started with £5 and the loan of a horse and cart to bring stone from a nearby quarry. Working with mallets, chisels, ropes, chains and pulleys – but without hardhats or protective clothing – this handful of men succeeded in raising a large twelfth century-style Gothic church in 32 years.

Why did monks build on such a scale? Lay brothers ate separately from the 'choir' monks, so a separate refectory was needed. They had their own dormitory, too, customarily in the upper storey of the range on the west side of the cloister. (There may have been a separate dorter parallel with the monks' dormitory). For the same reason the abbey church had to be sub-divided, as well as being of a size fitting to the majesty of God. The poor had to be fed every week, the sick cared for, travellers lodged and refuge provided for the populace in times

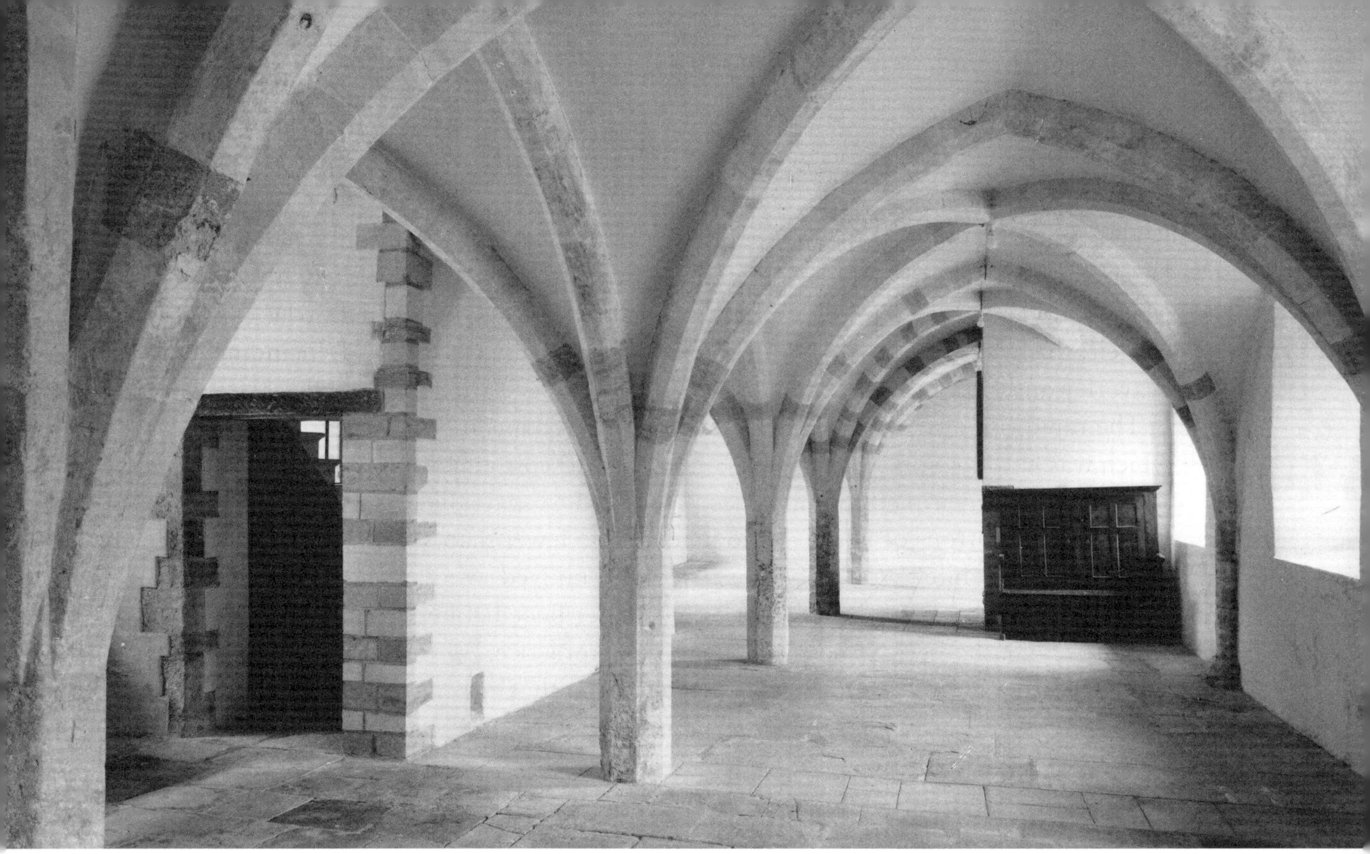

View of the Undercroft, the oldest part of the building, now converted into a restaurant

of trouble – not least during the current reign of King Stephen when civil strife was raging outside the walls. Moreover, the monks were spiritually ambitious, at least to begin with, and wanted to recruit as many men as possible.

A Cistercian Wave

Such attitudes were typical of the times, and motivated also the generosity of donors like Adelicia and her brother Richard. Everyone, rich and poor alike, was caught up in the great resurgence of religious faith that swept Europe at the end of the eleventh century. Instigated by the reforming Pope Gregory VII (1073-1085) and the militant Pope Urban II, sponsor of the First Crusade, it was spread by inspirational preachers such as Bernard of Clairvaux, the dominant figure of the period who was said to have the ear of every prince in Europe.

Even without Bernard's rhetoric, the people of those days believed implicitly in the existence of God and took seriously the task of saving their souls. Young men and women of all ranks flocked to the religious life. Those for whom the seclusion of convent or monastery was unappealing – and who were rich enough – could win earthly merit and heavenly approval by getting others to pray for them. That said, the Cistercians were reluctant at first to become, like the

Benedictines, mere intercessories, acquiring land in exchange for votive masses. Donors were keen especially to put village churches under the care of an abbey. Many founders, like Richard de Brionne at Brightley, were motivated by lack of an heir: this was true of a third of early Cistercian houses in England, including Waverley and Rievaulx.

The rapid rise of the Cistercian order was helped by its monks preferring land which was hard to work, making gifts of such land a cost-effective way for donors to demonstrate their piety. Some, indeed, had land to spare, like the Pomeroys of Devon – later patrons of Forde – who inherited no fewer than 58 estates.

Known as 'white' monks because of their undyed woollen cassocks, the Cistercians had broken away from the much older Benedictine, or 'black' monks whom they felt had grown soft in their spiritual practice. As we have seen, their austerity was handsomely repaid in this age of faith. Between 1098, when the movement began in France, and the death of Saint Bernard in 1153, some 280 houses were founded. By 1200, the high water mark of the Cistercian advance, they had 80 monasteries and 30 nunneries in England alone.

The architect of this great movement was an Englishman – a local man, as it happens. Stephen Harding was born in Sherborne, not 20 miles away. As a young boy he had been sent to the Benedictine abbey of Sherborne. Instead of taking holy orders when he came of age he left to go travelling. After visits to

Stephen Harding the Dorset man who founded the Cistercian order.

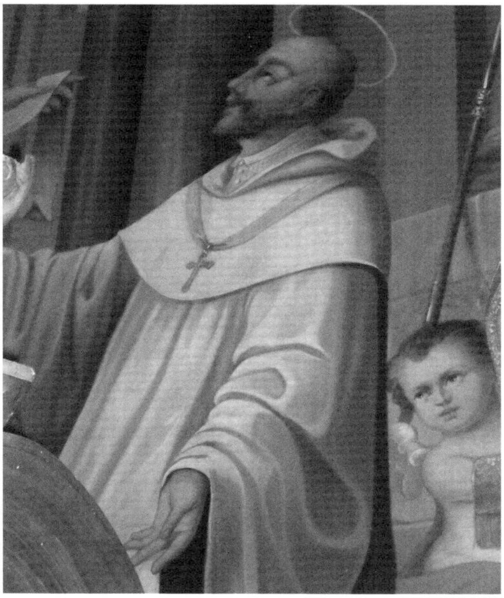

Scotland, Paris and Rome he finally enrolled as a monk at the Benedictine abbey of Molesme in Burgundy, where he became abbot.

Stephen regarded the luxurious life at Molesme as a betrayal of the Rule written 500 years before by Saint Benedict of Nursia. With 23 fellow dissidents he retreated to Citeaux, a marshy wilderness about 15 miles from Dijon, to live a life closer to that prescribed by the founder of western monasticism. A house was built for them by Count Odo of Burgundy, where Stephen was made abbot in 1109. And with the arrival of Bernard two years later, Citeaux became mother to a growing brood of daughter houses, of which the most influential was Bernard's foundation of Clairvaux, and chief of all the communities of 'white' monks. Citeaux replaced the vast Benedictine abbey of Cluny as the spiritual powerhouse of western Europe.

Work and Prayer

The monks' lives were centred on the divine office. Six or seven times in 24 hours they would chant the liturgy in the abbey church, with further hours of private prayer and study. By the time Forde was founded, the Benedictines were delegating much of the routine work to servants and hired hands. The Cistercians were determined to reintroduce the manual labour – seven or eight hours a day – specified in the Rule of St. Benedict. They reduced the time spent in prayer and delegated much of the farm work to their lay brothers, thus circumventing the prohibition on hired labour and the employment of serfs.

Life at Forde was rigorous, but not necessarily disagreeable. Rooms were sparsely furnished and the church was devoid of elaborate decoration. The monks were not permitted to wear cloaks and warm hoods, shirts or long drawers. For warmth they were allowed to spend a limited time in the 'calefactory', a room with a fire. They slept at first in an open dormitory with curtains between the beds, the abbot being in the middle of the row guarding a nightlight. Later, cells were created with low partitions. Bedspreads were banned, and so were combs. The food consisted of fish, fowl and vegetables: no meat or fat. Ailred of Rievaulx voiced the feelings of his monks:

> 'Our food is scanty, our garments rough; our drink is from the stream and our sleep often upon our book. Under our tired limbs there is but a hard mat; when sleep is sweetest we must rise at a bell's bidding. Self-will has no scope; there is no moment for idleness or dissipation. Everywhere peace, everywhere serenity, and a marvellous freedom from the tumult of the world. Such unity and concord is there among the brethren, that each thing seems to belong to all, and all to each.'[4]

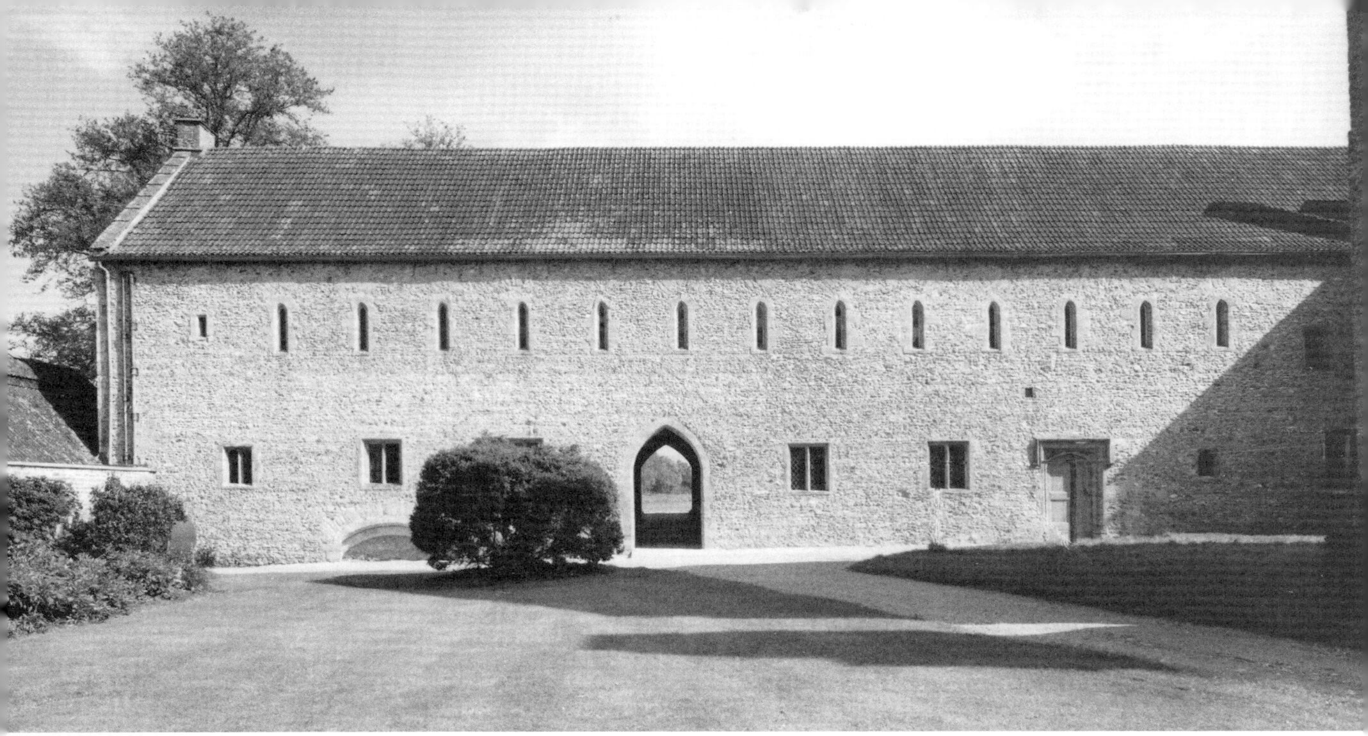

The monks' dormitory, with the 13 original windows (one for each founder monk). The *cloaca* or main drain is just visible to the left of the small tree.

According to the charter written personally by Stephen Harding, religious artefacts had to be of the simplest: painted wood for crucifixes, iron for candelabra, copper for the thuribles in which the incense was burned. Priestly vestments had to be made of linen, not silk; chalices could be silver, but not gold. Harding was determined to banish the luxuries which had crept into monastic life. Bernard of Clairvaux reinforced the ban on decoration. All this, however, was to go by the board in the coming centuries.

In the country around Forde in 1150 farming was still at a primitive level. Cultivable land was worked by people for their own needs, with only a small surplus for sale. Everyone grew the same crops and livestock, while fodder and grazing-land were shared. Almost everything – bread, beer, milk, cheese, pork, lard and eggs – was locally produced.

But the monks began to specialise. They bred horses, dairy cattle, and – on a huge scale – sheep. Monks had kept flocks in the past, and the Benedictines were already active sheepfarmers in Dorset. But it was the Cistercians who turned sheep farming into a sophisticated export business and for 100 years dominated the trade which was to make England so wealthy in the later Middle Ages.

As the abbey's estate expanded, lay brothers were stationed at outlying farms known as granges, usually built in places which were too far from the monastery for a man to reach and still do a full day's work. The work involved clearing the forests and turning wasteland into fertile fields for arable and pasture under the supervision of a professed monk. Granges were in effect the sub-stations of a central management system controlled by the 'cellarer' monk at the monastery. An example is Burstock Grange, five miles from Forde, built in the fifteenth century as a high, one-storey farmhouse with three partitioned rooms and a through passage, heated by an open fire. Burstock Grange was later converted into a two-storey farmhouse with the insertion of a floor and a separate staircase: the smoke-blackened timbers of the old hall roof are still visible.

The Cistercian system of land management was different from the Benedictine. David Knowles, the leading historian of monastic England, has likened the Benedictine model to 'the property of a great corporation such as Trinity College, Cambridge, which comprises farms, fields, cottage holdings, city houses, glebe, advowsons, and funds of all kinds,' while the Cistercian estate was more like 'the vast single area of a cattle or sheep ranch in the Argentine, with its one ranch house and its scattered and isolated huts, stores and byres.'[5] This distinction became increasingly blurred over time (but Knowles's reference to the Argentine was, as we shall see, prophetic).

Gifts and bequests of land from noble benefactors, patrons, local squires and yeomen helped the young monastery to grow rapidly. Forde benefited in particular from its connection to the ancient Norman family of Courtenay. Adelicia's daughter Alice had a grand-daughter Matilda who married into the family who later inherited the Earldom of Devon (another branch holds the title today), and took over as patrons of Forde. The liaison suited both parties: the Courtenay support set an example to other benefactors while the monastery's growing political influence added to the family's prestige.

Not all acquisitions were charitable. To maintain easy access across their estates, the monks would not scruple to buy rights to a farm or village and 'reduce it to a grange' (*redigere in grangiam*), removing the people and pulling down their cottages, rather as aristocratic English landowners were wont to do in the eighteenth and nineteenth centuries.

The population of the abbey grew rapidly with lay brothers outnumbering ordained monks by two to one. As early as 1172 there must have been at least 60 choir monks. That was the establishment required before a Cistercian monastery could found a daughter house, and in that year Forde founded Bindon near Wool on the Isle of Purbeck in Dorset. By 1200 the mother house had again grown large enough to found a second offshoot, at Dunkeswell north of Honiton in Devon. Today only traces of Bindon abbey can be found, but substantial ruins are preserved at Dunkeswell.

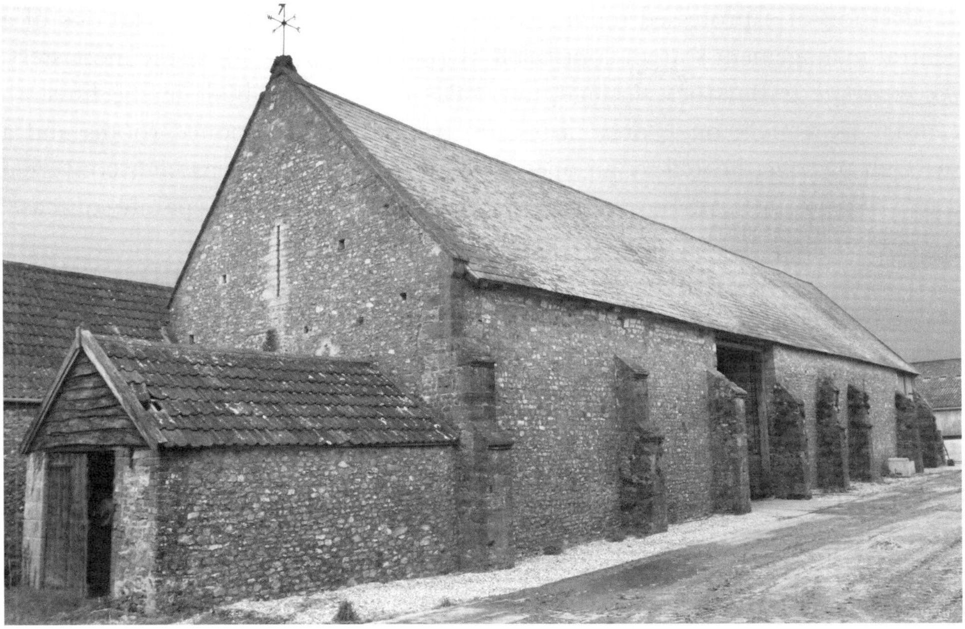

The thirteenth-century tithe barn at Forde Grange: built originally for the monastery farm, it would later have housed crops exacted as tax from tenants.

Burstock Grange, once one of the outlying farms belonging to the abbey.

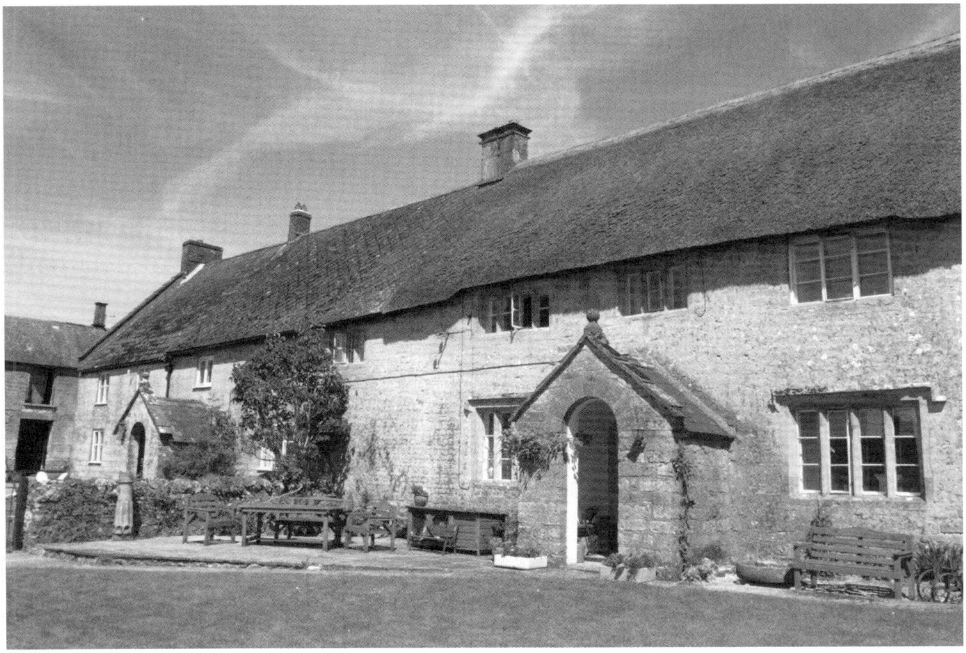

The Powerhouse

As the abbey grew, so its influence spread. In spite of the Cistercian rule which condemned study and writing as distractions from spiritual self-improvement, Forde became recognized as a centre of intellectual excellence. Cistercians were not artists: they produced no dazzling illuminated manuscripts like the Benedictines. But the prohibition on writing was breached by Bernard of Clairvaux himself, and two early abbots of Forde made their mark nationally as theologians, writers and political advisers.

The path to this intellectual summit was opened by Baldwin, the third abbot and the first character in the story of Forde of whom we have a contemporary portrait. A local man, born in Exeter in about 1125, Baldwin rose to become Archbishop of Canterbury where he became entangled in a row with its monks that reverberated throughout Europe. His religious writings – theological essays and sermons – are still studied by academics.

Baldwin was an ambiguous character: a precocious scholar but a weak administrator, an honest and virtuous man who was happiest as a monk yet could not refuse the rapid promotion that his education put in his way. He may have owed his ascent partly to the efforts of the Courtenay family whose star was rising and who may have seen in him a useful ambassador at court.

In appearance Baldwin was 'swarthy, with an honest, venerable face, only moderately tall, of good physique and inclined to be thin rather than corpulent,' according to his friend the historian Gerald of Wales, who travelled with him through the principality in 1188 mobilising support for the Third Crusade.[6] At the age of 65 he joined the vanguard of the Crusade, setting sail for Tyre and reaching Acre where he fell ill and died in 1190.

He was a modest man, more stubborn perhaps than courageous. His character was famously summed up by Pope Urban III in a personal letter addressed to 'a most fervent monk, warm abbot, tepid bishop and negligent archbishop' (*monacho ferventissimo, abbati calido, episcopo tepido, archiepiscopo remisso*). But the pope acknowledged his piety, comparing him favourably with his predecessor as Archbishop of Canterbury, Thomas Becket. At the end of a journey, he said, the first place Thomas would go was the dining hall, but for Baldwin it was always the church.

Baldwin was the son of an archdeacon. He went to school at Glastonbury abbey, then to Bologna to study canon law under the future Pope Urban III, and was appointed by Pope Eugenius III – the first Cistercian pontiff – as tutor to his nephew. Back in Exeter, be became a teacher and a protégé of Bartholomew, the bishop, who made him archdeacon of Totnes.

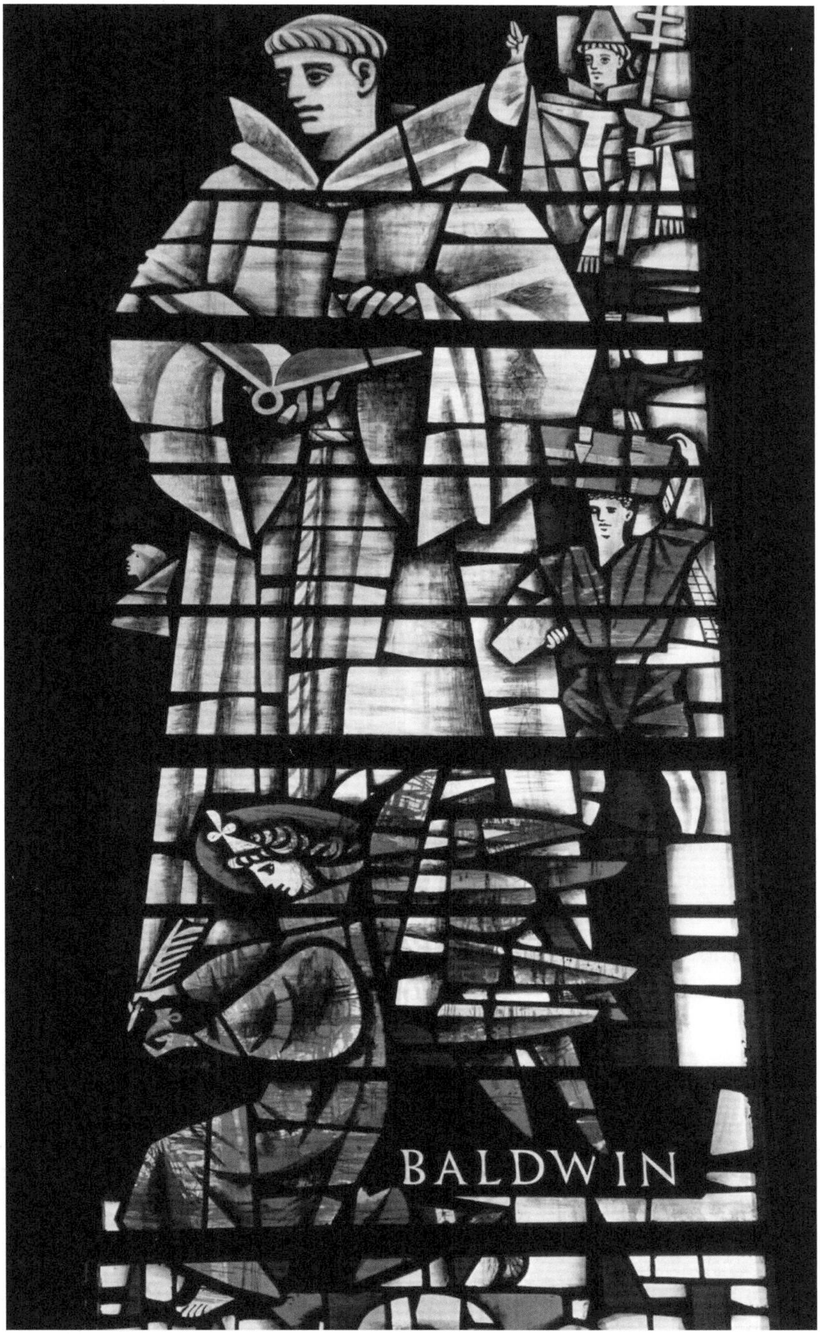

Baldwin, abbot of Forde and Archbishop of Canterbury: a modern image from Canterbury Cathedral.

In about 1170 he decided that his vocation lay not in church politics but in the cloister, and he joined the community at Forde Abbey. Within a year or two he was elected abbot and found himself delegated by the Vatican to act as a judge. A submission was made to have him promoted cardinal by Pope Alexander III, another Bologna graduate, who had described Baldwin and Bartholomew as 'the two candlesticks of the English church.' But King Henry II anticipated the move by making him Bishop of Worcester. An incident four years later seems to have confirmed Henry's respect: Baldwin intervened to postpone the hanging of a thief condemned by the king's own court to die on a religious feast day. With the bishops in support, he became the king's candidate for the See of Canterbury. As the new primate, he crowned Richard I in 1189 before 'the Lionheart' went off to the wars.

Having reached the summit, Baldwin found himself in a hornet's nest. The monks of Canterbury Cathedral insisted on their right to choose the primate, and had three worthy candidates lined up. Baldwin thought the monks were over-reaching themselves and tried to put them in their place, first by confiscating some of their properties, then by proposing to found a rival collegiate church at Hackington, in the suburbs of the city, that would be under the control of the secular – that is, non-monastic – clergy. The affair ended with a compromise devised by King Richard, but left Baldwin's reputation seriously damaged.

The austere, spiritual Baldwin may have lacked political judgement and managerial skill, but he attracted to Forde Abbey a circle of writers and thinkers which turned the monastery into a hub of intellectual life rivalled in England only by Rievaulx in north Yorkshire. The second half of the 12th century was the golden age of the Cistercians in England, and Forde was a shining example. It had 'more learning therein than three convents [monasteries] of the same bigness,' said Thomas Fuller, the seventeenth century historian (also, incidentally, rector of Broadwindsor).[7]

Of the great intellects at the abbey Baldwin was the most powerful, according to Christopher Holdsworth, a mediaeval historian at Exeter University who has made a special study of Forde. During his 14 years at the monastery the abbot was a prolific author of devotional works: sermons, letters, and theological commentaries.[8] Among his followers three younger monks made names for themselves.

One was Maurice ('Maurinus') Somerset, who came to notice under Baldwin's successor Abbot Robert. His chief extant work is a 550-line poem in Latin verse on the life of Thomas Becket, whose murder in 1170 on the altar of Canterbury Cathedral had stunned the nation and brought thousands of pilgrims to his

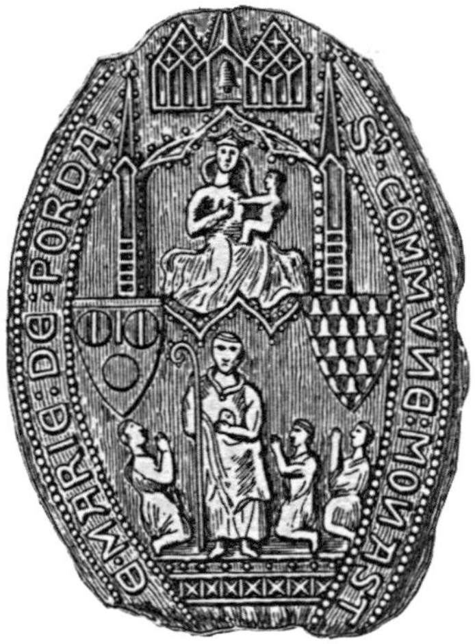

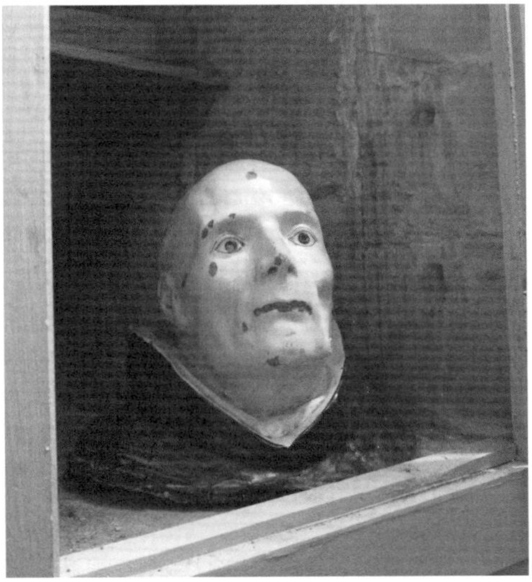

Above left: The Forde Abbey seal. At top under a steeple and bell, the Virgin and Child; below, an abbot with crosier and book. (From Oliver's *Monasticon*).

Above right: Ceramic effigy of a monk. Of unknown date and origin, it is kept in a niche off the stone stair inside the Chard Tower.

shrine. Maurice also wrote prayers and hymns about Becket. His poem 'The long-hidden voice of the seer' (*Vox vatis velata diu*) told of an obscure prophetic riddle attributed to the mythical wizard Merlin that England would have two kings and one of them would kill his father in his mother's womb. Another of Maurice's poems, on papal forms of doctrine (*de schemate pontificali*), is said to have earned him applause at the fledgling university of Oxford. He later became abbot of Wells.

A greater poet, however, was Maurice's friend (and probably Baldwin's pupil) Roger. He made his name while travelling in Germany with an account of the visionary nun Elizabeth (c.1129-1164) who lived in the convent of Schönau near Limburg in the Rhineland-Palatinate. He sent his report of her visions – she claimed to have seen the assumption of the Virgin Mary into heaven – back to England, dedicating the book to Baldwin on his election as abbot of Forde. At the same time he asked him to make a readable version for his – Baldwin's – mother who, like many widows of that time, had become a nun herself.

To this document Roger attached an unfinished 288-line poem of his own in praise of the Blessed Virgin. In one stanza he asks why, when she provided a model of sobriety in feeding the infant Jesus, his fellow monks should have been allowed to grow enormous pot-bellies from their carousing.[9] Roger suggested

Maurice might like to finish the poem for him, and listed eight miracles of the Virgin for him to set to verse. He also wrote the story of St. Ursula, a woman from Devon or Cornwall, and the 11,000 virgins massacred at Cologne.

Other members of the community worth a mention are William, first abbot of the daughter house Bindon, who shared Roger's interest in the miracles of the Virgin; and Alexander, reputedly a great bibliophile, who became abbot of Meaux in the East Riding of Yorkshire where, rashly, he crossed swords with King John.

John and the Holy Man of Haselbury

None of these monks of Forde was a great writer in our sense of the word. But one of them came close. He was John of Devon, or John of Ford – named, it seems, not after the monastery but the village near Axminster where he was born about the year 1150. Forgotten for many years, John's reputation as a writer was restored in the twentieth century by the rediscovery of his life of the famous miracle-worker, hermit and seer, Wulfric of Haselbury Plucknett.

Like his superior Baldwin, John suffered from divided allegiances. At heart he wanted only to write but his piety and intelligence took him away from the cloister, first to Bindon as its abbot, then to the court of King John to be the monarch's confessor and dispenser of alms to the poor. There was an historical irony here: Baldwin had crowned John's elder brother Richard I; now another abbot of Forde found himself on intimate terms with Richard's unpopular successor.

To hear the sins of a king whose reputation for bad behaviour has survived to this day must have been hard enough; to find yourself so close to a ruler who had his eye on your community's assets surely worse. King John was desperate for money. He wanted to recover Normandy which he had lost in 1202-4; and in order to seal a peace treaty with the French king he demanded the sum of 30,000 marks from the Cistercian abbeys. He was opposed by another monk from Forde, the abbot Alexander of Meaux already mentioned, as well as by the General Chapter of the Cistercian order in France which had authority over all the houses and claimed exemption from such levies. When, however, King John came back for more money to finance his campaign in Ireland, Alexander was the only one to resist. His Yorkshire monastery was seized and brought close to ruin. Alexander took refuge at Forde where he spent the last two years of his life in bitter retirement. Nor did Forde escape: in about 1210 the abbey was forced to sell many of its assets to meet the royal demands.

John was primarily a theologian. He was said to have been educated in Paris – more probably it was Exeter – and joined the monastery at Forde in about 1170. An intellectual who attracted scholars from the new universitites to the monastic life, he became prior in 1184 and soon after was sent as abbot to the new daughter house of Bindon. He returned to be elected abbot of Forde in 1191, a position he held until his death in 1220.

Known for his spirituality and piety, he was asked to complete a famous work of the age, a commentary on the *Song of Songs* begun by the great St. Bernard of Clairvaux. [10] John's additions were said to be 'full of expressions of regret for the tensions he felt between what he wanted to do and what he actually did.'[11]

Other religious commentaries, treatises and sermons of his survive. But the reputation enjoyed by Abbot John today is mainly due to a monk of Downside Abbey, Dom Maurice Bell, who in the 1930s wrote a long introduction to the Latin text of John's extraordinary biography of the 'holy man' Wulfric which, as he put it, had been 'lying in manuscript for about 750 years'.

Born around 1090 to a middle-class family in Compton Martin near Bristol, Wulfric became a hunting-and-hawking priest in Wiltshire until a chance encounter with a beggar made him reconsider. He was recalled to Compton Martin by its lord, William FitzWalter, but soon sought permission to become an anchorite – an enclosed hermit – at Haselbury Plucknett, near Yeovil. There he became well known to some of the older monks of Forde, about seven miles away.

John's biography brings to life the little world of the mediaeval village: the parish priest and his son the errand boy, the scroungers and petty thieves, the daily squabbles. Then there is Wulfric himself, locked in a cell on the north side of the parish church, praying all night, scourging himself against the promptings of the flesh, while at his window appears an endless line of visitors seeking a word of comfort, a miraculous cure – or just taking a look.

Despite its conventional pieties and Biblical references, John's account is a precursor of modern biography. There are humorous asides, Latin puns, frequent reference to sources and – for the more extravagant miracle stories – expressions of authorial doubt. His imagery could be homely. He commented on the behaviour of a local youth who, fearing the holy man had foreseen an early death for him, suddenly gave up his airs and graces: 'Like boys when the rain begins to fall, he put an end to his playing.'

John wrote the biography between 1180 and 1186, somehow finding time between the routine of work and worship to set down a few paragraphs each day. 'That's all I have time for today', he exclaims at one point. Wulfric had been dead for only 30 years and John interviewed many of the hermit's friends and followers.

During his lifetime, Wulfric's fame spread across Europe. He has been called 'the most celebrated anchorite of mediaeval England.'[12] Like the fifth-century ascetic Simeon Stylites on his pillar in Syria, he attracted not only gawping tourists but kings and nobles seeking his advice. King Henry I, prompted by his wife Adelicia, came to the window one day in 1130 to get the saint's blessing. He wanted a cure for Drogo de Munci, a courtier of his who had been mysteriously paralysed after suggesting that Wulfric was hoarding illegal coins in his cell. Wulfric duly obliged. Three years later, he heard that Henry was planning to go to Normandy. Wulfric – acting now more like the Delphic Oracle – prophesied that the king would not return alive. Not only was he proved right but on 2nd December 1135, distant though he was, he was able to announce that the king had died the previous day.

Henry's successor, the young Stephen, was hailed as the future king on his first visit to Haselbury. On his second visit the holy man criticised him for the turbulent rule which was tearing the country apart. On the third occasion Stephen made his confession, wept, and was absolved for a secret sin which, he said, was the cause of his failure as a monarch.

St. Bernard himself had asked for Wulfric's advice and prayers through a close friend of the anchorite's, Henry abbot of Tintern. This Henry was one of Wulfric's converts – in a former life he had belonged to a band of robbers – and one of his biggest admirers. He told the Pope all about the holy man over a long meal in Rome, reporting afterwards that the pontiff had been 'a passionate listener', and he provided John with much of his information.

Some of that information was not credible, as John himself admits. Among the more 'conventional' miracles – a stolen loaf turning to stone in the thief's hands, water turning to wine in church, cases of 'second sight' – there are three that stand out. The first concerns the tunic of chain mail that Wulfric wore to mortify the flesh (a hair shirt not being enough). The tunic had to be shortened to make kneeling possible. William FitzWalter offered to have the tunic altered in London, or in Exeter. No, said the saint, we'll do it here. He gave the knight a pair of shears, saying 'I'll go and recommend this business to God' and went over to the window to pray. FitzWalter thought Wulfric had gone mad, but obeyed. A seventeenth-century translator takes up the story:

> 'The one falls to his prayers, the other endeavours with iron and steele to cutt iron and steele: when both their labours took prosperous effect...For the knight in his cutting worke seemed rather to divide a peece of cloath than a peece of iron, with soe great facilitie the shears ranne through that steele garment.' As a result 'the glorie and sweete odour of his sainctitie was blowne ouer all parts of the Kingdom.[13]

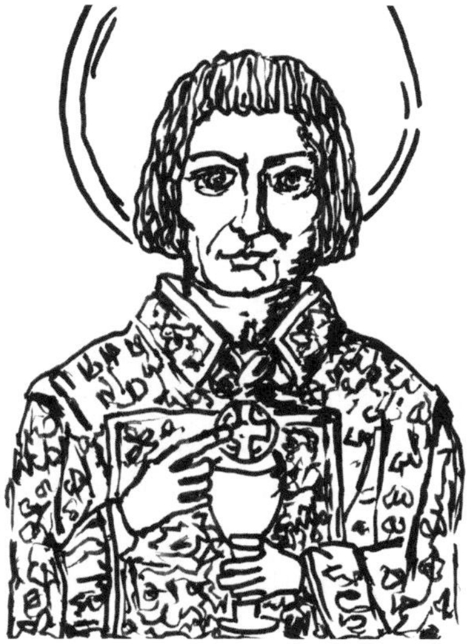

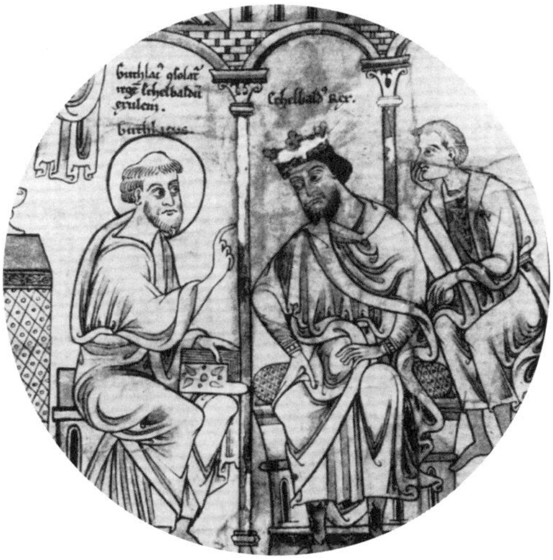

Above left: The holy man 'Saint' Wulfric, from a portrayal in the church of his birthplace, Compton Martin. Drawn by Sandra Oakins.

Above right: A king taking counsel from a hermit. Both Henry I and King Stephen visited Wulfric for his blessing and advice.

On another occasion Wulfric noticed that his coat had been nibbled by a mouse. He cursed the mouse, which promptly ran out of its hole and fell dead at his feet. When Brictric the local priest suggested he might like to perform the same trick on all the mice in the area, Wulfric refused: 'I wouldn't dream of it,' he replied. 'On the contrary, if it were not insulting to God I should have asked Him to bring the mouse back to life.'[14]

John was told by the guestmaster of Forde, a good friend of the hermit's, that Brictric had been much more upset when he heard that Wulfric had cured a dumb man so effectively that he burst into both French and English. 'Here am I who has looked after you for years, and you give a complete stranger not one, but two languages; while I am reduced to virtual silence when I'm with the bishop and archdeacon because you never gave me the use of French!'[15]

When Wulfric died on the 20th February 1154, the monks of Montacute priory claimed his body and sent a party of men to take the corpse away, hoping to profit from the hermit's fame. The villagers fought them off and Wulfric was buried in his cell (though its present whereabouts are not known). It took another 30 years for the cult of 'Saint' Wulfric (the title was unofficial) to catch on. Few *post morten* miracles were reported before John of Forde set to work in the 1180s. By 1235 they were too numerous to count, and the pilgrims were streaming in. The Reformation put an end to all that; but today Wulfric's fame is spreading once more, thanks to the historians' rediscovery of his biographer, John of Forde.

The World Intrudes

Roger of Forde's complaint about the pot-bellies of his brother monks was prophetic. By the beginning of the thirteenth century the ascetic rigour and spiritual intensity of the Cistercians had weakened, the intellectual vigour shown by Forde's early abbots and theologians had faltered, and the abbey's independence was increasingly challenged by the king, the secular church – even its own patrons.

The energy which the monks had put into prayer and work was diverted into managing their estates and building up their wool exports. Already in the early thirteenth century Abbot John was regretting the amount of time he was having to spend on administration and business trips. His monks, he complained, spent more time talking about 'the potency of bulls and rams, harvests, territorial disputes, lawsuits, and the doings of kings and princes than they did about the teaching of Jesus and the Songs of Sion.'[16]

A modern historian lamented that by the mid-thirteenth century Cistercian abbeys like Forde 'had sunk into the countryside and lost for ever that compelling charm which had once made them seem like outposts of Jerusalem, the vision of peace.'[17] It is tempting to see this as the beginning of a long decline stretching over the subsequent three centuries, accelerated by the Black Death and reaching its inevitable end with the Dissolution under Henry VIII.

But this is the wisdom of hindsight. Today's historians have a more nuanced view. Professor James Clark of Exeter University, an expert on the period, argues that after a brief 'heroic age', the monks of Forde merely adopted a more conventional form of spiritual life, and became, like the Benedictines, integrated into the local economy. Their fortunes ebbed and flowed. The turmoil of the Black Death and its subsequent recession were overcome, with the monks' help. And there was a monastic Indian summer before the unforeseen long winter of the Dissolution.

Certainly, the Cistercians faced competition from the new orders of friars, and Benedictine dominance of the new universities of Oxford and Cambridge. (The Cistercians did not have their own Oxford college, St. Bernard's – now St. John's – until 1446). And it is true that monastic writing of history, biography and letters declined in the later Middle Ages, obliging today's scholars to rely on official records or the chance survival of documents like the Forde Abbey cartulary.[18]

Yet the abbots of Forde continued to wield political power, to command the ear of kings while their estates expanded into Dorset, Somerset, across Devon and into Cornwall. By the time of the Dissolution they held a large portfolio of church 'livings', of villages, buildings and mills, of tithes and rents, and held sway over some 30,000 acres.

Economic success was bound to attract competition and envy. The more efficient the Cistercian monks became, the more scope there was for arguments with the neighbours, especially for a monastery like Forde situated in a populous area. The abbey was vulnerable not only to the erratic weather of the West Country (to this day a chief arbiter of its fortunes) but also to outside economic factors – inflation, which was rampant in the time of King John, the cost of debt, the price of labour, the price of wool – not to mention the demands of successive kings for money to finance their various wars.

Eventually, of course, the material wealth of the monasteries was to be their undoing. It left them open to the criticism that they had a bigger stake in this world than in the next, a criticism that was to be employed to devastating effect by Henry VIII's cunning and ruthless minister, Thomas Cromwell.

Challenges from Outside

An early presage of conflicts to come was the abbey's failure to avoid paying its share of the huge ransom of 100,000 pounds of silver (more than twice England's total yearly revenue) demanded for the release of King Richard I. Because the Cistercians had no gold, silver or jewellery they were taxed a year's harvest of sheep's wool instead. They pleaded exemption, and Richard's brother King John, formerly well-disposed towards the Cistercians, turned against them and imposed a fine on Forde of 750 marks (one mark was 13s.4d, or 68p) even though Abbot John had urged his monks to pay up.

The monks' privileged status, including exemption from tithes paid to Rome, was much resented by the secular clergy, and especially the bishops. They clashed continually with the monasteries over jurisdiction. (The King and his ministers could not interfere because the independence of the church had been guaranteed by Magna Carta in 1215.)[19]

A graphic instance of this rivalry, fully documented, occurred in 1275 when Bishop Bronescombe of Exeter challenged Forde's autonomy and was excommunicated by the then abbot, William of Crewkerne. The Bishop retaliated by excommunicating the abbot in turn, and took the case to court. Two canon law professors heard the evidence at Westminster in 1276, when the abbot felt it prudent to apologize and offer £500 in compensation. But the court deferred judgment until the following Easter. Meanwhile William appealed to the king, Edward I, enlisting other abbots in his support.

The result was a technical victory for the bishop. Abbot William was ordered to lift the excommunication, fined a thousand marks and given an extra penance: on the coming feast of St. John the Baptist, he and his monks were to process from the cemetery of St. Peter's, Exeter (now the Cathedral) to the door of the church 'bare-headed and bare-footed, and loosely dressed' where they would receive a 'discipline', or talking-to, from the bishop. But the sting of the verdict was drawn when the court added that the bishop for his part must apologize for retaliating, would receive only 100 marks of the thousand-mark fine, and should forget the penitential march prescribed for the abbot and monks.

By this time, even the Courtenay patrons of Forde were beginning to question the generous terms of the grant made 150 years by its founder Adelicia. Early patrons of Forde had been routinely praised by the old chroniclers, and their generosity and pious lives rewarded with solemn burial by the high altar of the abbey church (where they still lie today, somewhere under the croquet lawn).

A particular favourite of the monks had been the thirteenth-century John de Courtenay. The feeling was mutual, for John was convinced the monks had saved his life. He had been caught one night in a storm at sea which threatened to wreck his ship. When the sailors around him panicked, John told them to take heart and hold fast for another hour. 'By that time,' he said, 'my monks of Forde will be risen to their prayers, and will intercede for me to the Lord, so that no storms, or winds or waves shall be able to shipwreck us.'[20] John then raised his arms and asked God to listen to the monks. The storm abated and the ship was saved. John was so grateful he later joined the monastery himself; and there he died and was buried in 1273.

The benevolence of John de Courtenay did not, however, pass to his son and grandson, both of them named Hugh. They wanted more in return for their patronage. As the anonymous historian writes:

> 'The Lord Hugh de Courtenay did not follow the example of his father in piety towards God and tenderness towards the monks of Ford, but did much infest and trouble them. He affirmed (untruly) that the abbey of Ford, which was founded by his progenitors in the nature of a free, pure, and perpetual alms, ought to be holden of him by these services, viz., when any war should happen, to find him horses and furniture and arms and other accoutrements, and to keep for him two palfreys and

one greyhound bitch, with her whelps every year, until the whelps should be a year old.'[21]

These were the obligations, he claimed, which Abbot William of Crewkerne had reneged on. He reinforced his demand by 'coming with a great multitude of people thither' and driving away to Dartmoor all the cattle and ploughing oxen they found at Westford and Orchard granges. The monks sued for the return of their animals, and a truce was arranged. But two years later, in 1290, Hugh turned up again with a posse of cattle-rustlers. This time he was driven off by the abbey servants, armed with bow and arrows, 'who threatened to shoot him, so that he took no cattle away'. On the way home, however, he called again at Westford and took a bull, 12 cows, four oxen and four heifers as ransom. The abbot decided to ignore the provocation and let the lawsuit drop.

Hugh's son, later Earl of Devon, maintained his father's campaign against the monks by means of what the chronicle calls 'three evils' (*tria mala*): he demanded 'severe and burthensome services' of the abbey; appropriated the rights and rents of their estate at Tale, near Honiton; and encouraged the rector of Crewkerne church to sue the abbey for payment of a tithe of 50 shillings a year. The community resented these attacks so much that they stopped, at least for a time, recording the Courtenay family's births, marriages and deaths. The Courtenays were perhaps indifferent: they had shifted their patronage to the Cluniac priory at Cowick, Exeter, and the Benedictine abbbey at Tavistock.

Dealing with the Neighbours

Relations with local landowners, farmers and smallholders seem to have been more equable, if occasionally complicated. The abbey's cartulary, a painstaking (though incomplete) register of grants, leases and legal cases up to the year 1445, gives a fascinating insight into the complexity of mediaeval land management. The time of the monastery's greatest territorial expansion was the first 80 years, but the cartulary records a steady stream of donations to 'the abbot and convent' over three and a half centuries. It is a rare record of everyday life in old Wessex.

Some of the 690 entries show the monastery being forgiven rents due on land it has leased, or land it has bought being converted into a gift. Some are about rights of way specifying what livestock and carts the monks may drive over them, and what compensation they must pay for any damage done. We read of the monks getting permission to build dams and millponds; of the amicable settlement of a dispute in 1305 between the abbot and the dean of Wells about

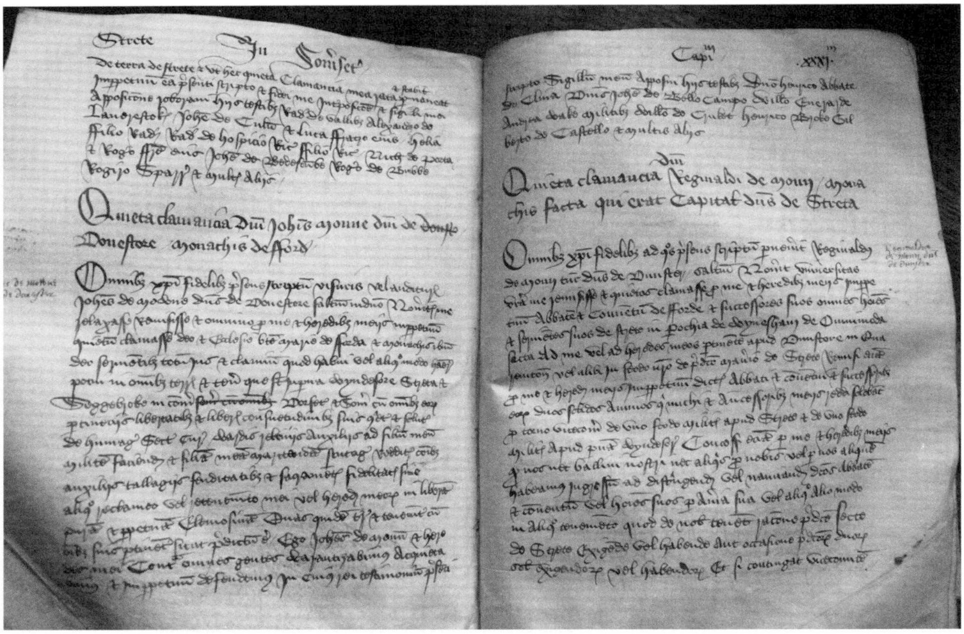

The Forde Abbey cartulary, an invaluable record of the monastery's dealings. These pages refer to the estate of Street on the other side of the River Axe.

flooding at Winsham; and use of the footpath between Winsham and Shedrick (it still exists) on land which the dean owned. Land is measured in perches, furlongs and acres, but also in virgates (about 30 acres) and in carucates, the area of land that could be tilled by one plough and eight oxen in a year. Boundaries are defined not only by streams and valleys, but by ditches, hedges, fences, even individual trees. The detail of these deeds is extraordinary.

Disputes were also logged. John de Wraxall was accused of holding two of the abbot's draught animals to ransom – cattle-rustling seems to have been a common form of retaliation. The cartulary records cases of the abbot being sued for rent overdue, and of him chasing up defaulters in his turn. But relations with the community seem, in general, to have been good.

Rent was often paid in kind, and often it was token. The cartulary contains examples of the 'peppercorn rent'. A deed of 1293 required the monks to pay one peppercorn a year at Christmas in return for an income of 20 shillings from a property in Crewkerne. Other payments in kind included spices – especially pepper and cumin – wax for candles, a pair of white gloves, or a single red rose. Rents could be more substantial. For the use of land between Chaffeigh and Drimpton, Jocelin of Winsham gave Robert Burnell a pair of gilt spurs, a palfrey, a mewed sparrowhawk, seven shillings and a gold coin for his wife. There were 29 witnesses to the deed, including Walter the clerk. (Some recurrent witness names, such as Raleigh and Churchill, are familiar).

The Forde Abbey cartulary reminds us that the monasteries provided in exchange the benefits of a welfare state: they were hostels, retirement homes, hospitals and hospices, schools and libraries. In 1260, for example, Henry of Sandpits near Drimpton gave a farm of five perches 'to provide alms for paupers at the door of the monks' house, to be distributed by the porter.' Like all religious houses that followed the Rule of Benedict, Forde would throw open its western gate once a week to feed the hungry.

Hospitality was another requirement of the Rule. The monks put up travellers, whether private individuals or kings and nobles with large retinues. They taught local children, kept and stored historical and legal records. They admitted old people close to death as 'novices' so that they could die within the walls. Former abbots and officials, retired servants, local pensioners and other dependants were offered 'corrodies'. These might include board and lodging in a small apartment, and stabling and forage for a horse in exchange for a gift of land or – at a later date – payment in advance. Some of these pensioners were foisted on the monastery by the local bishop, by the patronal family, or even by the king himself.

All this cost money. Like any business, Forde would have incurred debts and expenses, especially in bad farming years. On the other hand, houses like Forde generated large surpluses of wool, even if prices were volatile. When the price was rising, wool traders representing clients in Flanders, Brabant, Lombardy and Tuscany would call at the abbey gate with ready cash. Exports to Italy began around the end of the 13th century; we know that by 1315 Florence was an important customer for the abbeys of Forde, its neighbour Newenham at Axminster, Torre and Buckfast. (The abbot and monks of Buckfast had been enrolled as members of the Merchants' Guild of Totnes back in 1236).

The wool trade went on growing until about 1330. In the later fourteenth century prices collapsed and in the aggressive new business climate monasteries would sell their wool forward, being paid for so many sacks a few years in advance. Cistercians could not at first spare money from rents, leases and tithes to meet emergencies or satisfy their need for ever larger premises. So they borrowed from Italian or Flemish bankers (and from English Jews until King Edward I expelled them in 1290), then found themselves unable to repay. Such contracts could become a nightmare for heads of houses.[22] We know that the abbot of Forde struggled to maintain the fabric of his church and monastic buildings, and that repairs had to be made to the abbey church in 1354. It may have been at this time that Hey Farm across the valley acquired its handsome cinquefoil windows: the farm's recent owners believe a crafty predecessor bribed the carters to drop a few off as they passed by on the road from the Ham Hill quarry.

There was commercial competition from other sheep-farming monasteries in the south-west like Wilton, Shaftesbury and especially Glastonbury, which had flocks, granges and farm buildings all over Somerset. There was spiritual competition from the new orders of friars that were arriving in the towns, and from the big new parish churches being built at Axminster, Chard and Crewkerne. 'The High Street church was luring customers away from the out-of-town spiritual supermarket,' as Professor Clark put it. And there was commercial competition from the new towns like Honiton sponsored by former monastic patrons such as the Courtenays.[23]

Of all the changes of these times, the greatest was the disappearance of the lay brothers. At the Dissolution only three granges are recorded of the seven which Forde Abbey boasted in the mid-thirteenth century. The clear implication is that instead of farming the land themselves, the monks had increasingly been forced by economic presssure or lack of recruits to lease out the lands they owned.

As we have seen, lay brothers, or '*conversi*', had been essential to the original model of Cistercian life. But living as they did up to 20 miles from the mother house, they became increasingly independent, in some cases even rebellious. They turned themselves into farm managers, hiring others to do the labour. Sometimes the monks supposedly in charge gave up living there. Even if they stayed, discipline in these self-contained communities slackened. Besides, there were other opportunities: farm wages had risen and there were affordable plots of land for rent. Monastic life began to look much less attractive.

The Black Death, the rat-borne plague which landed at Melcombe Regis only 30 miles from the abbey, was a great shock but not a fatal blow. It put an end to the old economy but did not– as has been argued – send the monasteries into terminal decline. There is no record of how many monks Forde may have lost in that first epidemic of 1348 (the plague returned twice more in the 1360s). At Newenham Abbey, a few miles down the road, 20 of the 22 monks and three lay brothers died. Walter the abbot survived.[24] Between a quarter and a third of the general populace of five or six million were killed. The death rate was higher among the religious – up to half in the case of monks – because although they were healthier and stronger than the common people they were also vulnerable, being conscientious about ministering to the sick.

The labour shortage caused by the Black Death drove wages rates even higher, making unpaid work for monasteries less attractive still. Large areas of land fell into disuse and labourers migrated to the towns. But even before the plague, the number of lay brothers with farming skills was falling, and the monks may have been partly responsible for discouraging young men from signing up. Instead of recruiting from the towns they preferred to follow Benedictine practice and employ domestic servants.[25] By the end of the 14th century, most of the monastery land beyond the home farm was let, and all the lay brothers had gone.

* * *

Meanwhile the home life of the monks was becoming easier, and their abbot ever more preoccupied with business affairs, just as John of Forde had prophesied.

The ban on meat-eating was relaxed by Pope Benedict XII in 1336 to allow the healthy as well as the ill to eat meat, so long as it was in the infirmary. Second refectories for meat-eaters began to appear – some of them described as extensions to the infirmary – usually adjacent to the existing dining room. Twenty years later the concession was extended by Pope John XXII to allow meat three times a week. By the early fifteenth century the ban had lapsed entirely. Forde seems to have been slow off the mark. It did not get a separate refectory until about 1465, a date suggested by examination of the roof timbers, when an upper floor was created above the refectory. The upper dining room is now a library, where traces remain of the niche from which devotional works were read to the monks while they ate. We have no information about mediaeval drinking habits at Forde, but wine was first allowed to Cistercians in 1350. Knowles suggests that, for the black monks at least, the single glass of beer or wine in the evening permitted by the Rule soon became two glasses, especially if there were visitors.

Perhaps these concessions were part of a recruitment drive. As an historian of Buckfast Abbey wrote: 'The days had gone by when monks were content to live on beans and vetches, when they would rarely see such luxuries as eggs, cheese, or fish. Still less would they have thought of eking out their fare with beech-leaves' [as St. Bernard and his colleagues are said to have done.[26]] Also relaxed – and this applied to all monasteries – was the rule barring women from the precincts. Female servants were now employed. The hours allowed to the monks for conversation were gradually extended. Some houses even allowed them to take holidays – small groups would enjoy a short break in a cottage on the estate where, after saying their daily office, they would go for walks and perhaps indulge in a bit of sport: jumping hedges was popular.[27]

Lord of the Manor

Yet houses like Forde continued to enjoy local patronage. And if their spiritual and intellectual powers were dimmed and recruits harder to win, they remained what Knowles calls 'a great social force' with estates and buildings that no landowner, not even the king, could match.[28] Nothing illustrated this more than the status of the abbot. While his monks adopted a more comfortable lifestyle, the abbot had already left them far behind. Ever more detached from his community, he had mutated from spiritual father to feudal lord. In some instances, the title was literal: abbot Walter of Burstock, a man of modest family from a little hamlet five miles to the east, became lord of the manor of Burstock in the 1380s. The abbot acquired a retinue of advisers and servants, dressed finely, entertained handsomely, and travelled with a large escort. Long regarded under civil law as solely responsible for his house, he had nobody within to restrain him and had become deaf to edicts from distant Citeaux and the even more distant Pope. The most glaring excesses, however, would be picked up by the Cistercians' system of periodic inspections, or visits by the local bishop; cases are recorded from this time of abbots being suspended for gross overspending or keeping a mistress.

The grander the abbot became, the grander his lodgings. Nowhere is this more apparent than at Forde. Early incumbents may have been from wealthy backgrounds, but they lived cheek-by-jowl with their brothers and slept in the monks' dormitory at the east end. Later abbots were usually local men, like Walter, from poorer backgrounds. But they lived in a separate apartment above the west side of the cloister and had their own dining room, supposedly to prevent their brethren being disturbed by the carousing of the abbot's guests. The final move was to lodgings attached to the west end of the Great Hall built by Thomas Chard, last of the line of about 30 abbots, and the most ambitious of them all.

The Master Builder

If not the most distinguished Cistercian, Thomas Chard was – in the opinion of most commentators – one of the greatest builders of his day.[29] His extravagant and beautiful additions to the monastery were begun in 1522. A sumptuous late Gothic tower was added at the north-west corner of the cloister; from it grew a Great Hall some 80 feet long, 28 feet wide and 28 feet high extending over six bays, one of the largest in southern England. Beyond it were the new abbot's

Opposite page: The Great Hall built by Thomas Chard, the last abbot.

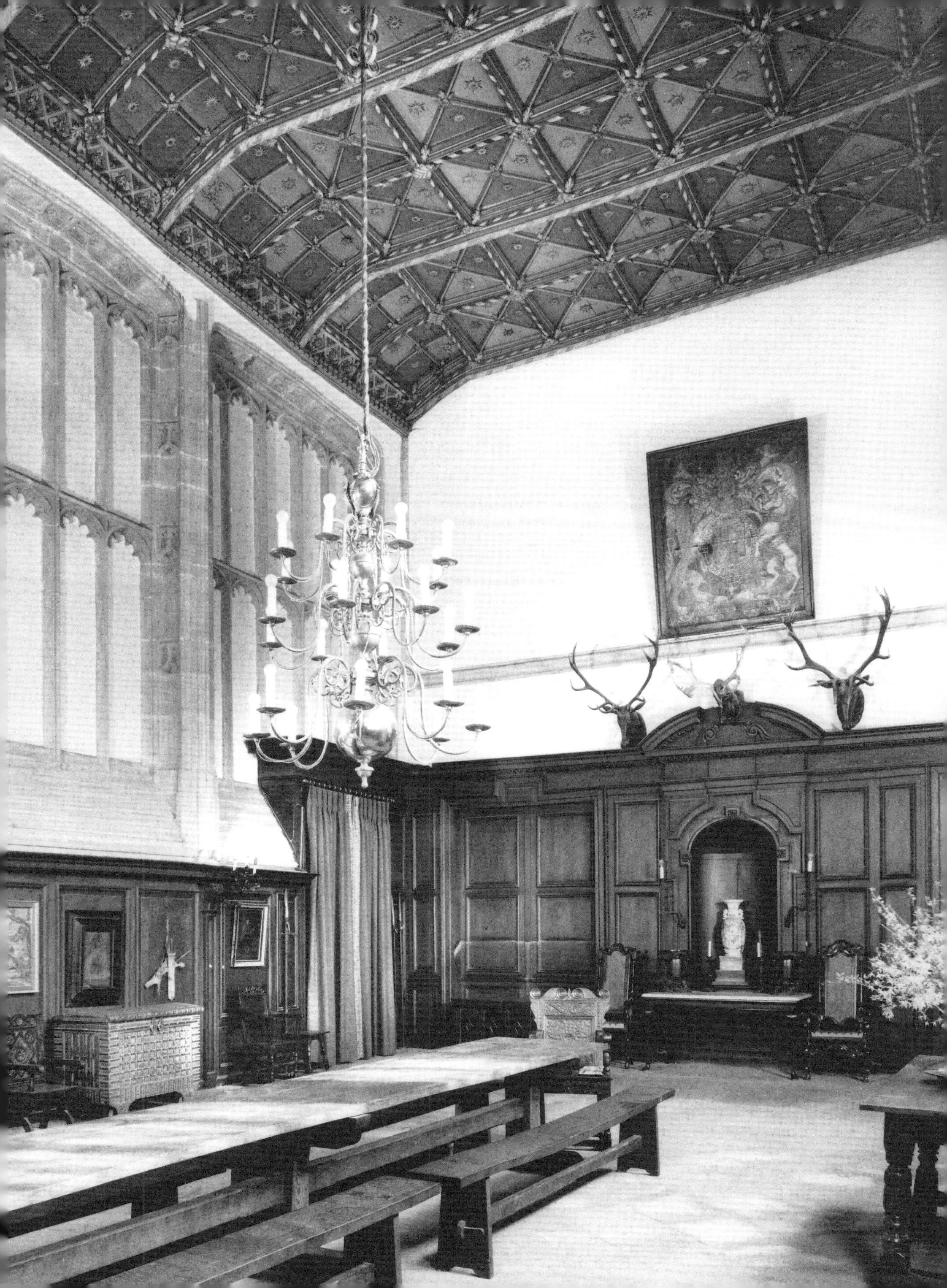

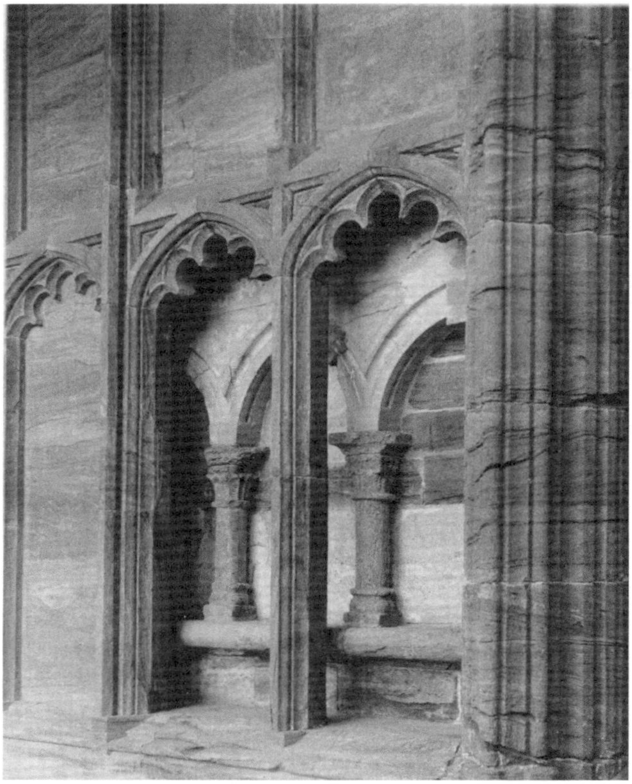

Section of the existing cloister, showing the original twelfth-century work behind Chard's remodelling.

lodgings. The old cloister was removed and rebuilt. Only the north side of its replacement has survived, contained within the east wing of the present house. (It is not clear whether Chard's cloister was left unfinished – or if it was, when the other three sides of it were removed).

John Leland the antiquarian, visiting the abbey in the 1530s during his tour of monastic libraries, described how abbot John of Forde had been 'buried without great pomp in his monastery which the abbot [Chard] is now restoring most magnificently, at quite incredible expense.'[30]

All this was planned more than a decade after Henry VIII had come to the throne and less than 15 years before the Dissolution began. Why did Abbot Chard, along with so many others, embark on this grand project with such a threat looming over his monastery? Did he not guess what was coming? Was it prudence that made him convert the abbey's moveable assets into stone and plaster before they could be seized for the king? Did he calculate that by turning

Forde into a desirable residence for courtiers he could ward off the fate which reduced other English monasteries to picturesque ruins? A Victorian visitor, echoing Leland, marvelled that Forde should have been suppressed 'just as it was apparently rising, with renewed life, and with buildings surpassing in splendour all it had before possessed.'[31] Such theories are attractive, but probably wrong. There is another and better explanation. Thomas Chard was reacting not to some future disaster, but to present prosperity.

In spite of the ravages of the Black Death and falling recruitment, the English monasteries were enjoying a revival, an Indian summer that had started in the early fifteenth century under the benign monarch Henry V and continued largely undisturbed by the fratricidal Wars of the Roses from 1455 to 1487. The country was getting rich from foreign trade; magnates were building themselves country houses, nobles were converting their fortress-like castles and the monasteries were not be left out. Most of those in the south-west set about upgrading their premises: the nave of Sherborne abbey was rebuilt with its astonishing stone fan-vaulted ceiling; Glastonbury expanded; new living quarters were built at Cleeve, Muchelney and Montacute in Somerset; and the abbey of Bath was still rebuilding when the Dissolution came.

The end of the English monasteries was totally unforeseen. Thomas Chard, like the abbots of all the bigger monasteries, had no idea that the large houses would be shut down, even after the closure of the smaller ones began in 1536. Nor, for that matter, did King Henry VIII himself nor his chief minister Thomas Cromwell. As we shall see, policy was being made on the hoof. If there had been any sign of what was to happen, the abbot would surely have detected it. After all, he was no peasant monk, but a well-educated man from a family of clerics, a man of the world.

Chard was born in about 1470 at Tracey Hayes outside Honiton. In 1505 he was sent to the newly-founded Cistercian college of St. Bernard's in Oxford where he was acclaimed 'a shining example of virtue and learning' (*vir magna doctrina et virtute clarus*). He acquired a series of preferments or 'livings' in Devon and Cornwall, most of which he seems to have given up before he was elected abbot of Forde in 1521.

Such perks were normal for the times, and not merely a sign of greed. On the contrary, Chard was a generous donor to the building fund of his old college, which thanked him by inscribing his coat of arms in the college windows. He was also patron of a leper hospital, St. Margaret's, near Honiton. Proof of his probity, perhaps, is that from 1513 to 1527 he was an official inspector of the English Cistercian houses, appointed by Citeaux. It is not clear at what point he

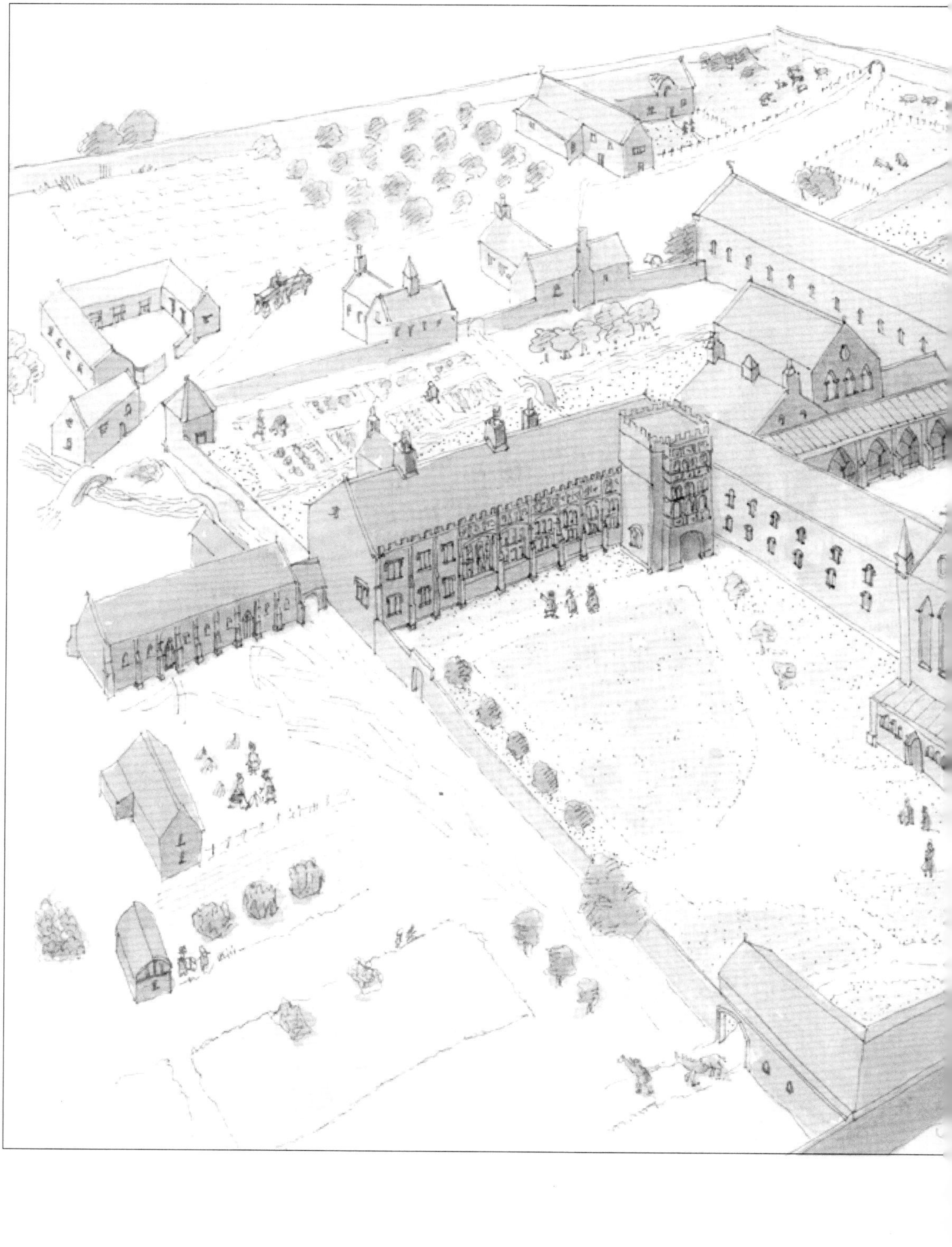

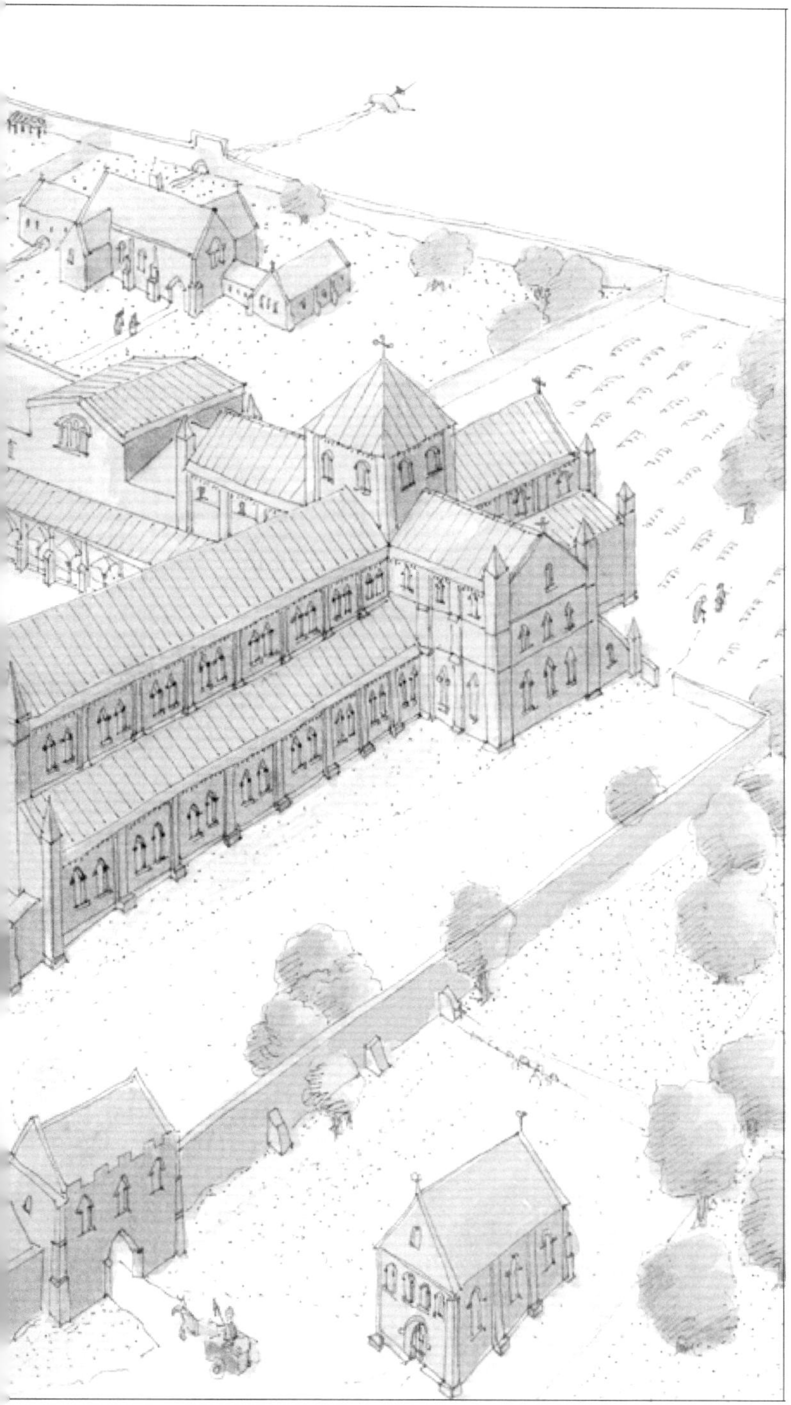

A bird's eye view of how the abbey may have looked in 1530 after Chard's additions, as seen from the south.

Note (*left*) the mediaeval barn outside the perimeter wall opposite the new abbot's lodging and Great Hall, and behind it the main drain running off to the river; the infirmary with its chapel (*top right*) beyond the monks' dormitory; the outer chapel by the gatehouse (*bottom right*); and the lay brothers' dormitory (*centre*) running between Chard's Tower and the abbey church.

The chapter house (now a chapel) is next to the north transept of the church.

Drawing by Sandra Oakins.

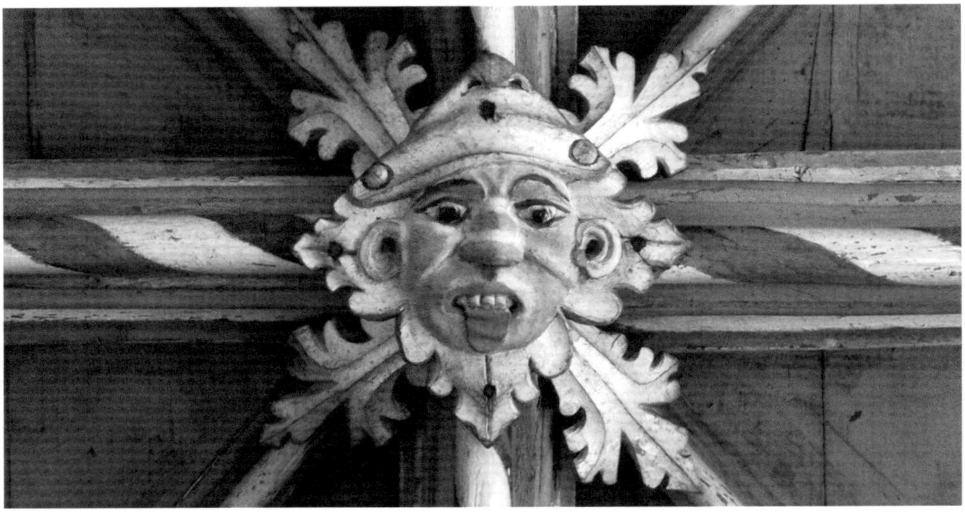

Boss in the wooden vault of the Great Hall.

became a monk at Forde; it may have been shortly before his election as abbot.

Work on the new buildings seems to have ended in 1528. We know the date because it appears with Chard's name inscribed in Latin under the battlement of the tower. This reads: *Año (anno) Doñi (Domini) millesimo quingesimo vigo (viginti) octo. A dno (domino) factum est Toma Chard, Abb.*

It seems, however, that the work was not completed, for reasons unknown. For example, the Great Hall was probably destined to have a stone vaulted ceiling, like that of Sherborne Abbey. The wood panelled vault seen today was installed later. The new cloister, as we have seen, is incomplete. And there is an odd omission: the boss of the vault inside the entrance to Chard's tower seems to have lost – if it ever had – its decoration. Perhaps he ran out of money. Perhaps he did indeed become fearful for the future and called a halt.

A year after work stopped Chard became – fortuitously, as it was to prove – titular vicar of Thorncombe. Another appointment freighted with historic irony was his choice of a local magnate, Sir Amias Poulett of Hinton St. George, and his son Hugh, as abbey stewards. For generations the growing size and complexity of the monastic estates had made it necessary – as well as politically prudent – to involve big local landowners in their management, and many abbots did so. These, however, look like special preparations for an uncertain future. Quite how uncertain, Thomas Chard cannot have known. But the skies were certainly darkening over the monasteries of England.

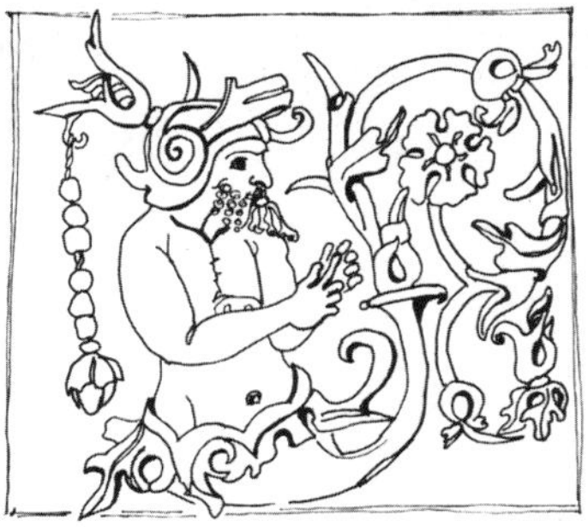

TWO

Dissolution and Decay

THE FIRST RUMBLE of the storm that was brewing reached Thomas Chard on the last day of January 1535. He learned that his appointment as inspector of Cistercian monasteries in the south-west had been revoked by Thomas Cromwell, soon to become the king's 'vice-regent in spirituals', or minister for church affairs.

Chard may have been vexed at the news. The post had been offered to him the previous year and confirmed by Cromwell only a few days earlier. But he cannot have guessed the full significance of the decision. Cromwell had decided to send out a team of valuers to make a rapid survey of the wealth of the English monasteries. The Dissolution of the Monasteries had begun.

The financial inspectors appointed in January 1535 were drawn from the gentry and bishops. They were given only five months to complete their survey, whose ostensible purpose was to discover whether monasteries were paying the right amount of tax – formerly due to the Pope but now appropriated to the king. The real purpose of the survey, called the *Valor Ecclesiasticus*, would become clear only later.

The inspectors worked hard, and by all accounts fairly: if anything they underestimated the value of the religious estates. But the process must have alarmed the abbeys, and may explain why Thomas Chard began leasing land and bringing in sympathetic local gentry as stewards. The survey reckoned Forde's net income at £335 a year from an estate of 12,400 acres – presumably only the lands contiguous with the abbey. This put it among the richer, but not richest, houses in the region.

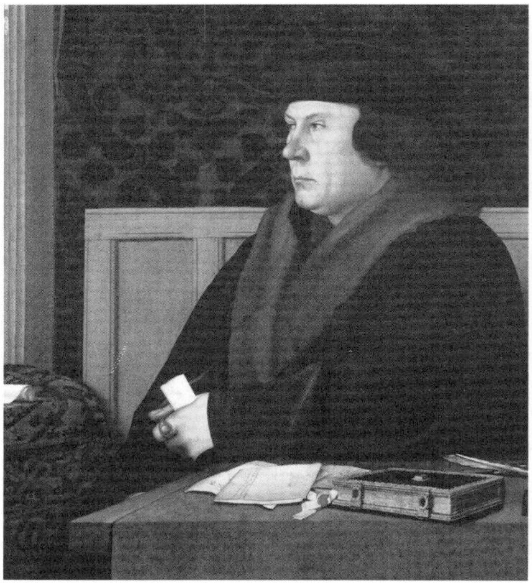

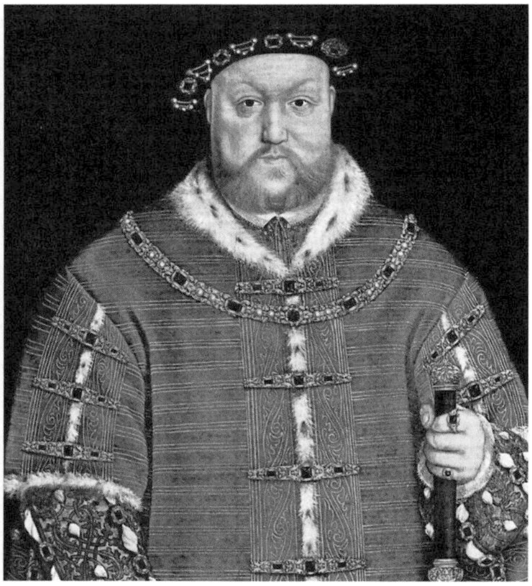

Above left: Hans Holbein's portrait of Thomas Cromwell, Henry VIII's cunning minister, who masterminded the expropriation of the monasteries.

Above right: Henry VIII, desperate for money and a male heir, broke with Rome before moving against the church (from the portrait by Hans Holbein).

The idea of raiding the wealth of the church as a way of paying the king's mounting bills had been in Cromwell's mind for some years. Henry VIII was anxious to appease his rebellious courtiers and did not want to alienate the common people with yet more taxes. But he needed money for defence, for palaces, and for a planned campaign to regain lands lost in France. And he felt affronted by the monasteries' wealth: as he confided in 1533 to Eustace Chapuys, the ambassador of the Holy Roman Emperor, he wanted to take back the goods 'which the churchmen held of the king.'[1]

But neither the king nor Cromwell felt free to move until they had settled the problem of the Pope's refusal to sanction Henry's divorce from Catherine of Aragon and marriage to Anne Boleyn. Their solution was to break with Rome. In 1534 a submissive parliament passed the Act of Supremacy endorsing Henry's claim to be head of the Church in England. Now Henry could annul his own marriage. And Cromwell could set about reforming – as he put it – the Church.

If Thomas Chard was not yet aware of the machinations at court, he soon would be. In 1535 he and his monks were paid a visit by two or more 'royal visitors' requiring them to renounce the authority of the Pope and sign oaths of submission to Henry as head of the Church. These visitors, legally trained laymen and secular clergy, were appointed to carry out the suppression of the monasteries. The job of the team preparing the *Valor Ecclesiasticus* was to dig out the financial information; the job of the royal visitors was to give Cromwell an excuse for seizing the assets, and then carry out the expropriation.

By now it must have become apparent to the abbots that the king had designs on their assets. In 1537 and 1538 Thomas Chard made a number of grants to local people, including members of his mother's family. John Tybbes, a clerk, got an annuity of £5. John Chidley of Thorncombe, a relation by marriage, was granted the lease of Oathill Grange and a 'tithe of sheaf' (a tenth of the cut corn) from Burstock for life. The two men were made stewards of abbey estates at Thorncombe, Burstock, Little Windsor, Street and Tale. Meanwhile a Ralphe Tybbes and his son Thomas became bailiffs of abbey land at Charmouth; another John Tybbes, along with Thomas Marker, received 40 years' worth of tithes at Payhembury.[2]

While the royal visitors were making their tour, Cromwell was secretly preparing to close down all houses containing fewer than 13 monks or nuns, put the monks of the richer houses on a fixed stipend, and seize the rest of their income for the king. Ignorant of what Cromwell was planning, the abbot and monks of Forde would have signed the oath of Supremacy however much it grated on their consciences. The Pope could not help them now, and the alternative to swearing allegiance was death.

Inevitably, the financial survey due to be completed in May 1535 took longer than expected; it was still only half completed when in late July the impatient Cromwell sent out his royal visitors again. This time their mission was more aggressive, even hostile. Although there is no firm evidence that Cromwell demanded it, they seemed determined to get the monks and nuns to incriminate themselves so that a catalogue of misdemeanours could be drafted to justify closing the monasteries down. It is clear from their reports (known as *comperta*) that the interrogators found it easy to get dissident monks to report on their superiors. Naïve young monks were persuaded to admit to the sin of self-abuse. Nuns were drawn into confessing youthful affairs or the birth of a baby – though many were by now in their sixties or seventies.

No record survives of what the inquisitors had to say about the moral regime at Forde. It seems unlikely there was much to report given the high standing of its abbot, even in Cromwell's eyes. Of course there were rumours, as everywhere else, some of which persist to this day – that the monks used farm buildings to lodge their mistresses and illegitimate children; that there were tunnels leading from the abbey to nearby villages for illicit nights out (hard though it is to imagine tunnels being dug under the river). Nor was there any sign of grievances held against the abbot, as at some monasteries in the area where Cromwell's invitation to report bad behaviour directly to him was enthusiastically taken up.

The investigators brought with them lists of 'injunctions', rules governing the daily life of the monasteries which had been drawn up by Cromwell in advance. Thomas Chard's letter of protest was one of many complaining that the rules were so restrictive that they would prevent anybody from stepping outside the monastery at all.

Early in 1536, as soon as the *Valor Ecclesiasticus* was completed but well before the abbeys and convents had had time to reply to, or comply with, the findings of the moral inspection, Cromwell drafted – and Parliament quickly passed – the Act of Suppression, closing down every house with a net 'temporal' income of less than £200 a year.[3]

The Act stipulated that the inmates of houses with fewer than 12 people would be sent to the bigger abbeys where they would be 'compelled to live religiously for the Reformation of their Lives'. Their property would go to the king. In its preamble the Act made the most of the moral depravity allegedly uncovered: 'Forasmuch as manifest synne, vicious, carnal and abominable living is dayly used and committed commonly in such little and small Abbeys, Priories and

The undercroft of Waverley Abbey, Forde's mother house, which like most English monastic buildings was left in ruins after the Dissolution. Its stone was used to rebuild Loseley Park for Sir William More.

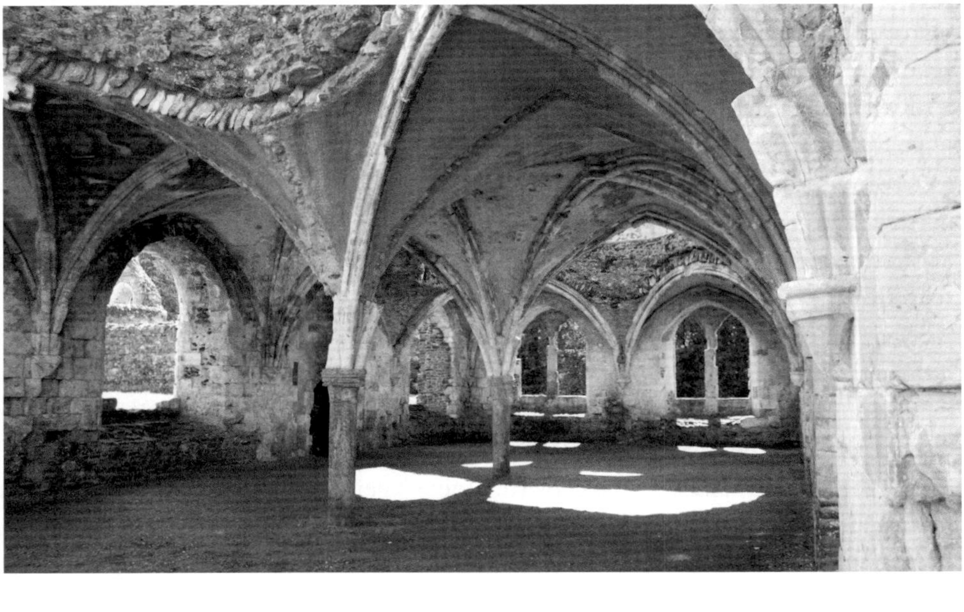

other Religious Houses,' going on to accuse their heads of utterly wasting their assets and failing to reform despite two hundred years of visitations. Reading this, abbots of large monasteries had every reason to breathe a sigh of relief. Not only were their houses spared, they were praised as 'great and honourable monasteries of Religion wherein (Thanks be to God) Religion is right well kept and observed.'

The royal visitors set about their task. It must have been painful for Thomas Chard and his community to learn of the closure of their mother house at Waverley in Surrey, now reduced to only 6,500 acres with remittances of £180 a year. Vulnerable, too, was Forde's daughter house at Bindon in Dorset, the only monastery in that county small enough to fall under the Act since its income was assessed at £147 per annum on an estate of some 6,000 acres. But the abbot of Bindon bought Cromwell off – temporarily at least – with a bribe of £300.

Thomas Chard cannot have been too worried about his own abbey. For in the following year he set up a generous live-in pension scheme for William Tyler of Axminster, a university graduate who had been of service to Forde. Tyler was awarded an annuity of £3 6s 8d, a new gown each year made of four yards of broadcloth costing 5s a yard, a furnished room at the abbey and meals with the monks. In return he would teach grammar to the boys in the monastery and, when required, expound the scriptures to the monks at mealtimes.[4]

Once started, Cromwell moved at speed. But at this stage he did not know how far or fast he could go. And indeed, he and the king were now stopped in their tracks by a popular uprising in the north of England. Starting in Lincolnshire in October 1536, and quickly spreading to Yorkshire, the rebellion of an estimated 30,000 people was a protest at the economic and religious policies of the king – or rather of Thomas Cromwell – set alight by the closure of the monasteries. Henry did not have the soldiers to put the rebels down and was obliged to make concessions to their leaders to persuade them to go home. Then he took his revenge, executing some 200 of the ringleaders including a dozen abbots, aristocrats and gentry. The Pilgrimage of Grace, as it was called, was the biggest revolt of the Tudor age.

With that threat removed, Cromwell turned to the bigger prize. Exactly when he decided to go after the remaining monasteries is not known.[5] But now his team of royal visitors set off again round England, threatening and cajoling their abbots in the hope – largely justified – that they would surrender without fuss.

In general, says Knowles, the visitors were 'men of intelligence who made for themselves careers of some distinction and considerable profit' but were also 'grasping, worldly and without a trace of spiritual feeling.' Some were worse than others. Richard Layton, their leader and the only priest on the team, was closest to Thomas Cromwell. Knowles describes him as diligent, witty, unprincipled and salacious. Thomas Legh was seen as cold, gross and humourless; John Price was shrewd and anti-religious; John Tregonwell, from a notable Cornish family, was independent-minded; while Thomas Bedyll, who acted for the king in his divorce of Anne Boleyn, was 'obsequious and repellent.'[6] These men headed the team responsible for closing most of the monasteries – and the big convent of nuns at Shaftesbury – in the south-west. Three of them, William Petre and the brothers Hugh and Richard Pollard, are central to the story.

* * *

Richard Pollard was one of the brightest and most energetic of the royal visitors, a rising star in the Tudor administration and a man of particular interest to us: for his reward at the end of the campaign was Forde Abbey.

What kind of man was he? Let us survey his career to date.

Born in 1505, he was the second son of Sir Lewis Pollard of King's Nympton in north Devon, MP for Totnes and Justice of the Common Pleas (the court handling disputes not involving the monarch). The family was well-connected and Richard's education and natural abilities carried him even further. As a teenager he was sent to study law at the Middle Temple, where he later practised. He came to Cromwell's notice while employed in the household of Sir William Courtenay, a distant cousin and a courtier who kept Cromwell informed about recalcitrant abbots in the west. Pollard was one of the young lawyers consulted on how canon law should be treated after the Act of Supremacy.

In 1535 he made his mark with Henry VIII by acting for the Crown in the successful prosecution of Lord Dacre for tax-avoidance, a test case which resulted in a big rise in the king's revenues.[7] By 1537 he was not only an important member of the *Valor Ecclesiasticus* survey team but a senior member of the Court of Augmentations, the body set up to collect and disburse the gold, silver, jewellery and plate seized from the monasteries. The court was headed by Richard Rich, who had a reputation as the most treacherous man in England – and an enthusiastic torturer. In that year Richard Pollard was busy shutting the smaller monasteries of Kent, Surrey, Sussex and Yorkshire. The following year he and colleagues were stripping the shrines of the saints at Bury St. Edmunds, Winchester and Canterbury.

Pollard's despoliation of Thomas Becket's shrine at Cantebury, the most popular in England, was a spectacular demonstration of his zeal. Working with Thomas Wriothesley and William Petre, he supervised the removal of two huge chests of treasure. The chests were so heavy with pilgrims' offerings they reportedly required six or seven men to lift them. It is hard to tell whether Pollard was motivated by scorn for religion, personal ambition or puritanical disgust. A satirical account of the episode was given by John Husee to the wife of his master, Lord Lisle, governor of Calais:

> 'As touching Mr Pollard, he hath been so busied, both night and day, in prayer, with offering unto St. Thomas' shrine and head, with other dead relics, that he could have no idle worldly time to peruse your ladyship's book for the draft of your ladyship's letters. Howbeit, when his spiritual devotion is past I doubt not he will at one time or another apply his worldly causes accustomed.'[8]

Husee's heavy irony does not leave much room for a more charitable interpretation – that the ambitious young civil servant may have been genuinely torn between private faith and public duty. When clearing out St Swithun's shrine at Winchester at three o'clock in the morning, he claimed that he had swept up all the rotten bones in case it was thought that 'we came more for the treasure than for avoiding of the abomination of idolatry.'

In spite of the warning signs, many abbeys still refused to believe they were in danger. There was no Act of Parliament to authorize their suppression – that was to come in May 1539 as retrospective legislation – and they felt secure enough. Land was fetching high prices, their building programmes were in full swing and their supporters among the local gentry were now closely involved in helping to manage their estates. An ill omen had been the surrender of the big Cluniac priory of Lewes in Sussex back in November 1537, and worrying rumours began to circulate. But even as the royal visitors were heading south-west, the abbot of Forde received a letter from Cromwell written in the king's name and addressed to the heads of all the big houses denying that a general suppression was under way.

The Axe Falls

Led by John Tregonwell and William Petre, the commissioners opened their south-west campaign in the cold and muddy January of 1535. Starting in Wiltshire, they rode down through Somerset to Devon and Cornwall and back again to the Devon-Dorset border, closing no fewer than 40 monasteries on their way. Forde's daughter house of Dunkeswell, north of Honiton, surrendered to Tregonwell in February 1539. The monastery owned nearly 10,000 acres and enjoyed business receipts of about £260 a year. Here, as in the great majority of houses, the abbot and monks gave up without a fight in return for the promise of a pension.

Early in March, assistant commissioner William Petre accompanied by Richard Pollard's older brother Hugh arrived at the gates of Forde Abbey. No account of the visit has survived; but it is unlikely to have been hostile. Thomas Chard, as we have seen, enjoyed a high status among Cistercian abbots and apart from one letter of complaint had done nothing to antagonize Cromwell. No doubt Hugh Pollard cast an appreciative eye over the splendid new buildings which Chard had added. Perhaps he knew the place already, for his younger sister Philippa had married – or was about to marry – Hugh Poulett, recently appointed a steward of the abbey.

Proceedings were probably polite and straightforward. For William Petre and Hugh Pollard it was just another couple of days' work, while the abbot and his monks must by now have been fully prepared for what was to happen. Meeting in the chapter house – today the chapel – Petre presented them with a standard form of surrender, neatly inscribed in Latin in his own flowery hand on parchment.

We have only one brief contemporary note of this pivotal moment in the long history of Forde Abbey, contained in a letter written by Petre and Pollard to Cromwell two days later. But the deed of surrender itself has survived. Signed by the abbot with his seal on behalf of himself, the prior and 11 monks, it declares:

> 'Know ye that we, the Abbot and convent, by our unanimous assent and consent, with our deliberate minds, right knowledge and mere motion, from certain just and reasonable causes especially moving our minds and consciences, have freely and of our own accord given and granted, and by these presents do give, grant, surrender and confirm to our most illustrious prince Henry VIII, by the grace of God King of England, Lord of Ireland, supreme head of the Church of England in this land, all our said Monastery or Abbacy of Ford aforesaid, and also all and singular manors, lordships, messuages.'

There follows a long list of assets, includings mills, serfs and bondsmen, fairs, markets, warrens and fishponds, livings, vicarages, chapels and chantries, tithes and rights owned by the abbey in Devon, Somerset and Dorset or anywhere in England and Wales, conferring on the king the right to use or dispose of them as he wishes. The deed is confirmed and dated 8th March 1539 by William Petre, 'one of the clerks'.[9]

Pensions for the abbot and 13 monks were allotted by the Court of Augmentations. The list was signed by Petre and John Tregonwell. Half of the

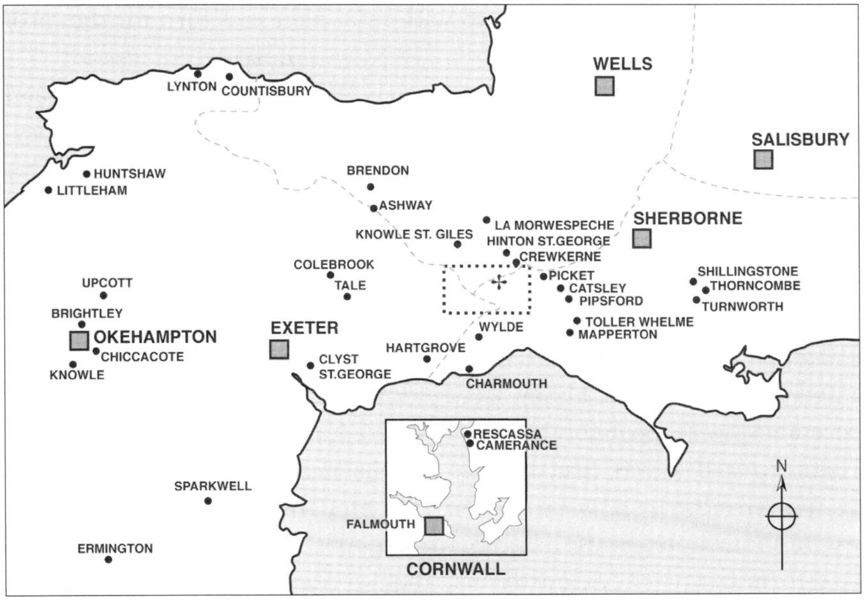

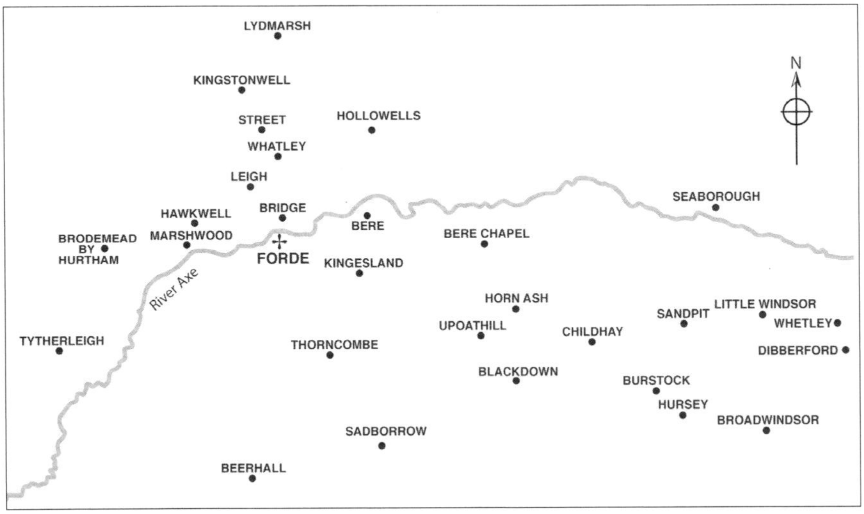

Two maps showing the reach of the Forde estates. By the time of the Dissolution, the abbey controlled some 30,000 acres.

entire annuity for the abbey went to Thomas Chard: £80 a year, and in addition 'forty wain-loads of firewood, to be taken yearly during his life out of such woods being no part of demesnes of the late house.'

The rest was allotted as follows: William Sherneborne (alias Reade), the prior, was awarded £8 a year, as were Richard Exmester (alias Wear) and John

Bridgewater (alias Stone). Robert Ilmester (Rowse) and Ellis Olescum (Potter) got £7; John Cousins £6 13s 4d; John Newman £6; John Fawell, Thomas Stafford (Bate) and William Green £5 6s 8d; William Winsor (Hyde), William Denington (Wilshire) and Richard Kingsbury (Sherman) £5 each. The total came to £161 13s 4d. Nationally, the average pension paid to monks was £5 10s, the annual earnings of an unskilled labourer.[10] Some of the monks found jobs as secular clergy in local parishes, others went to live with relatives or gave up the priesthood for civilian employment. No provision was made for the abbey servants – cooks, maids, cleaners, equerries and tradesmen of various kinds – who must have numbered 50 or more. Pensioners living in the monastery would have been evicted, to find homes where they could.

On 10th March, Hugh Pollard and William Petre wrote to Thomas Cromwell, announcing that they had taken Forde (they had closed the Cistercian abbey of Newenham near Axminster on the same day) and were now at the Cluniac priory of Montacute trying to persuade the obstinate prior to surrender. They suspected this prior of conspiring to frustrate them 'in privy conference' with the equally recalcitrant abbot of Bruton whom they had visited in February. 'Before our coming', they told Cromwell, 'he [the prior] had leased almost all his demesnes to divers persons.'[11]

If Montacute held out, though only for ten days, why did Forde surrender so readily? The short answer is that Thomas Chard had done what he could to protect his house and was left with no real alternative. Thanks to its size and wealth – not to mention Chard's own additions – Forde was just too big a target. The mother house had gone, and the two daughter houses. Devon's richest monastery Buckfast had been shut down a year before. Besides, the abbot was nearly 70 years old, he had been promised a large pension and already had a good berth waiting for his retirement. He went up the hill to become vicar of Thorncombe, the estate upon which his monastery had been founded by Adelicia almost exactly 400 years before. There he died a few years later, in late 1543 or early 1544.

The alternative was to resist, but resistance would have been fatal. In the two years before Forde's dissolution six rebellious abbots had been executed for treason. The previous year a special example was made of Robert Hobbes of Woburn Abbey for doubting the king's supremacy: after execution his dead body was hung from a tree in the abbey grounds. Closer to home, the 78-year-old abbot of Glastonbury was to suffer an even uglier fate. Richard Whiting was head of the last surviving monastery in Somerset, and the richest in England; its 130,000 acres overlapped the Forde estates and its taxable income had been assessed by the *Valor Ecclesiasticus* at nearly £3,000. Whiting said nothing to offend the king or Cromwell – indeed, he sent them presents. But he refused to surrender.

In September 1539 he was confronted by three royal visitors sent by Thomas Cromwell: the priest Richard Layton, Thomas Moyle – and the ubiquitous, indefatigable Richard Pollard. The commissioners accused him of hiding treasures that now belonged to the king. When that had no effect, Whiting was taken up to London and put in the Tower for interrogation by Cromwell himself. Now the charge was treason: among the loads of valuables the commissioners had seized from the abbey was found – so it was said – a book arguing that the now-divorced Catherine of Aragon was the rightful queen of England.

Cromwell, as Lord Privy Seal, ordered that Whiting be tried and executed at Glastonbury; Pollard, Moyle and one other testified for the prosecution. Pollard took the old abbot back to Wells in Somerset, where on 14th November a makeshift court convicted him of robbing his own abbey church. The next day, a Saturday,Whiting with two of his fellow monks, John Thorne and Roger James, was taken back to the monastery and there tied to hurdles and dragged by horses from the abbey gate through the town and up to Glastonbury Tor. Before the sentence was carried out, Pollard pressed the old man again to give him names of other accomplices and and the hiding place of other treasures. Whiting replied that he alone was to blame for any offence to the king. He refused to confess to hiding any gold or silver. According to Pollard in a letter to his master Cromwell the following day he 'asked God's mercy and the kyng for his great offence towards his highness' and 'took his death very patiently.' In an act of barbarity which defies our understanding, the three men were hanged, drawn and dismembered – the execution reserved for traitors. Whiting was decapitated and his head posted over the west gate of his abbey while his arms and legs were distributed for display at Wells, Bath, Ilchester and Bridgwater.

During these unpleasant proceedings, Pollard was collecting his prize for faithful service: Forde Abbey.

Given his strategic role at the heart of the Dissolution, this was not surprising. And Pollard was by no means the first to reap such a reward. Even before the Act of 1536 rumours of a monastic property bonanza had courtiers begging for favours. The above-mentioned Lord Lisle, illegitimate son of Edward IV and governor of Calais, wrote to Cromwell 'beseeching you to help me to some old abbey in mine old days.' Lisle was running out of money and had his eye on Beaulieu, near his Hampshire estates, but it was already spoken for. He looked at Waverley, Forde's mother house. Finally, after meeting Henry VIII and with help from Richard Pollard, he was granted Frithelstock Priory in Devon.

Jane Seymour's sister Elizabeth, about to marry Cromwell's son Gregory, was another who asked for 'one those abbeys, if they go down.' The couple got Launde Priory in Leicestershire which Cromwell had wanted for himself but did not survive to enjoy: he was executed for treason in 1540. The commissioner John Tregonwell was awarded Milton Abbey in Dorset, which he converted into a mansion, turning the church into a private chapel. It is now a school.

By the time Richard Pollard acquired Forde, the abbey church would have had the lead removed from its roof, the roof itself torn off and the stairs hacked away to prevent it ever being used again. Cromwell was afraid of a counter-Reformation. While the monks were packing up their few belongings, all the plate and other valuables would have been sent to the king's treasury. The books in the monastery library, including 29 owned by John of Forde – a collection good enough to be noted by John Leland the antiquary – were sold or destroyed. Everything else, vestments, candlesticks, furniture, gates, locks, even tiles and paving stones would have been auctioned off in the cloister or chapter house. The bells would have been sold separately, though it is possible that one at Forde survived – the small bell on the kitchen roof, cast by the Norwich firm of Brasyer, and carrying an inscription: *Fac Margareta Nobis Nec Numera Leta.* ('Be of help to us, Margaret, and don't count the deaths').

New owners were required to demolish abbey churches within a certain time. As a privileged insider, Richard Pollard may have been able to ignore

The pagoda created with pillars from the vanished abbey church discovered recently in a barn on the estate.

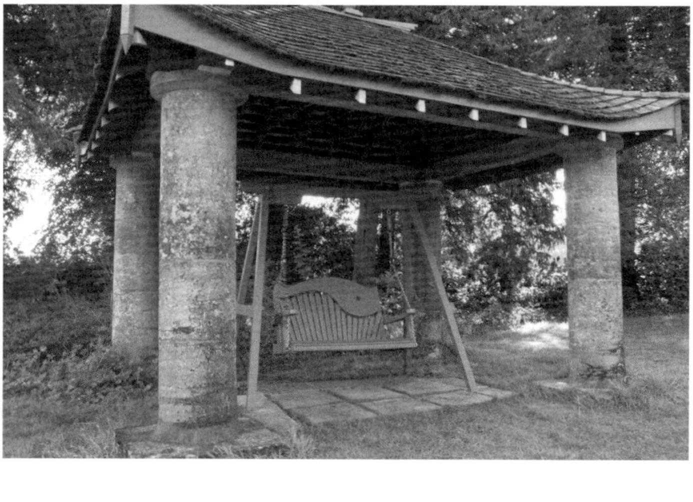

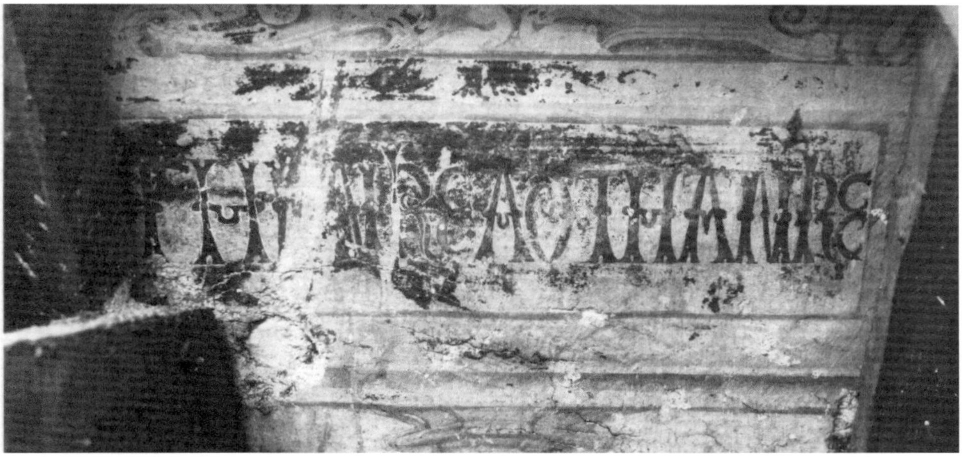

Inscription found, along with other sixteenth-century decorations, behind the plaster on the north wall of the Saloon, in what was once the abbot's office. The letters 'THINREADTHANRE' have been deciphered as '...(wi)thin read then re(pent).'

that requirement. Demolition was not cheap, so the shell of the church may have hired out as an architectural salvage yard. Local farmers could come and buy stone for barns or mills and the poor could pick over what remained. Even the monks' friends did not scruple to take advantage. Asked years later why he had bought timber from a desecrated abbey church, one man said: 'I did see all would away. And therefore I did as others did.' And who can blame him?[12] Much the stone may have been re-used on the house or the estate. Columns thought to have come from Forde abbey church were recently discovered during alterations to a barn at the Home Farm; they now support a pagoda beside the Mermaid Pond. Hamstone pillars were discovered in a cart shed at Chaffeigh, and suspiciously large stone blocks can be seen in ruined cottages along the Synderford River below it.[13]

Pollard's acquisition occurred in three steps. Immediately after the surrender he bought part of the abbey and rented farmland attached to the granges of Orchard and Street and the site of the former chapel of St. Mary Magdalene for £42 17s 10d a year. In October that was converted into a 21-year lease at the same rent. The following May he was allowed to buy from the king these properties, plus woods in Somerset, for £417. The deed of sale was signed by the infamous Richard Rich, head of the Court of Augmentations and later Lord Chancellor.[14] Part of the abbey's Thorncombe estate he acquired later from Sir Richard Williams, a nephew of Thomas Cromwell and great-grandfather of the future Lord Protector, Oliver Cromwell.

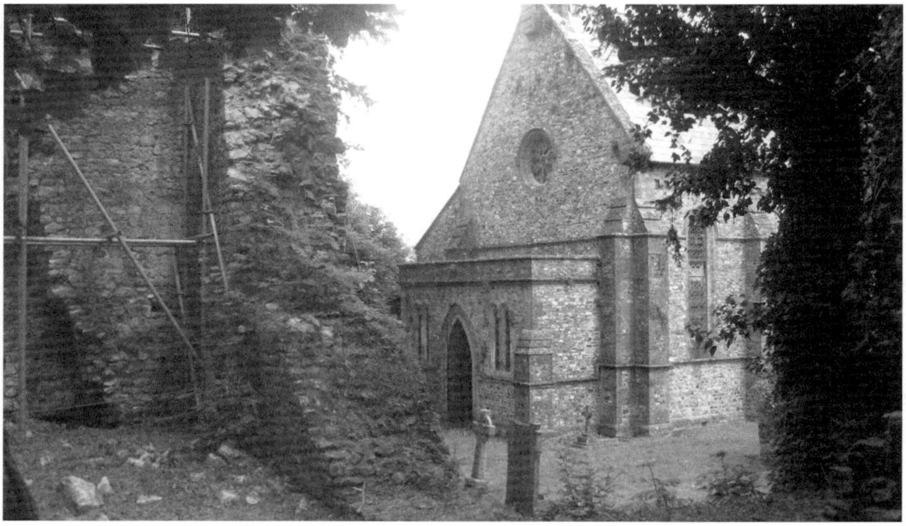

Ruins of the abbot's lodgings at Dunkeswell, daughter house of Forde. The parish church beyond was built on the site of the original abbey church.

More distant parts of the Forde property empire including estates in Exeter, mid Devon and at Lynton and Countisbury on the north Devon coast, were also distributed. The estate of Dunkeswell, closed a month before Forde, went to the most powerful man in the south-west, the baron John Russell (later 1st Earl of Bedford). Its abbey was quickly demolished; all that remains is part of the gatehouse, an end wall of the cellarer's range on the west side of the cloister and some masonry incorporated into the early Victorian parish church which was built on the site of the old church. Russell was head of the Council of the South-West, the king's minister for the region, and responsible for putting down the so-called Prayer Book Rebellion ten years later. One of his first appointees to the Council was none other than Richard Pollard, the new master of Forde.

The Impact and the Verdict

Although the field labourers in the Axe valley could no longer hear the sound of bells as they worked, things appeared to go on much the same. The change of owner – an absentee landlord replacing a remote abbot – would hardly have been noticed by most of the tenant farmers. Because monastery ownership had become what Knowles described as 'an affair of parchment only' the tenant found himself dealing with the same bailiff as before. All but the most recent leases were honoured: so William Tyler the university graduate got his pension (though it was reduced to £3). Local villagers were able to take back ownership of parish churches which had been donated to the abbey or 'appropriated', like Thorncombe's, by the monks. The hamlet of Burstock whose priests had been supplied by the abbey since 1226 was not so lucky: it lost its current priest John Higgen, and there was no replacement for over 120 years, while the church fell into disrepair.

New landlords – especially those who had bought estates as a speculation – were more aggressive than the monastery ever was. The population was rising, and prices too; the local economy was booming. Keen to make the best of it the new men raised rents, took back manorial lands, enclosed common land and turned villagers' plots into pasture for sheep or cattle. Smallholders deprived of their livelihood sold themselves for hire as day-labourers, begged in the towns or joined the vagrants that swarmed over the countryside. Such exploitation was not new – the monasteries had been guilty of it too. But now there were no monasteries to hand out soup and bread to the hungry each week. The law forced 'sturdy' beggars into work and criminalized vagrants, until gradually over the next 50 years a system of parish relief was developed.[15]

The destruction of the monasteries in the south-west caused no general outcry at the time. But the introduction of the Book of Common Prayer ten years later under the boy-king Edward VI provoked a serious rebellion. The trouble began in June 1549 at Sampford Courtenay, Devon, where parishioners refused to allow the priest to use the new service or discard his vestments. They also demanded the return of abbey lands. The protest spread and a number of local magnates, including Sir Thomas Pomeroy and Sir Humphrey Arundell, led 10,000 armed rebels in a month-long siege of Exeter. The siege was lifted by Lord Russell who, short of militiamen, was forced to employ German and Italian mercenaries to help defeat the rebels at nearby Woodbury. His army then ravaged the countryside, burning villages and killing an estimated 4,000 people until the rebellion fizzled out at Plymouth in August.[16] There were more than 850 monasteries, convents and friaries in England before the Dissolution. By 1541 there were none (although five abbeys were saved to become cathedrals). The biggest revolution in the English property market since the Norman conquest saw four million acres of land change hands, more than a fifth of the country's cultivated terrain. Some 7,000 monks and nuns were evicted (there were 15,000 before 1536) and perhaps five times that number of servants. What began as a tax-raising measure turned into wholesale expropriation by the Crown. A campaign justified as religious reform, a war on monastic greed and vice, was itself motivated almost entirely by money. Instances of clerical immorality were gleefully highlighted. But the records show that vice was far less common than critics claimed.

Was the Dissolution a Good Thing? It is one of the best documented and most studied periods of English history, and professional opinion is still divided. Dissolution brought to an end a totally inappropriate regime in which dwindling numbers of monastics were running ever larger agribusinesses. The monasteries were not greedy. But they were unnecessarily rich, and the luxurious lifestyle of some abbots – the hunting, the wining and dining – was egregious. The monks' various roles, as spiritual counsellers, social workers, scholars, teachers and lawyers, had been taken up by others. Henry's wholesale confiscation was barely legal and clearly unjust; but it may have been inevitable.

The forced liquidation of monastic estates provided a social and economic stimulus as well as funds for the crown. About half the estates seized were sold off within a few years, and a new class of small landowners and farmers was created. On the other hand, little was done – and that not quickly enough – to help the poor and jobless. A few hospitals, grammar schools and splendid university colleges were built, but many equally splendid libraries had been scattered and their precious books destroyed. Some of the greatest buildings in England were reduced to mournful, if picturesque, ruins. Very few of them were to rise again from the ashes. Forde Abbey was a rare exception.

* * *

The first secular owner of Forde had used his wit to navigate the corrupt and despotic court of Henry VIII, and his career at the Court of Augmentations to make a fortune in property. Described as one of the outstanding civil servants of his time, Richard Pollard the lawyer became a justice of the peace, three times member of Parliament and Sheriff of Devon. He survived the disgrace and execution of his boss Cromwell to be knighted in 1542. But he did not enjoy his wealth and position for long. That same year he died, still in his forties.

How much time, if any, Pollard spent at Forde Abbey is not known. In his will he left to his eldest son John 'all my stuff of household, harness, bows and bills that shall happen to be at my house of Forde in the said county of Devonshire at the time of my decease (money and plate only excepted)...' But what of the house itself? Certainly it must have been maintained, but there is no record of his son – who was a minor – living in it. Pollard's other properties he left to his wife Jacquetta Bury who survived him by only three years: these were his estate at Combe Martin in north Devon and most of his 'stuff of household' in

London and Putney. His two younger sons got the estate of Merley in Dorset. A telling final gesture was his gift of a gold salt-cellar to his boss at the Court of Augmentations, Sir Richard Rich. After his death the Thorncombe estate formerly attached to Forde, along with its rectory and the rent from the living of the church, was divided. Part went to the king, part was leased to the Earl of Oxford, distantly connected to the Courtenay family.

John Pollard was about 14 years old when his father died. He was put under the protection first of his uncles Hugh Pollard and Hugh Poulett, then of Lord Russell until he was allowed to inherit in 1553. Russell, now Earl of Bedford, helped him to a knighthood and sponsored him as MP first for Plympton, then Barnstaple. In the Parliament of 1554 he was elected to Exeter and found himself sitting under a Speaker with the same name – for whom, it is said, he made life difficult.

Pollard's greatest distinction was his detention in the Tower of London for eight months in 1556, when he was indicted for his part in the failed attempt to put Lady Jane Grey on the throne instead of the Catholic Mary. He was released to join a campaign against the French in 1557, and pardoned early the following year. Either because of his arrest, or because he needed money to repay his debts, John Pollard sold Forde Abbey about this time.

The buyer has always been identified as Amias Poulett of Hinton St. George, Pollard's first cousin, near neighbour and son of Hugh who was steward of Forde before the Dissolution. But the truth is proabably more complicated. Amias may have only held the estate in trust. Meanwile John went to live at Trelawne in Cornwall; and although he was returned to Parliament under Queen Elizabeth he took little further part in public life and died in 1575.

* * *

The Poulett family (pronounced and formerly spelled 'Paulet') had strong connections with the Abbey. They lived only a few miles away and had been involved in its affairs for years as benefactors and stewards: the last abbot had the Poulett coat-of-arms engraved in stone on a shield outside the cloister. But the young Amias, born in 1532, cannot have been much involved. When he took charge of the estate he was in Jersey serving as lieutenant-governor of the island under his father. For the next 20 years he was mainly occupied in France, latterly as Queen Elizabeth's ambassador to Paris. His time in England was probably spent in London or at the family mansion at Hinton St George. A detailed history of the Poulett family makes only the briefest mentions of Forde Abbey.[17]

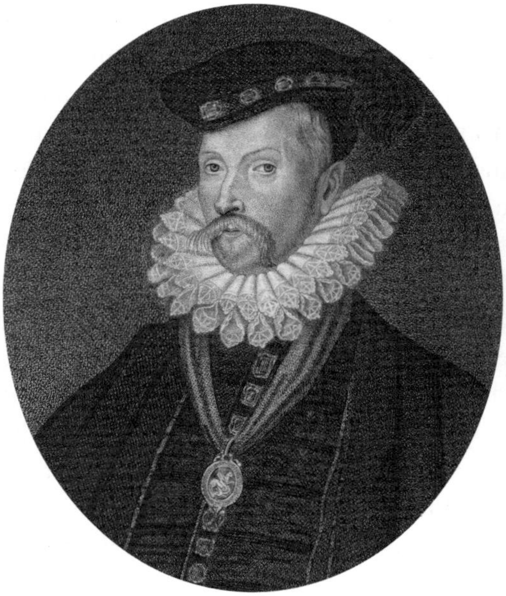

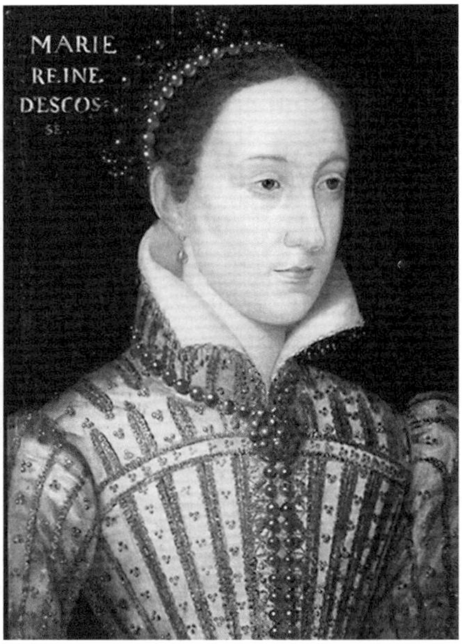

Above left: Sir Amias Poulett, a local magnate who held Forde Abbey in trust and became Mary Queen of Scots' jailer.

Above right: Mary Queen of Scots reputedly thanked Amias Poulett for his trouble as she was beheaded in 1587. The last house in which he had imprisoned her was later bought by a family connected to the present owners of Forde.

The Pouletts were big landowners in the south-west, and staunch Protestants. As 'knight-marshal' of Lord Russell's mercenary army, Amias's father had helped put down the Prayer Book Rebellion in 1549. His son Sir Amias is described as 'a high-principled Puritan'. He succeeded his father as governor of Jersey (where one of his staff was the young Francis Bacon), became MP for Somerset and a leading figure in Elizabethan politics. But his greatest claim to fame was his role as the last jailer of Mary Queen of Scots.

Amias left France in 1579 and was anxious to find a new job. He wrote to Queen Elizabeth's minister Walsingham: 'I am Jack-out-of-office, I thank God for it.' Nothing interesting turned up until the beginning of 1585 when out of the blue he was summoned to take over as Mary's 'guardian'. Amias was delighted. He had written many letters to the Queen warning her that Mary was a danger to the throne, and saw his appointment as God-given. He promised to be a strict jailer.

Mary was at this time under house arrest at Tutbury Castle in Staffordshire. Poulett cancelled her rides in the park, had all her letters read and the laundry baskets examined for secret messages. He burned her rosary and prayer cards. Tutbury was cold and damp and Mary was sickening, but her jailer seemed more worried about his gout – the pain of which may explain his vindictive behaviour.

He decided to move to a pleasanter and more secure house. In the autum of 1585 he found Chartley, a Tudor mansion 12 miles away belonging to Robert Devereux, Earl of Essex and built in the grounds of a ruined Norman keep. The mansion had a moat, which was good for defence and meant that Mary's maids could do her washing without having to leave the house. Poulett now devised a trap for his prisoner. The local brewer was a renegade Catholic and was paid by both sides to smuggle letters to and fro inside beer barrels. After a year at Chartley, Mary was arrested and taken to the fortress of Fotheringay in Northamptonshire. Paulett refused Walsingham's demand that he and his assistant should be responsible for executing their prisoner, saying that his conscience would not allow him to commit murder. But he was present when Mary was beheaded on 8th February 1587. According to an account attributed to Poulett himself, Mary turned to him as she knelt to the block and said: 'Thanks, Sir Amias. This will be the last trouble I shall give you.'

The jailer did not long survive his royal captive. Rewarded with various honours he died the following year at the age of 56, leaving no fewer than fourteen manors in Somerset, four in Devon and a large house in Clerkenwell. He was buried at St. Martin-in-the-Fields, and re-interred at Hinton St. George.

More than 300 years later, in 1904, by one of those coincidences which occur so frequently in history, the house at Chartley was bought by the Congreves of Staffordshire, a family related by marriage to the Ropers who inherited Forde at almost exactly the same time.[18]

The Rosewell Succession

Like many properties after the Dissolution, Forde had become a trophy asset, which explains its many changes of owner in the first 40 years. The conventional account is that Amias Poulett, having bought the house from John Pollard, sold it to William Rosewell, Queen Elizabeth's solicitor-general. But the dates don't allow this. It is more probable that Pollard junior sold Forde directly to William Rosewell in around 1556, and that Rosewell bequeathed it to his infant son, another William, but left it meanwhile in trust to Amias Poulett.

Rosewell, a lawyer like so many of his contemporaries, was Solicitor-General from February 1559 until his death in 1566. The family came from Loxton near Weston-super-Mare in north Somerset. Not much else is recorded of him.[19] With the help of his wife, a rich widow called Elizabeth Isham, he bought a large number of estates from people who had grabbed them at the Dissolution, and his will conferred these properties in trust to a number of friends, including 'Amice Pawlett'. His second son William was only five when his father died, and it seems he had to wait until he was about 20 before Amias Poulett was able to hand over to him the Forde estate – and presumably the house also – in 1580-1. The transaction was made a few years before Poulett was put in charge of the captive Mary Queen of Scots.

The Rosewells seemed destined to die young. The Solicitor-General was still in his mid-forties when he died in 1566. His first son Parry had died in his teens and his heir William was to die in his early thirties. (His daughter Philippa married a Speke of Whitelackington, a family of which we shall hear more). Young William married Anne Walkden and had settled Forde and its estates on her until their son Henry should come of age. With Henry's succession, the house seemed to have found stability at last: the heir lived to be 66.

But Henry Rosewell's career was blighted by lawsuits and rash investments in North American colonies. After Oxford University he studied at the Middle Temple and was knighted by King James I in about 1618. He married Mary Drake of the prominent Devon family which had produced Sir Francis Drake, round-the-world sailor and harrier of the Spanish fleet. The union was to produce no children but a good deal of legal trouble for Henry after his wife's death in 1643.

As a prominent local man (he was Sheriff of Devon in 1629-30) Henry was invited to join investors in the Massachusetts Bay Company to found a colony in New England. Some of these investors – it is not clear if Henry was among them – had been involved with the venture's predecessor, the Dorchester Company, which had collapsed after the failure of its colony at Cape Ann. The new settlement was successful, however, and about 20,000 Puritans crossed the Atlantic to start a new life in Massachusetts Bay. There may have been other ventures: there is a Rosewell Bay in Nova Scotia.

Henry's Puritan loyalties were to bring him trouble of a different kind. In 1634 a legal action was started against him by a Fleet Street haberdasher called Roger James who, motivated by some obscure feeling of outrage, had him charged with 'refusal to attend his parish church of Thorncombe, and for having a private chapel in his house to which others, not of his family, sometimes to the number of 20 or 30, have been known to resort.'

In other words, he was holding Puritan church services at home. When the case was finally decided, Henry was fined £100 with costs. For years he seems to have resisted paying these, because in 1640 an order was issued for his detention 'in safe custody' until he did so. Hard on the heels of this affair came a more

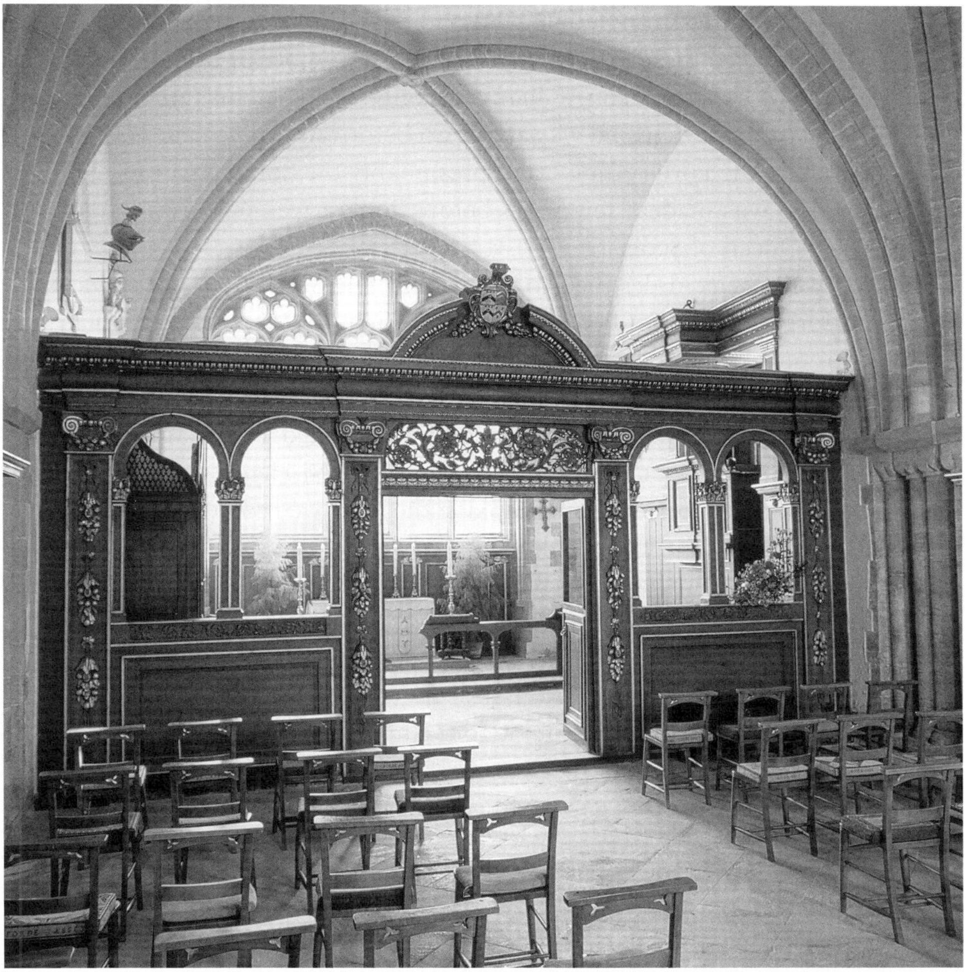

The Chapel, formerly the monastery chapter house. Henry Rosewell, the first of a succession of Puritan owners, was prosecuted for attending services there rather than in Thorncombe parish church.

vexing series of cases. Henry was an executor of his wife's brother Sir John Drake, and from 1641 was beset with suits in Chancery brought by Drake's daughters claiming they had not received their 'portions'.

Meanwhile the country was descending into civil war as a result of Charles I's illegal taxation of shipping and seaports and mishandling of a divided Parliament. Most of the landed gentry of the south-west were Royalists – though Somerset was evenly balanced – but Puritan sentiment was strong and there were militant pockets of Parliamentarian support at Lyme Regis which was besieged by the

King's troops in 1644, at Poole, Dorchester, Exeter and Plymouth. Sympathisers like the Rosewells were under pressure to play their part. Henry seems to have been reluctant to raise troops at first; but by 1640 there is a record of 'Sir Henry Rosewell's Regiment of the East Division of Devon', under the captaincy of William Fry.

What part Rosewell played in the subsequent skirmishing is not known. But at some point during the last phase of the war he must have decided he could no longer bear the pressure nor afford to maintain his house. In 1649, within months of the defeat, capture and execution of King Charles I, Henry sold Forde Abbey to a rising star of the new Commonwealth, Edmund Prideaux. He retired to Lymington in Hampshire then to Churston Ferrers near Brixham, where he was buried in 1656.

Better known for his troubles than his triumphs, Rosewell managed to leave a footnote in literary history as 'Sir Hudibras', the Quixotic hero of Samuel Butler's satirical poem which mocked Puritans, Presbyterians and other Roundheads and was a bestseller after the Restoration. Butler told a friend that his model was a West Country knight whom he had met at lodgings in Holborn.

Frances James concluded her 1888 monograph on Henry Rosewell with these words:

> The vast estates obtained by his grandfather seem to have borne the curse of ill-gotten gains snatched from the hands of the Church. The property had been partly wasted by William Rosewell, his father; and Sir Henry was obliged to part with more; lost probably in aiding his Parliamentarian friends, in unsuccessful ventures in America, while most likely a vast amount of it was spent in the Chancery proceedings in which he became involved, through, in an evil day, his having accepted the burdensome trust laid upon him by Sir John Drake.

Fate is often unkind. Henry Rosewell's misfortune was to bring nothing but good fortune to Forde Abbey, as we shall see in the next chapter.

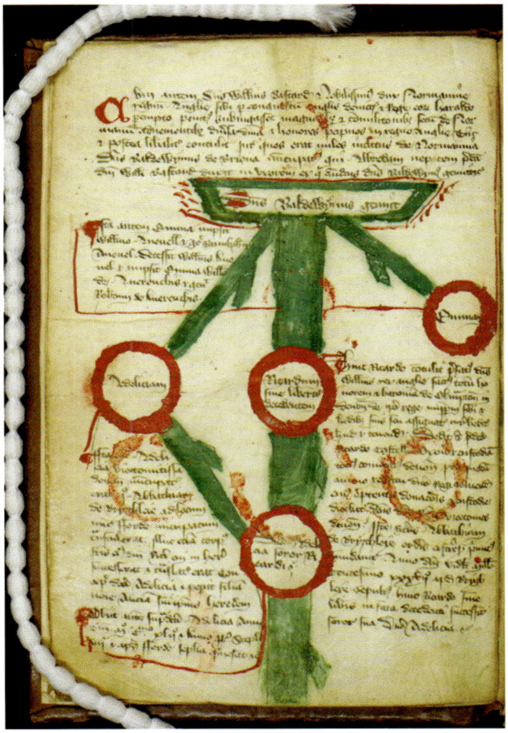

A mediaeval family tree of Adelicia's family, the de Brionnes, written in Latin. It reads (*from top*): 'The lord Baldwin begat'; (*below, left to right*), 'Adelicia', 'Richard, who died without children', and 'Emma'. Adelicia appears again at the foot of the tree as 'The lady Adelicia, sister of Richard'.

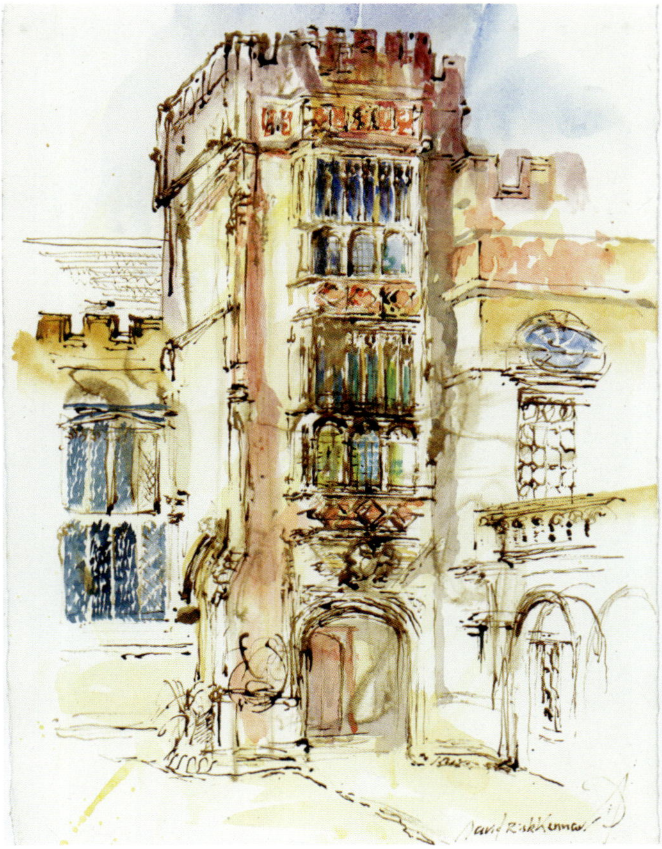

Above: The Chard Tower, watercolour by David Risk Kennard.

Below: The monks dorter from the kitchen garden.

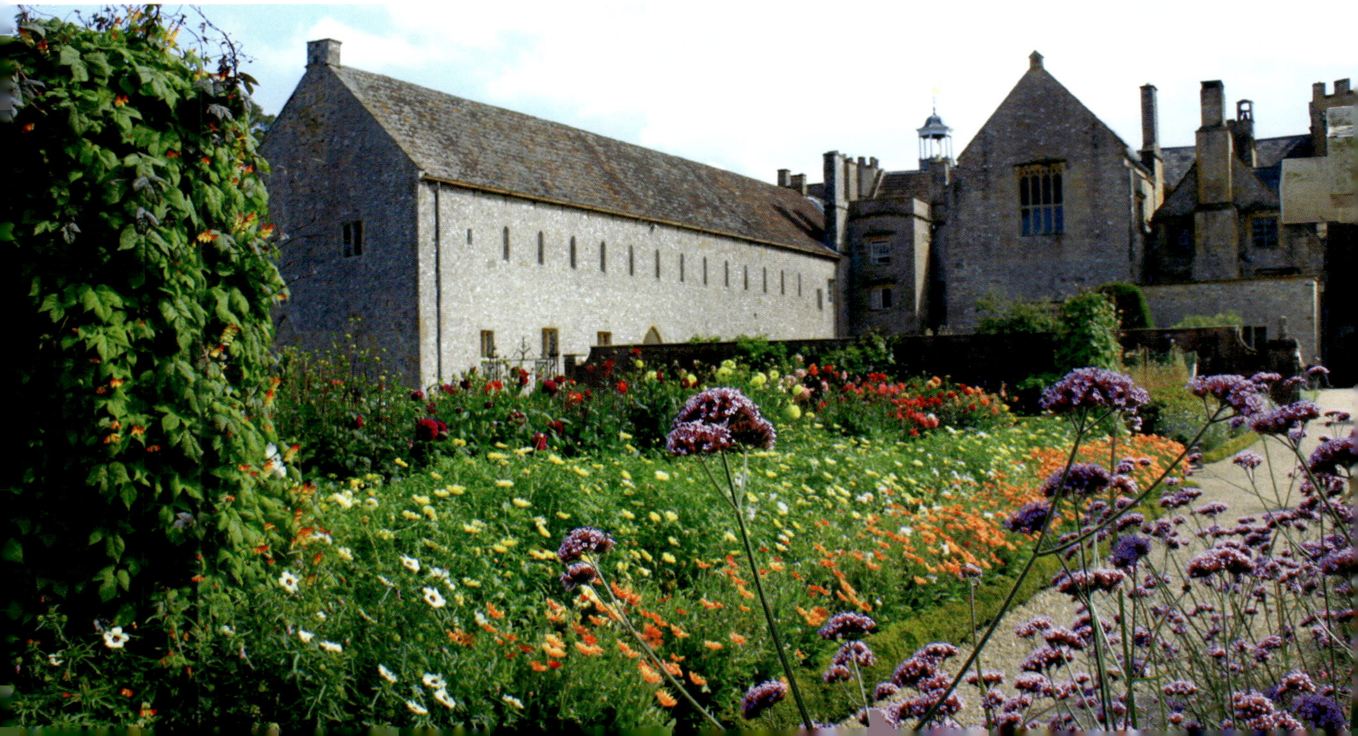

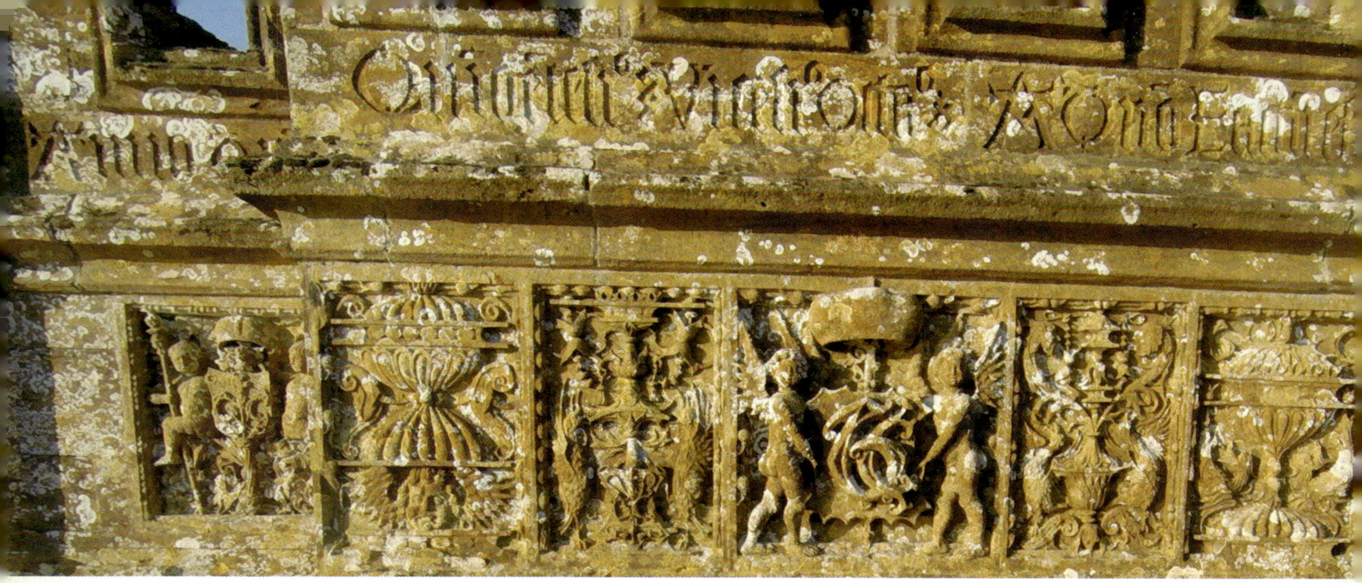

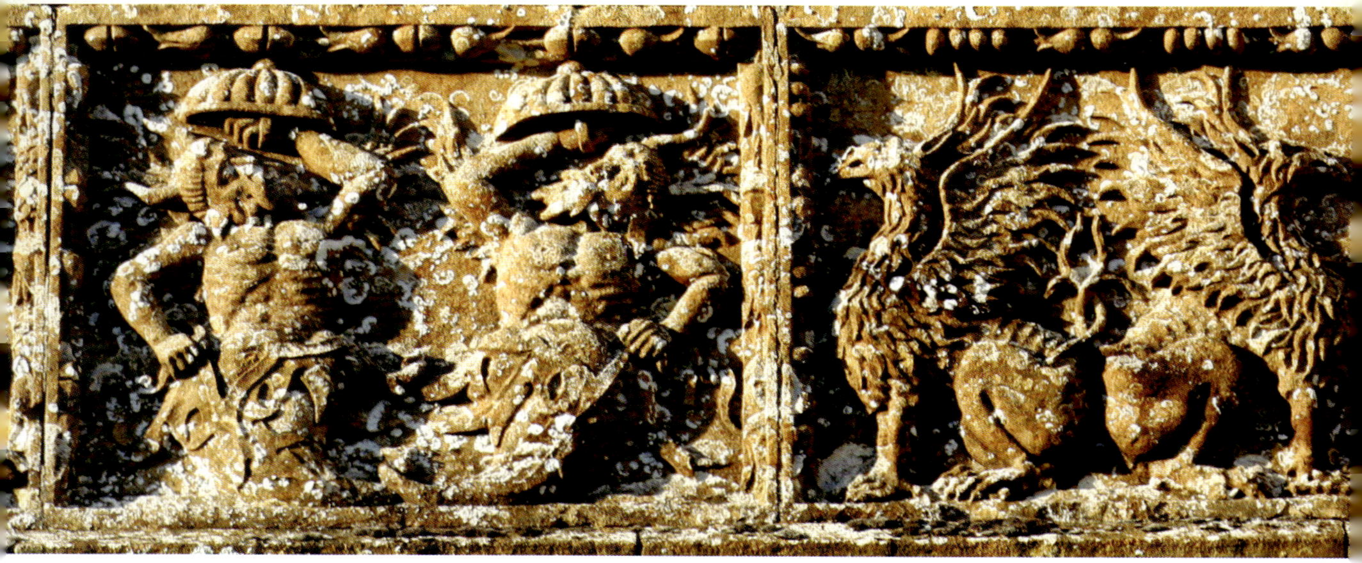

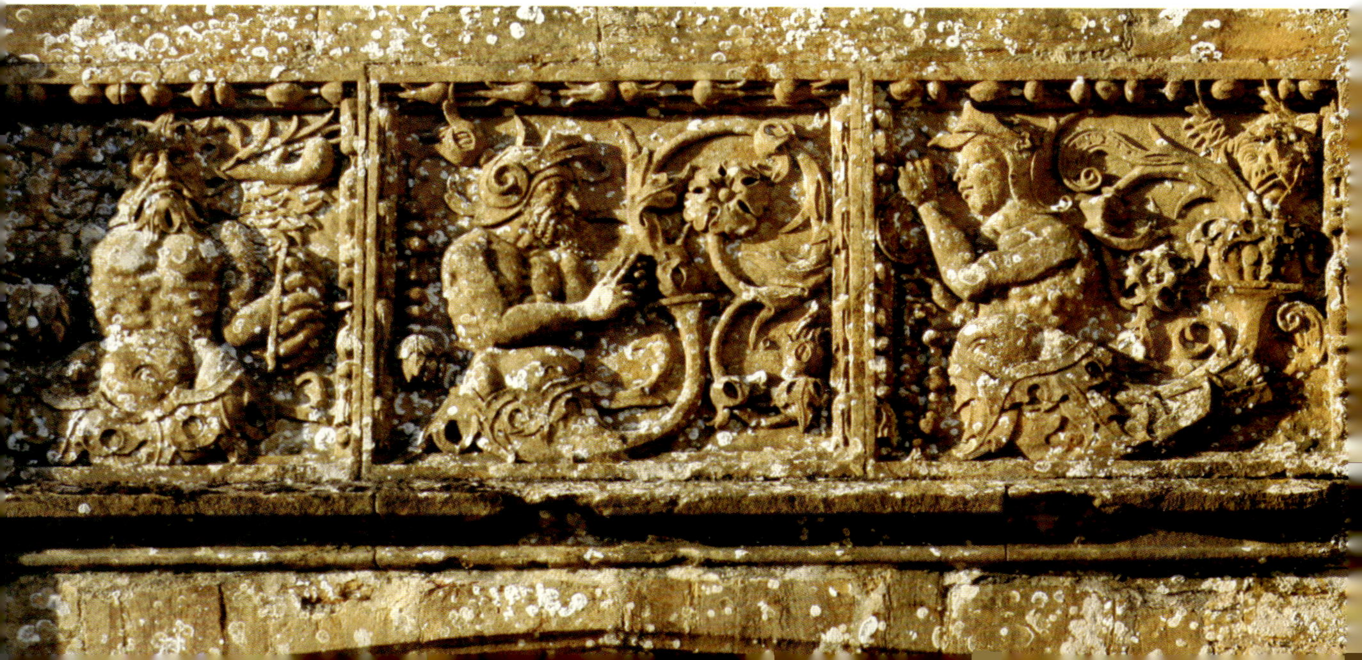

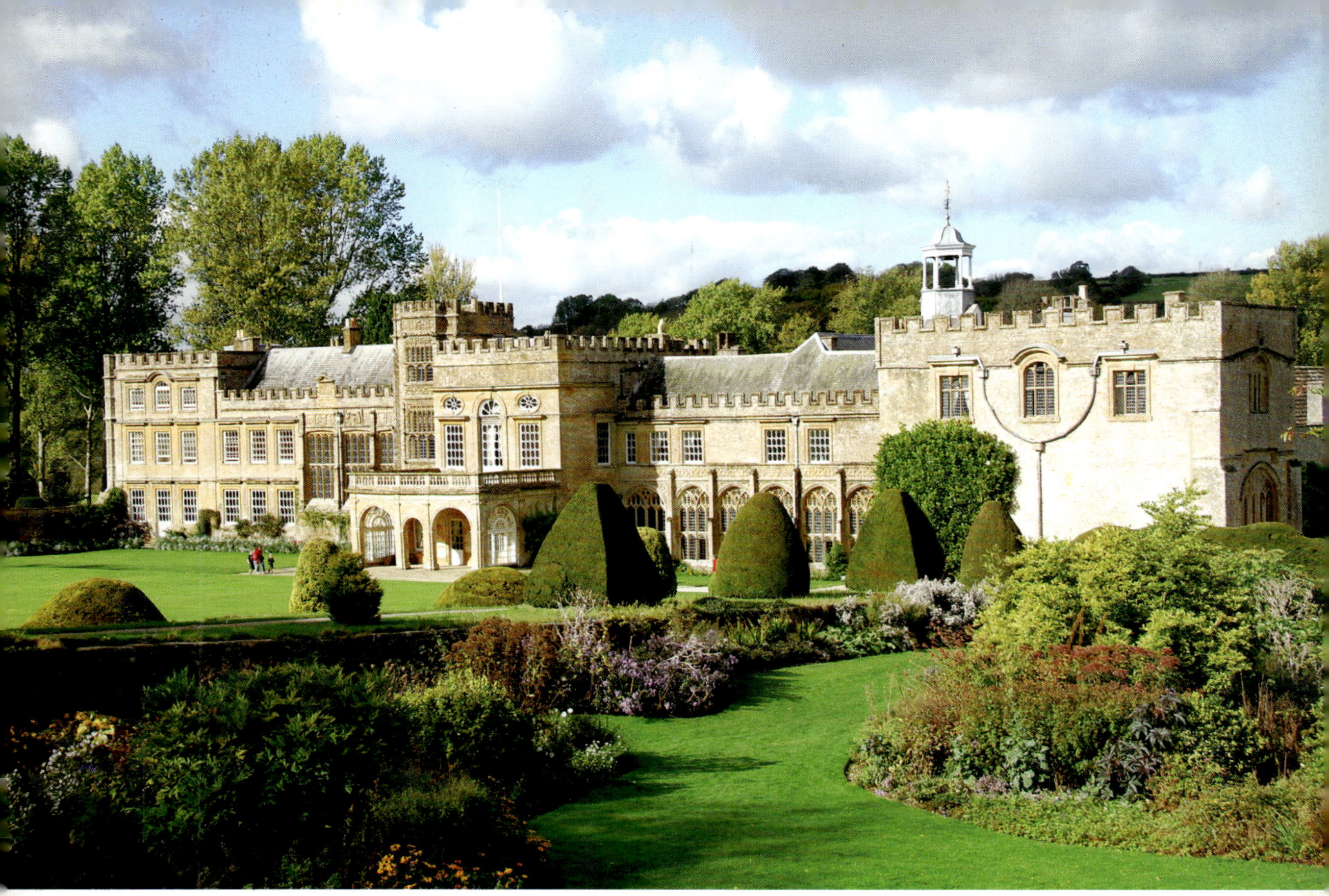

Opposite page: Three photographs of the decorative frieze at the top of the Chard Tower and the south face of the abbey.

Above: Forde Abbey from the south-east, showing Prideaux's reduction of the Great Hall, his Saloon over a classical portico, and state rooms above the remaining range of the cloister.

Right: Edmund Prideaux the elder, Cromwell's attorney-general, whose fortune saved and enhanced the abbey

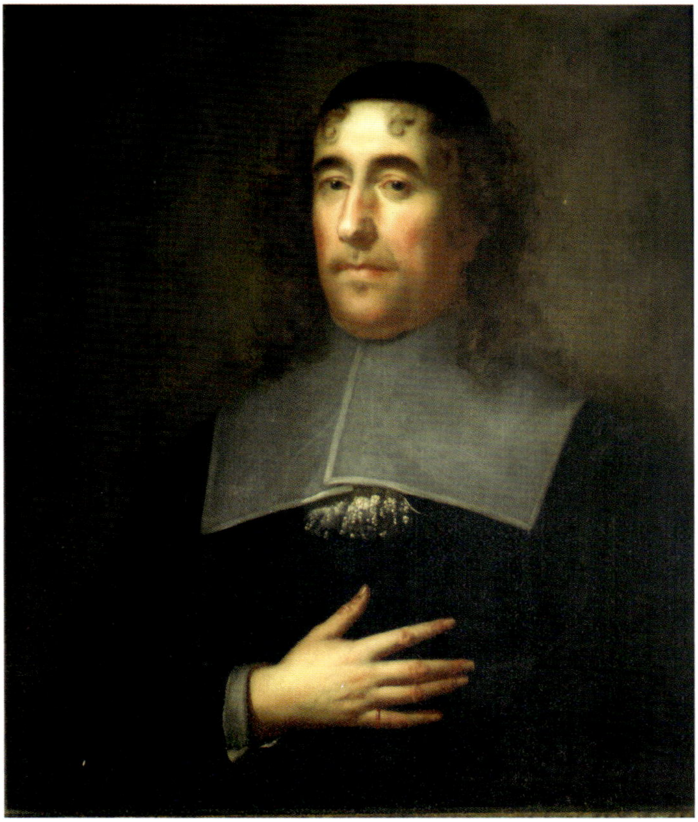

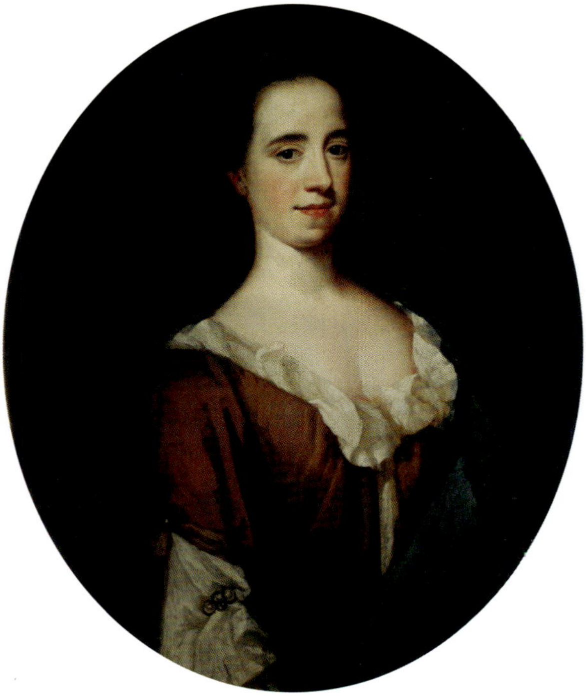

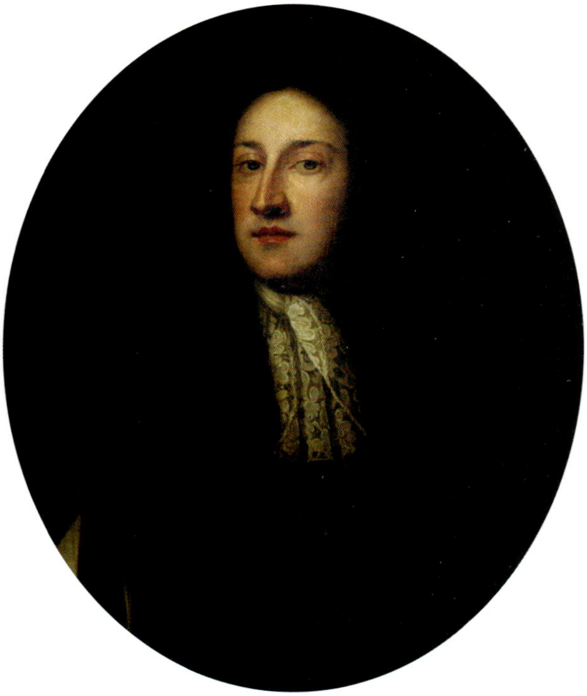

Above: Amy Fraunceis Prideaux and her husband Edmund Prideaux the younger. Amy saved him from imprisonment in the Tower of London.

Below: The Saloon where the Raphael tapestries from Mortlake hang.

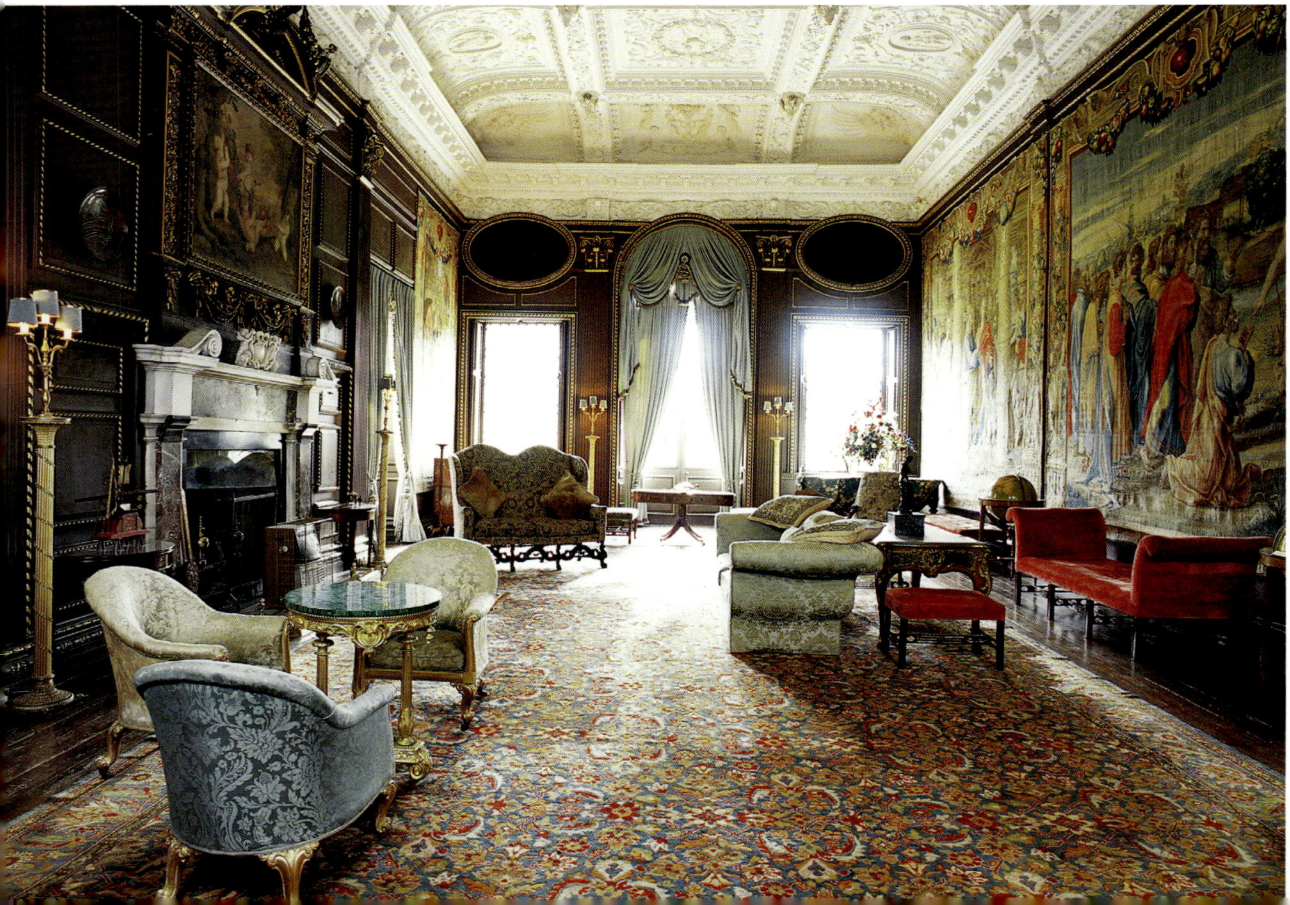

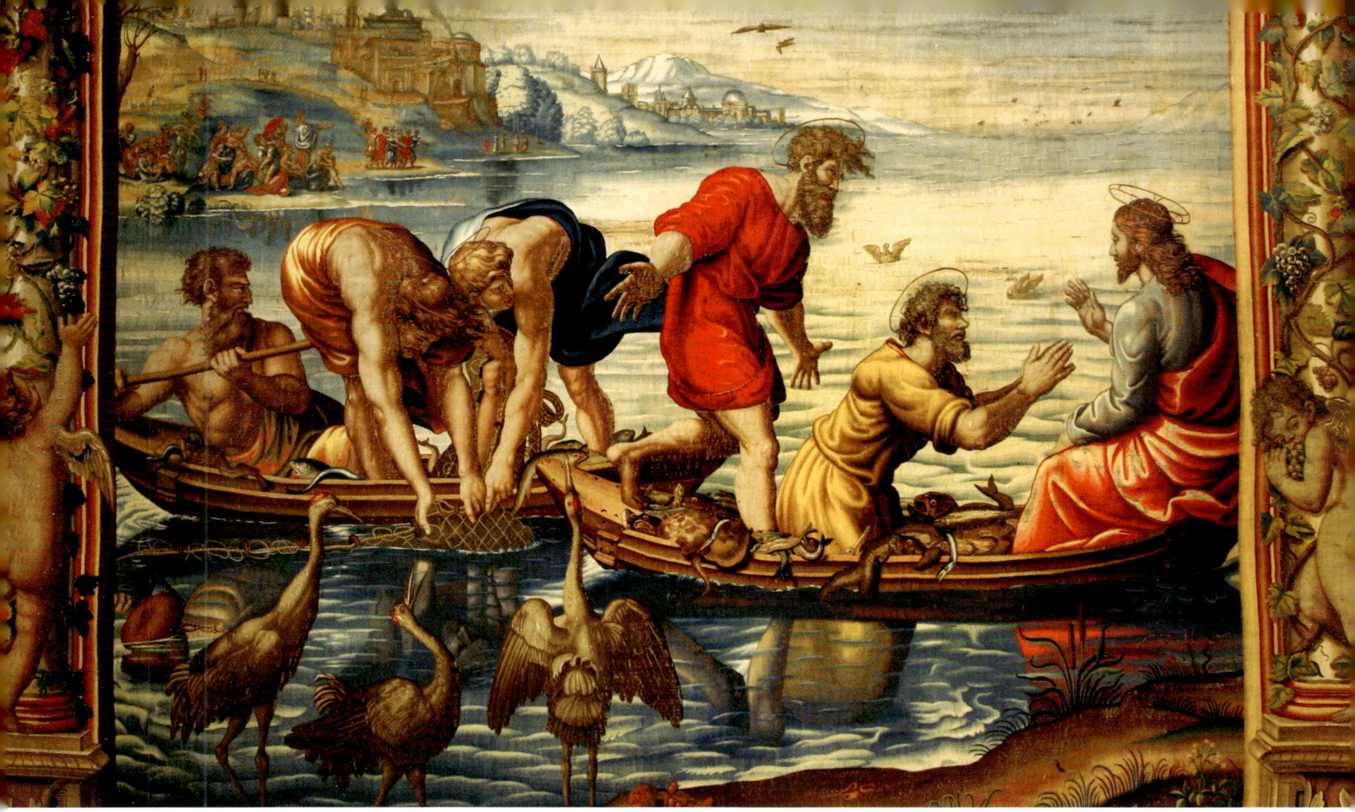

Details from two of the Mortlake tapestries. *Above:* 'The Miraculous Draught of Fishes': St. Peter kneeling, St. Andrew standing, and Ss. James and John hauling the net.

Below: 'Christ's Charge to St. Peter' who kneels with the other Apostles behind him.

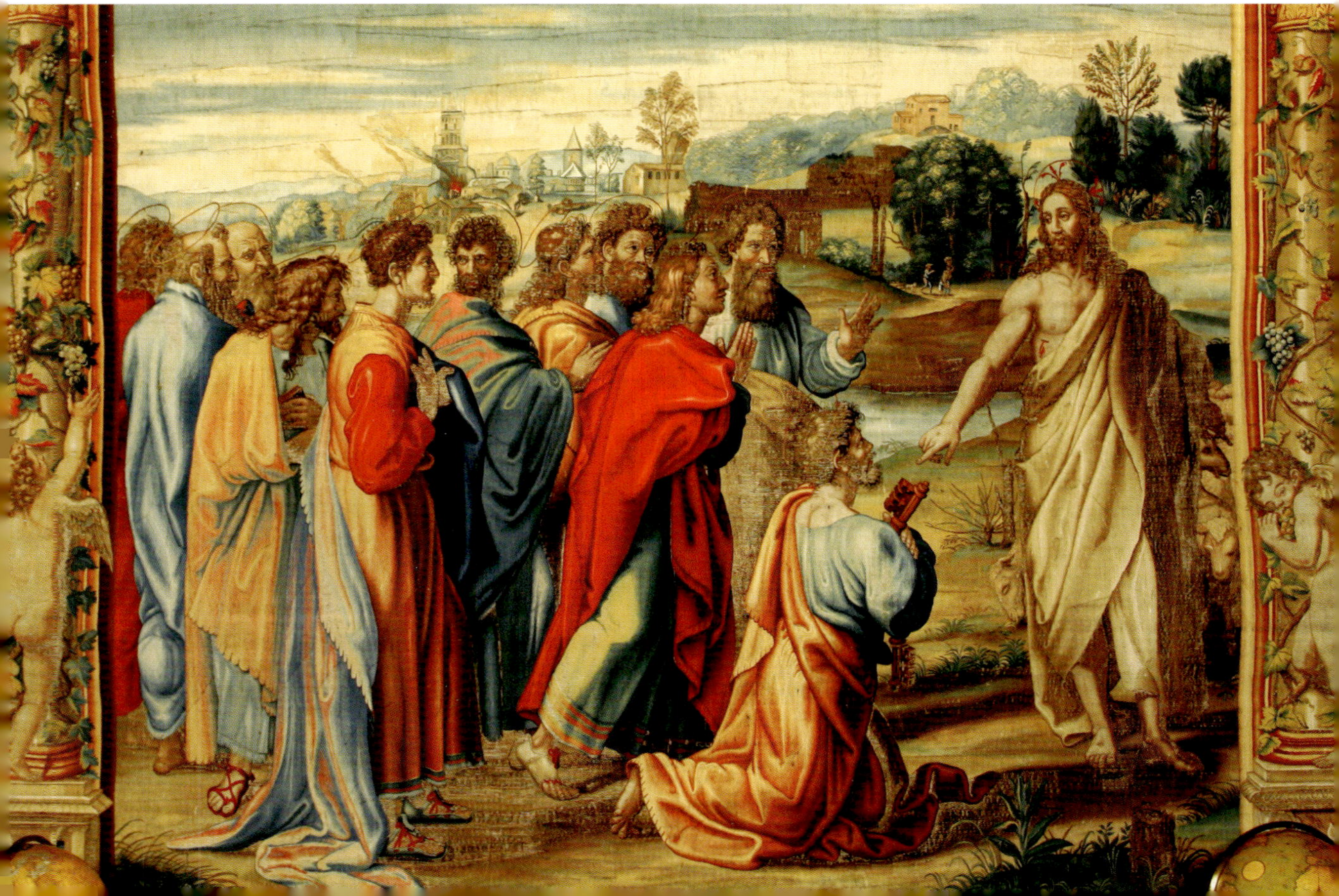

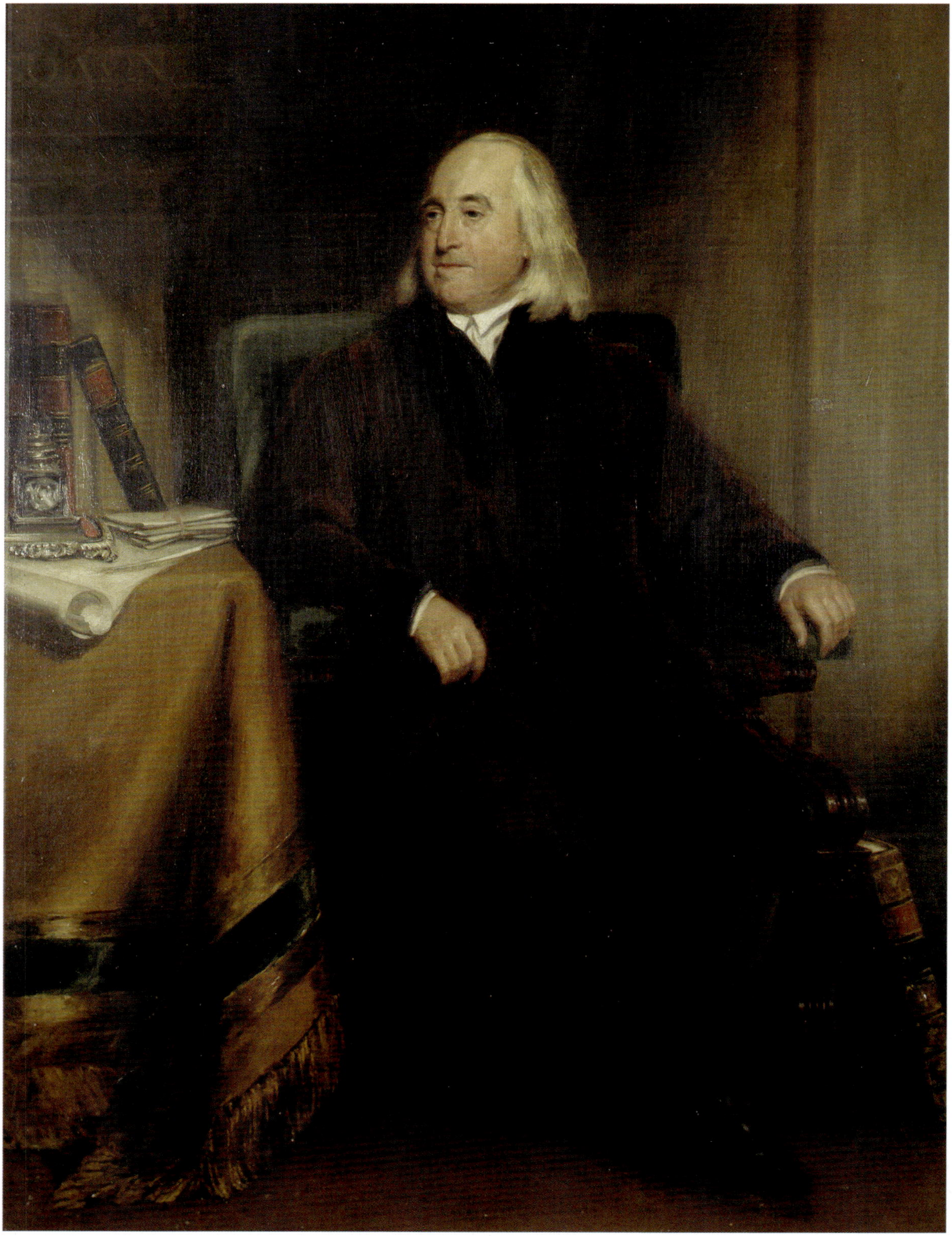

Jeremy Bentham, by Henry Pickersgill. The radical philosopher was tenant of the abbey for four years. He kept fit and covered 15 pages of manuscript every day.

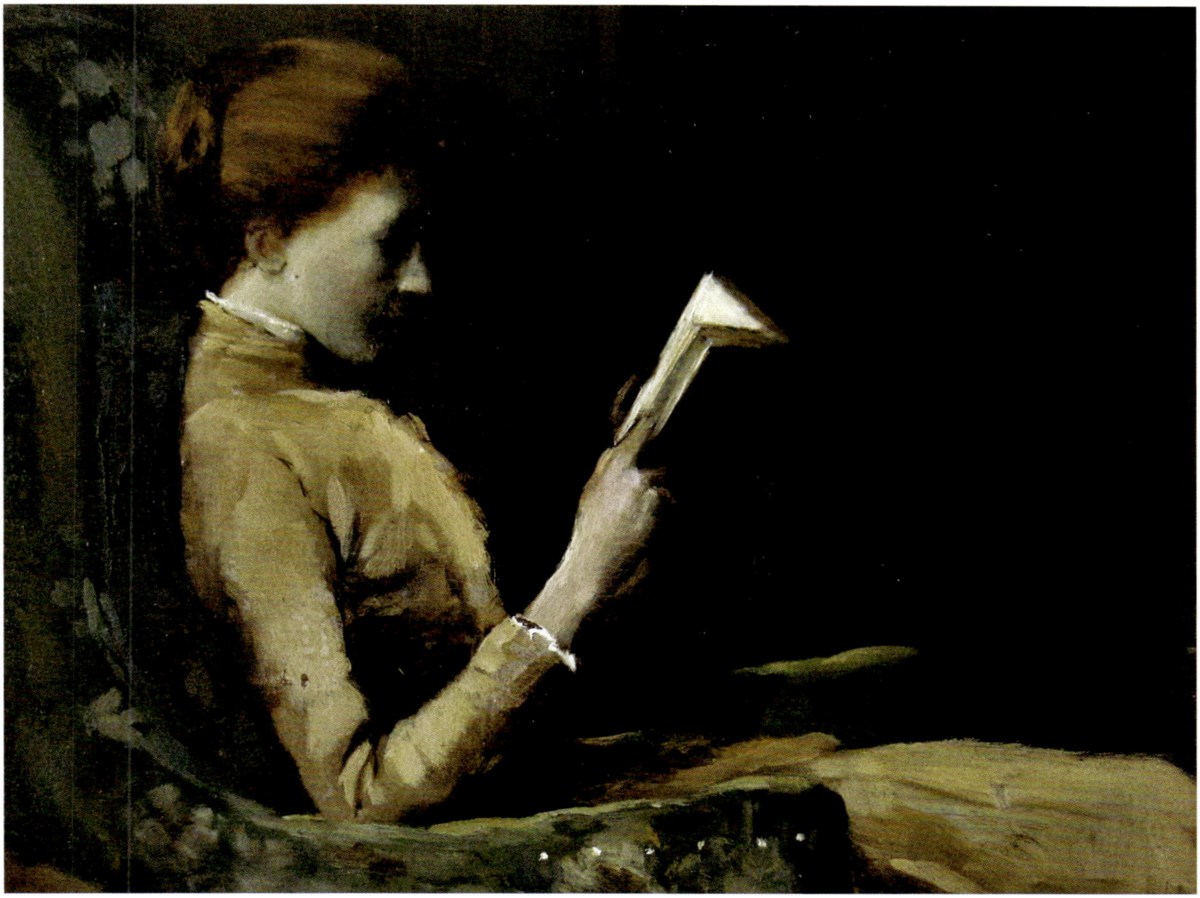

Above: Portrait of Elsie Fitzgerald, who inherited Forde and married Freeman Roper.

Right: Four-poster bed in the Crewel Room. The hangings were designed by Elsie and carried out by her son Geoffrey and daughter Kate.

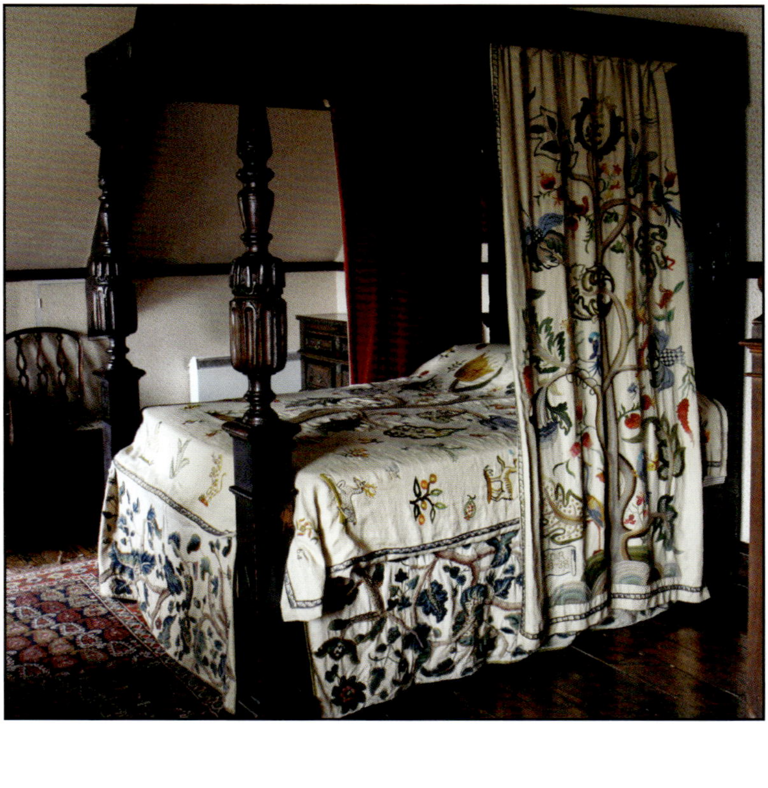

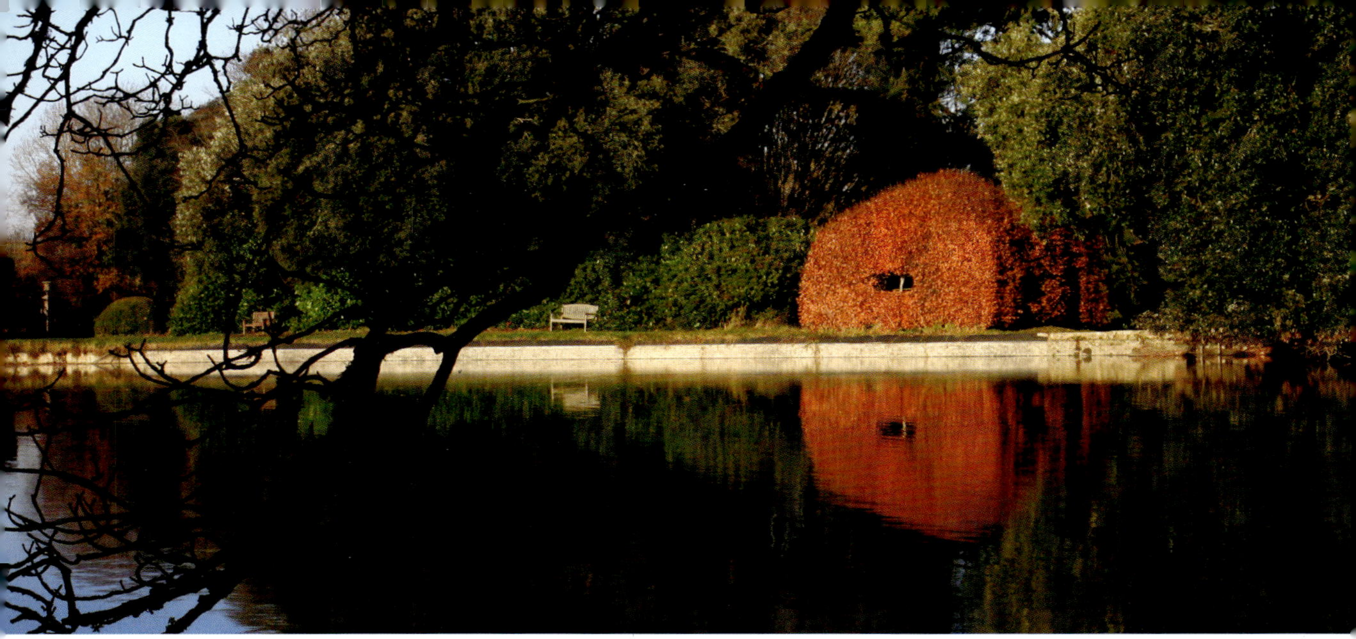

Above: The beech house on the Great Pond planted by Geoffrey at the birth of his first son, Mark.

Right: The Bog Garden, with Japanese bridge.

Below: Lisa Roper's herd of Devons.

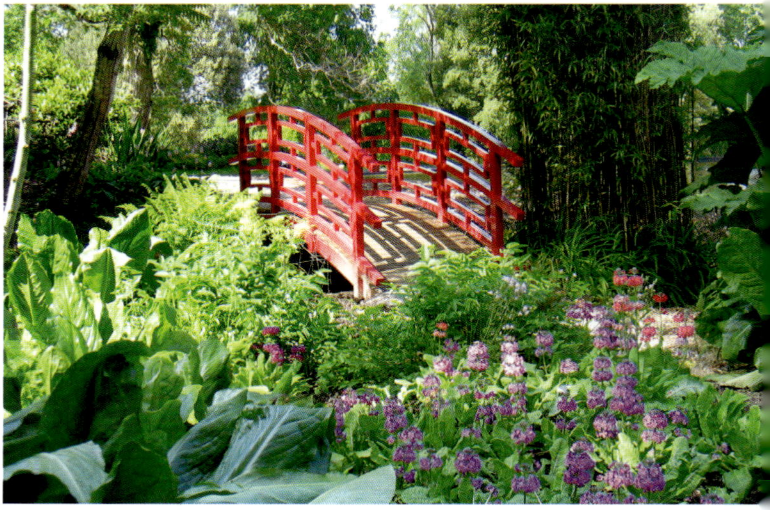

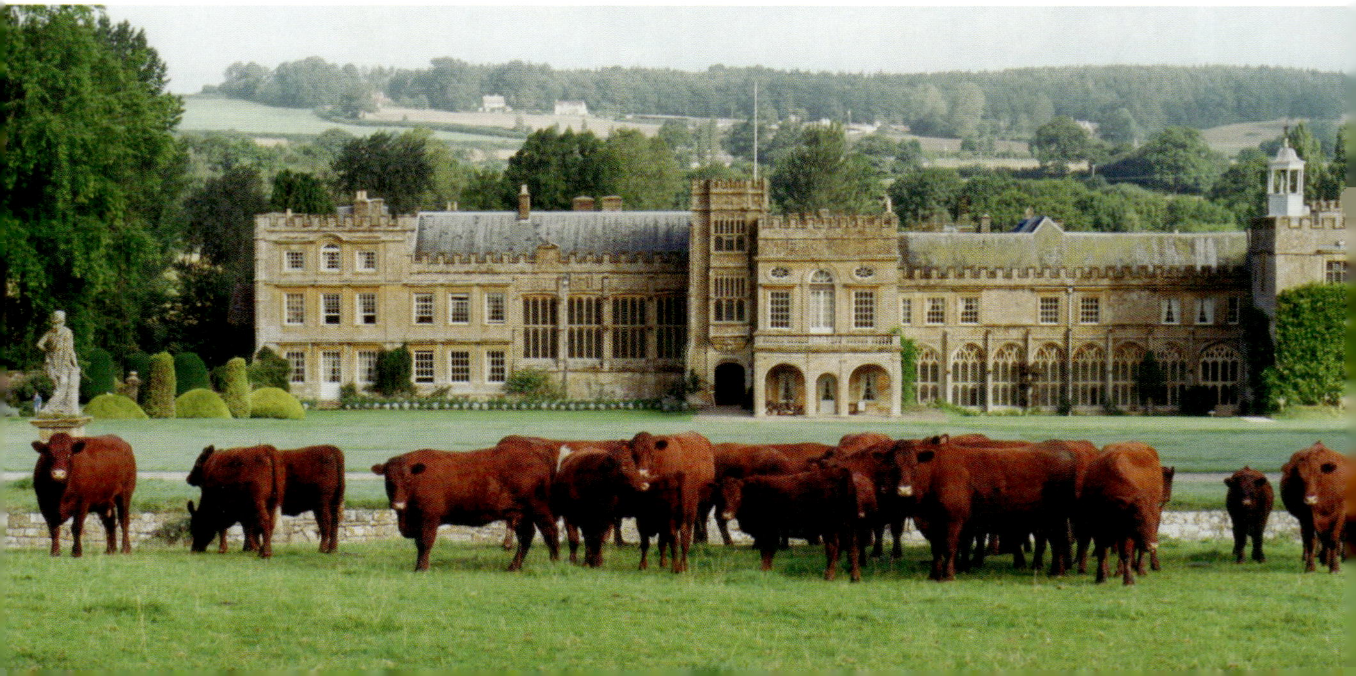

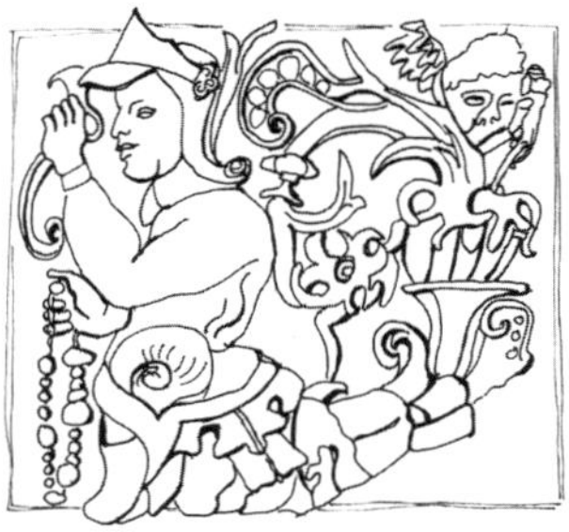

THREE

Restoration and Rebels

LIKE SO MANY of his successful contemporaries, Edmund Prideaux was a lawyer and politician. By the time he bought Forde Abbey, he had earned a fortune as a barrister and from his various offices as commissioner of the Great Seal, head of the postal service and chief legal adviser to the government. His combined income was rumoured to have peaked at over £20,000 a year – about £3m in present purchasing power, or £40m relative to average earnings – which put him in the same league as to-day's business moguls and investment bankers.

The Prideaux family came originally from Cornwall, claiming direct descent from William the Conqueror. By no means *nouveaux riches*, they were nonetheless quick to profit from the Dissolution. At that time a Nicholas Prideaux was legal adviser to the prior of Bodmin whom he helped sell leases of his estates before the priory was closed down by the Act of 1536. Nicholas then married his nephew to one of the leaseholders, who happened to be the prior's niece, and owner of Padstow. After the property had been wrested from King Henry VIII a great-nephew built Prideaux Place in 1591, the family seat to this day.

At about the same date Edmund's father, also called Edmund, bought an estate at Netherton at Farway near Honiton and it was here that our Edmund, the second son of a second wife, was born in 1601. (His elder brother Peter inherited Netherton and married Susan Poulett of Hinton St. George.). After Truro Grammar School and Cambridge University, Edmund was called to the bar. He became MP for Lyme Regis in the Long Parliament and in 1644 during the first phase of the civil war was put in charge of the postal service.

As Master of the Posts, Messengers and Couriers he was paid – or paid himself – £15,000 a year, an enormous income which put him in a European élite alongside people like the Thurn und Taxis family whose monopoly of the postal service in the Holy Roman Empire brought them a fortune which their descendants are enjoying to this day.

The job was no sinecure. Private mails had existed in the past – even the monks of Forde had been part of a European-wide network created by the Cistercian order. A public postal service was introduced in 1635; letters were carried by mounted youths between 'posts' and delivered to the local postmaster who would take out the letters for his area and hand the rest to another post-boy. Prideaux had chaired a committee to investigate the rates charged for inland letters. Now as postmaster general he set up regular weekly services: first to Hull and York, then to his consituency of Lyme Regis; then to Chester, Holyhead and Ireland; later to Bideford, Kendal and Carlisle. By 1649 the network covered most parts of England, replacing an *ad hoc* system of special messengers and relays of horses costing so much per mile.

Not surprisingly, Prideaux's job was the cause of great envy. Competitors sprang up, and Prideaux used all his legal – and not so legal – wiles to thwart them. After repeated challenges, however, Parliament decided to take control of the mails and in 1653 Prideaux was relieved of his post. One biographer says that the loss of the office and the business 'affected Prideaux little' since his legal practice 'continued to be large and lucrative.'[1]

As MP for the militantly Puritan borough of Lyme Regis, Prideaux could only watch helplessly as a Royalist force of 6,000 men lay siege to the town in 1644. (The siege was lifted before the Parliamentary army arrived). This was as close as the civil war came to Forde. But a local farmer, Roger Knight of Burstock Grange, did have his farm sequestered for failing to support the king against Cromwell: he later paid £185 to get it back. A committed Puritan himself, Prideaux sat through the Long Parliament (1640-60) and was appointed solicitor-general in 1648. But he resigned the post when he saw the trial and execution of King Charles looming: he had no wish to be numbered among the regicides.

Charles was executed on 30th January, 1649. In April, Prideaux was appointed Attorney-General to Oliver Cromwell, and in the same year he bought Forde Abbey.

* * *

The abbey could not have wished for a more energetic or lavish owner. Prideaux set about converting a property which had scarcely been touched for more

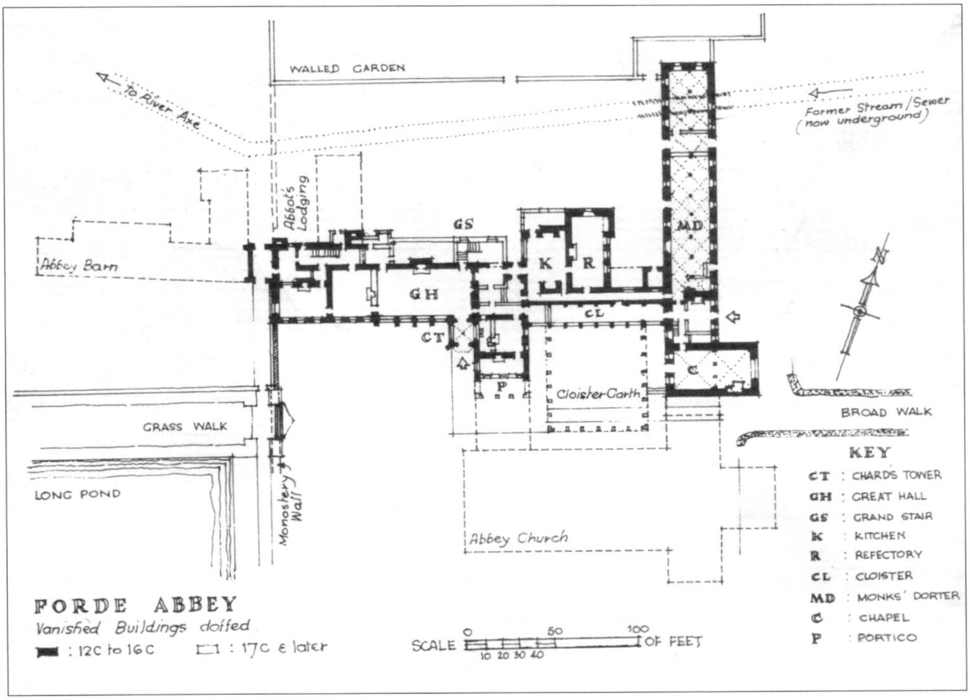

Ground floor plan, showing monastic buildings in bold, Prideaux and later additions are in double feint lines, lost buildings in single dotted lines.

than 100 years. His aim was an Italian-style palazzo, a style newly fashionable in England. By adding and altering rooms he used classical additions and decoration to merge the mediaeval monastery with Thomas Chard's extravagant Tudor extensions, and created a mansion fit for a wealthy seventeenth century family and its servants.

The 80-foot Great Hall was shortened by means of a dividing wall to create a private dining room in the space formerly occupied by the abbot's high table on its raised dais. The six window bays of the hall were thus reduced to four. This had become common practice: the original lay-out can still be seen in the dining halls of older university colleges. The windows on the north side of the Hall were filled in, a fireplace made and panelling installed. A bedroom was built into the space above the new dining room. Carvings taken from the windows of the Great Hall were set into the outside wall at the west end, where the former abbot's lodging was raised to three storeys.

Where the west range of the cloister had been, Prideaux enlarged a gallery on the first floor – the abbot's office – in order to make the Saloon. A double

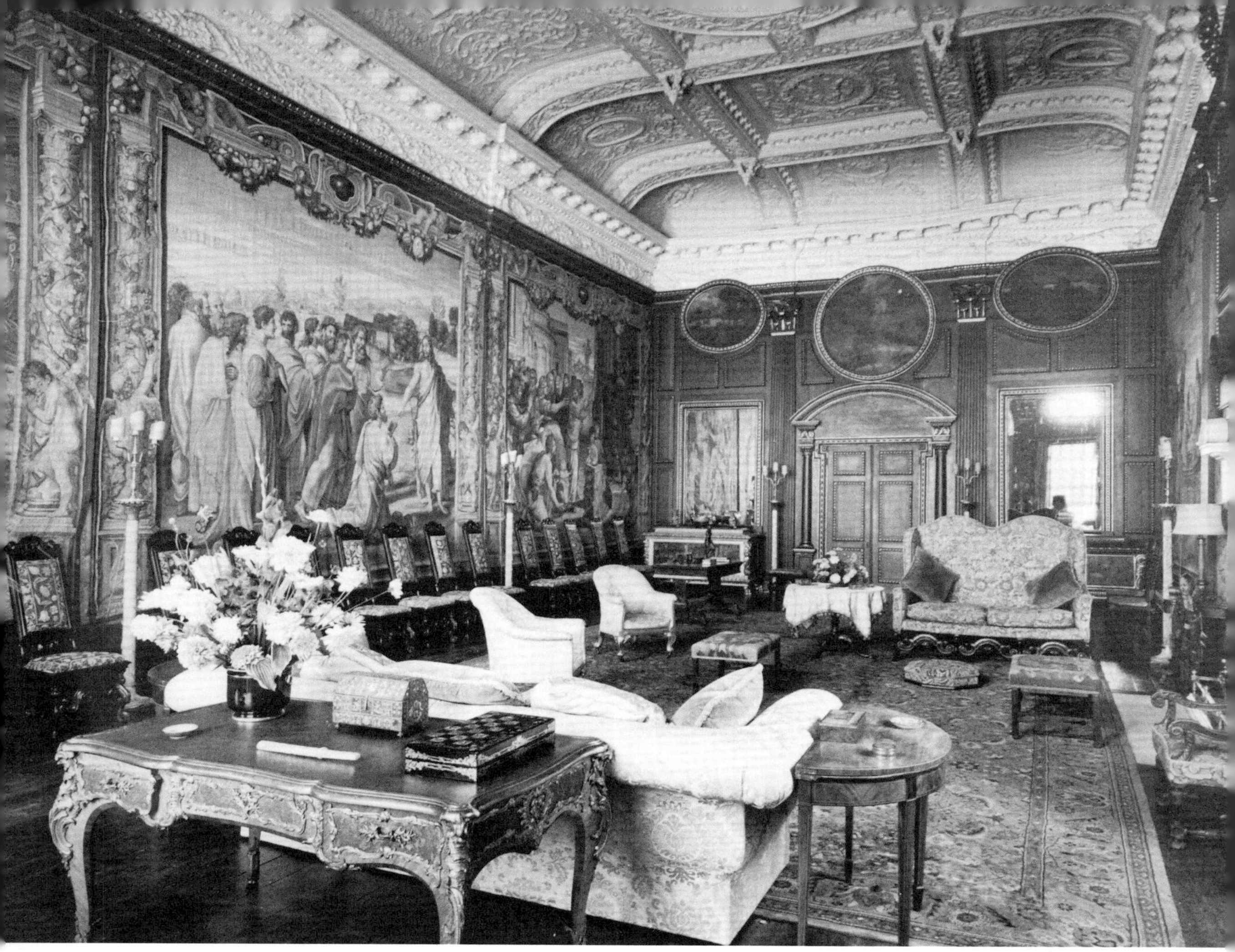

Prideaux's ornate Saloon replaced the abbot's office in the west range, occupying part of what had been the lay brothers' dormitory.

cube in proportions, it was decorated with an extravagant plaster ceiling with the Prideaux coat of arms in the middle. English workmen were employed for the work, hitherto seen as an Italian monopoly. The plasterwork is usually ascribed to the Abbott family of Frithelstock in north Devon, but an expert on the Abbotts has recently cast doubt on this.[2]

It is now almost certain that the Saloon was designed to house the famous set of Mortlake tapestries woven from Raphael's designs for the Pope in 1515 which Prideaux had either commissioned or been offered as a gift by Cromwell. The tapestries were not to arrive for some 50 years, however. Their story and the conflicting theories about them, will be told below. To reach the Saloon a grand staircase was installed with 'pierced luscious foliage panels instead of balusters' in the latest fashion. The date of its completion, 1658, is inscribed on the wall above.

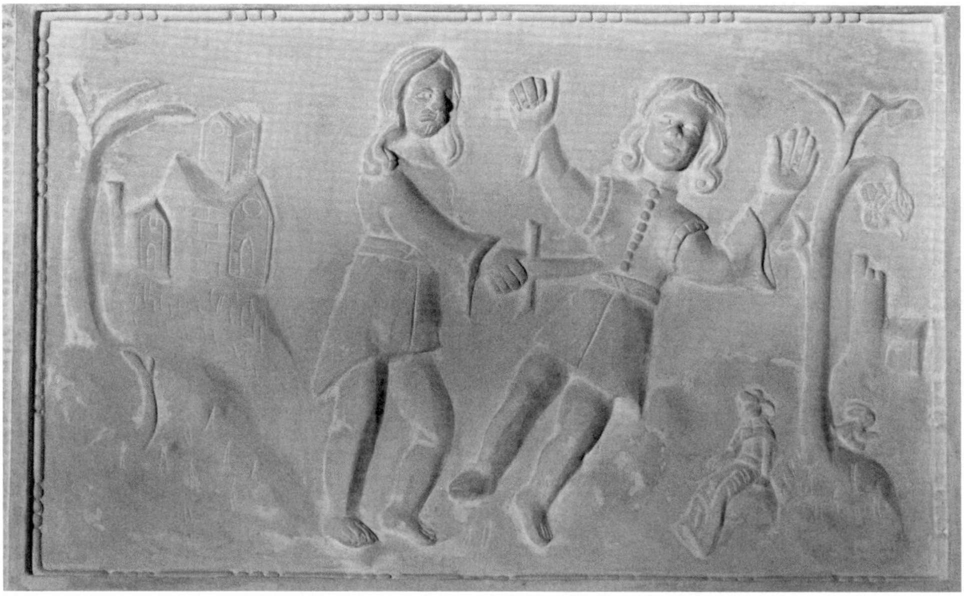

Cain killing Abel, in Carolean style: a plaster panel in the ceiling of Prideaux's Saloon.

Outside, below the Saloon was built a classical portico topped by a balustrade. Originally this portico opened to the west but was later re-orientated. The portico and saloon made a new centrepiece, jostling for attention with Chard's splendid oriel tower. Above what remained of the cloister, the north walk, three state bedrooms were installed on the first floor under the original roof.

The south face was decorated with windows in classical style (the 'Gothik' glazing bars were added 100 years later) and crenellated parapets were ranged along the whole length of the roof. Inside, Prideaux spared no expense on plaster ceilings – not only the magnificent example in the Saloon – or on panelling, tapestries and furnishings. Inside the old Chapter House, now converted into a private chapel, he installed the screen.

Until quite recently Prideaux's classical conversion of Forde Abbey was attributed to Inigo Jones, the most celebrated architect of the day. As the work of a pioneer of the English Renaissance, it was generally admired. But by the time the Gothic revival was in full swing the reaction was very different. Observers professed themselves shocked by the fusion of styles: 'Inigo Jones did not live to see his designs [at Forde] completed . . . and it is fortunate that the splendid front was not more mutilated,' wrote Maria Allen in 1846. The Rev. Gilpin complained that the sash windows 'glared over pointless arches'; that the cloister had been turned into a greenhouse; that the house was 'a ruin patched up into an awkward dwelling' in which the old and new were blended to the mutual disgrace of both.

The angling antiquarian George Pulman was equally censorious of Prideaux's portico, calling it 'Inigo Jones's incongruity, which projects from the main building as if trying to be as conspicuously ugly as possible.' Even Pulman had to concede that in spite of all, Forde was 'really a stately and magnificent pile – unapproachably the grandest not only in the Valley, but for many a mile in every direction.'[3]

Opinion has today swung firmly back in Prideaux's favour. The late Richard Tyler, architectural consultant at Forde Abbey for 20 years, wrote that the interest and charm of the building lay in the fact that its owners had resisted the temptation to keep up with fashion: most of the major work on the house was done before 1700. The Chard-Prideaux combination, he said, was 'unimaginable in any other country.' This was the verdict of a man whose career had been dedicated to the tactful modification of large country houses to make them habitable for a post-war generation of owners without servants:

> 'The abrupt collision of architectural styles must have seemed strange at first, but the patina of age, and the grey lichens on the Ham Hill stone, have drawn the buildings together to form a lively composition along the south front – there is even a hint of symmetry in the balance of the Chapter House at the east end and of the three-storey family rooms on the west, with Chard's Tower and the Saloon, a hundred and fifty years apart in date, forming together an unusual centrepiece.'[4]

Pevsner's *Dorset* agrees that the blend of styles is a happy one, a marriage of the finest examples in the country of late Gothic and early neo-classical elements.

One thing only remains to be said. Prideaux's architect was not Inigo Jones. Hundreds of country houses have been attributed to this English apostle of the Italian Renaissance and follower of Andrea Palladio; but Jones was involved – usually marginally – with very few of them. After the outbreak of the civil war Jones lost his practice (he had designed the Banqueting House in Whitehall, the Queen's House in Greenwich, St. Paul's Covent Garden, and various royal chapels); and he died about the time Prideaux was starting work on Forde.

Some have promoted the cause of Jones's nephew by marriage, John Webb (1611-1672), who assisted his uncle on a number of big houses and lived near Glastonbury. Another candidate was Edward Carter, who designed buildings for the Middle Temple. Today the design is usually attributed to Peter Mills, a London builder who worked for several of Prideaux's senior colleagues and died in 1670. Mill had worked with Inigo Jones on one London church and was among the surveyors appointed to supervise the rebuilding of London after the Great Fire of 1666.

* * *

To coincide with the completion of his palace, Edmund Prideaux was made a baronet by Oliver Cromwell in August, 1658. The citation noted 'his voluntary offer for the mainteyning [sic] of thirty foot-souldiers in his highnes [sic] army in Ireland.' On the 3rd September, the Lord Protector died. Edmund survived his master by only a year, denied the enjoyment that should have been his after years of hard work in London and the sumptuous restoration of Forde.

Prideaux is said to have been highly esteemed as a man of religion as well as learning. A 'commonplace book' which he began in 1655 does not shed much further light on his character – unless the miniscule writing offers a clue. There is a draft of his will at the front. Most of it is taken up with notes on various aspects of the law: 'riots, routs, unlawfull and rebellious assemblies,' on menaces, assault and battery, forcible entry, extortion, perjury and the suborning of witnesses. He has a list of law books with prices. The remainder is devoted to religious commentary and prayers.[5]

Prideaux's first wife was Jane Collins of Ottery St. Mary, who died in 1629 at the age of only 19. He was married again to Margaret Ivery of Cothay, who survived him, and left a son, another Edmund, and three daughters. Young Edmund's legacy included an excellent early education from John Tillotson, a Yorkshire Calvinist and fellow of Clare Hall in Cambridge, whom Prideaux had appointed tutor and chaplain. Tillotson became a famous preacher, dean of Canterbury and St. Paul's and finally, like Baldwin the third abbot of Forde, Archbishop of Canterbury. If young Edmund's education was assured – he became known as 'The Walking Encylopaedia' – so was his livelihood. His father reportedly left him the sum of £60,000: a fortune, but one that was to bring great misfortune.

* * *

Edmund the Second, 27 years old when he inherited in 1659, was more fervent a Puritan even than his father. He organized meetings for Dissenters in his cellar; and he refused to subscribe to a fund for ransoming European prisoners held in Turkey (presumably captured at the 1683 siege of Vienna) on the grounds that 'they were better to live in slavery under the Turk than to come home here where they must live under Popery.' This was reported by a neighbour in Lyme Regis, who described Edmund as 'the little Parliament man for Taunton' whose house was 'formerly an abbey and in it is a chapel where preaches a non-conformist. It is the receptical of all the fanatics.' [6]

At the Restoration of Charles II he was denied the baronetcy conferred on his father because it was a Cromwellian honour; and for the same reason, although elected MP for Taunton in 1681, Edmund was given no important government job.

Naturally, Edmund was a keen supporter of the Duke of Monmouth, the Protestant and illegimate son of Charles II who tried to seize the throne from his Catholic uncle James II. That support was to bring Edmund to the precipice of disaster – a disaster from which he was to be saved, very largely, by his wife.

She was Amy Fraunceis, daughter of John Fraunceis of Combe Florey in Somerset and a considerable property owner in her own right. They were married in 1655. Amy brought with her a half share of Combe Florey estate; the house itself, best known today as the home of the writer Evelyn Waugh, went to her sister. [7]

The Arrest of Edmund

'Ardent and intrepid on the field of battle, Monmouth was everywhere else effeminate and irresolute,' declared the historian Lord Macaulay. Yet all agree the pretender to the throne was charming, handsome and attractive, if rather spoilt. Exiled as a troublemaker, he returned in 1680 to conduct a 'royal progress' through the West Country in order to mobilise support.

His tour started at Wimborne St. Giles where lived the Earl of Shaftesbury, a Protestant sympathiser, founder of the Whigs and patron of the philosopher John Locke. From there Monmouth visited Thomas Thynne at Longleat where he was 'sumptuously' entertained. He called on Sir John Sydenham at Brympton d'Evercy, outside Yeovil, where he proved his royal descent by curing a woman called Elizabeth Parcet of the 'King's Evil' (scrofula). At Whitelackington, home of George Speke, leader of the opposition to the Duke of York, a banquet was served under a chestnut tree. (Its fallen trunk still lies outside the house). At Forde Abbey the young duke and his party were wined and dined by Edmund Prideaux, and given beds for the night before making their way to Exeter.

Everywhere the debonair rebel was rapturously received by the people. Lord Macaulay painted the scene: 'From Longleat to Exeter the hedges were lined with shouting spectators. The roads were strewn with boughs and flowers. The multitude, in their eagerness to see and touch their favourite, broke down the palings of parks, and besieged the mansions where he feasted. When he reached Chard his escort consisted of five thousand horsemen.'[8]

If the tour was a triumph for the Duke and his supporters, its consequences were mostly disastrous. The Duke would end up on the scaffold. Edmund would survive, having given what would turn out to be the most expensive dinner party in English history.

Prideaux first fell under suspicion, along with Shaftesbury and others, three years later when a plot to assassinate the king and his brother on their return from Newmarket to London (the Rye House Plot) was foiled. Some prominent suspects were executed, Monmouth was again arrested and exiled, while Prideaux was released for lack of evidence. According to his own notes, his house was searched in July 1683 and two muskets, a brass blunderbuss and several cases of pistols were removed.

Charles II died in February 1685 and his brother James duly succeeded. At dawn on the 11th June, three ships appeared in Lyme Bay a mile or so from the coast. A boat was lowered and made for the shore. It carried Thomas Dare, a militant Monmouth supporter and former goldsmith from Taunton, and Hugh Chamberlain. The two men were the advance guard of the Duke of Monmouth's invasion; they had been deputed to spread the word, spy out the land and collect weapons and horses.

Heading north, they called at Hawkchurch and then at Forde Abbey where, it seems, they found Edmund Prideaux at home. It was eight o'clock at night and (so it was alleged later) Edmund drank a toast to Monmouth's health when the two scouts told him the news. Witnesses denied this, claiming the toast was drunk by a certain Malachi Mallock from Axminster. Whatever the truth, Dare and Chamberlain seized, or were allowed to take, a number of horses from the abbey stables. About the same time a different group of rebels from Ilminster is said to have called on 'Esquire Pridicks' and with his permission search the house for weapons, taking a number of muskets, two carbines, two blunderbusses, some half-pikes and two rapiers.

Meanwhile the three ships had dropped anchor some distance off Lyme Regis. At sunset, the turn of the tide, about 80 armed men clambered from the ships into seven small boats and landed on the beach (now called Monmouth) to the west of the Cobb. The Duke was among them; he knelt on the shingle and prayed for success. For three days the little army waited, enlisting recruits and transport. Dare and Chamberlain appeared mounted on one of Prideaux's fine horses in a cavalcade of about 40 animals. Very shortly, however, Dare quarrelled with another of the Duke's lieutenants about which of them was to have the best mount. His antagonist promptly shot him dead. It was a bad start to a chaotic campaign. Recruits were plentiful, but their quality was poor: the cavalry consisted mainly of farm horses which could not stand the sound of gunfire, while the infantry were armed with scythe blades attached to poles. Less than a month later, although they fought courageously, Monmouth's peasant supporters were routed at Sedgemoor on the Somerset Levels. The Duke himself escaped on foot and was tracked down to a field of fern and brambles on Horton Heath by the Hampshire border, where he was discovered in a ditch wearing a shepherd's smock and a stubbly, prematurely grey beard.

Prideaux missed the fighting because he had been detained eight days after Monmouth's landing. News of Thomas Dare's visit to Forde reached London, a warrant was issued on 13th June and Edmund was arrested at home six days later. According to entries he made in his pocket-book, he was 'seized by a messenger, Mr. Saywell' and taken to his (Saywell's) house in London. On the 14th July, a week after Monmouth's defeat and a day before his execution,

A page from Edmund's diary, headed 'My Confinement'. The third entry reads: '14 Sep (85) carryed to ye Tower by Evans.'

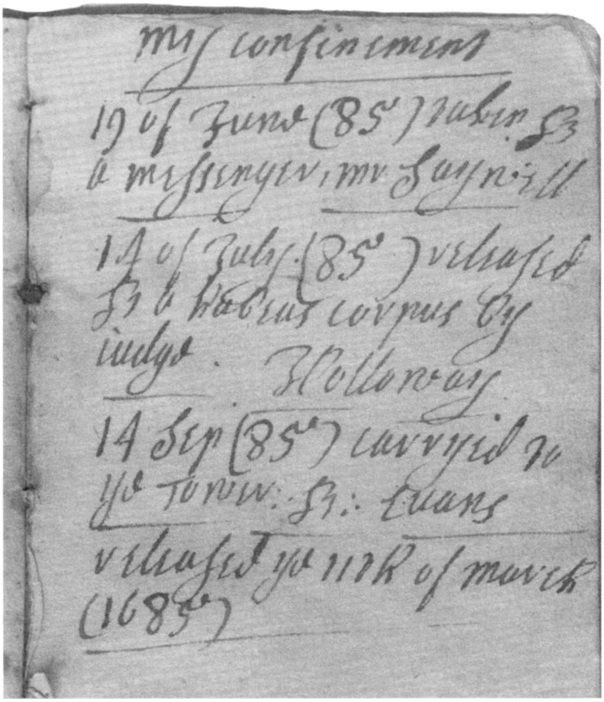
My confinement
19 of June (85) taken by a messenger, mr Saywell
14 of July (85) released by habeas corpus by iudge Holloway
14 Sep (85) carryed to ye Tower: by: Evans
released ye 11th of march (1685)

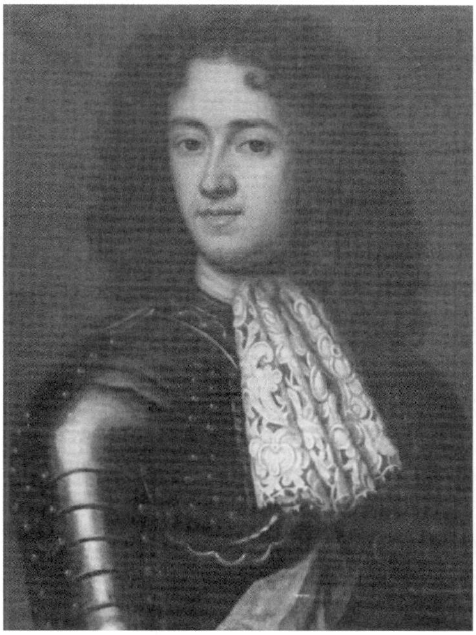

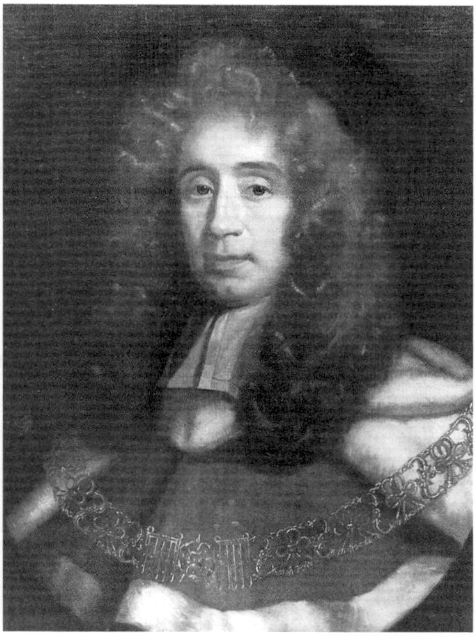

Above left: James Scott, Duke of Monmouth, whose rebellion led to the arrest of Edmund Prideaux the younger.

Above right: Judge Jeffreys: who demanded an enormous ransom for Prideaux. His indiscriminate hanging of supposed rebels in the South-West is still remembered by their descendants.

Edmund was released on bail under a writ of *habeas corpus*. The bail was set at £10,000, of which he himself put up £5,000 with an unnamed kinsman and a Mr. Craig vouching for the rest.

On 14th September he was 'carryed to ye Tower', as his diary puts it, and kept in close confinement. The charge was high treason. Because three days previously Malachi Mallock, the man at Forde on the night the toast was drunk, had turned King's Evidence. Mallock had been sentenced to death at Dorchester and was due to hang at Bridport. To save his neck he had testified that Edmund was in league with Monmouth.

Edmund was one of many trapped by the vicious campaign of revenge waged by King James against those who had dared to dispute his succession. The instrument of his revenge was the enthusiastic – many prefer the word 'bloodthirsty' – Judge Jeffreys, Lord Chief Justice and now Lord Chancellor. The brutality of Jeffreys Bloody Assizes is still remembered by descendants of those hundreds of men who were hanged on gibbets or trees along the roads of the West Country or deported as slaves to the islands of the Caribbean.[9] Most of the villages in West Dorset reported losses: anyone absent from their village at the time of Segdemoor was assumed by Jeffreys to be a rebel. A special example was made of 12 men at Lyme Regis who were hanged, drawn and quartered on Monmouth Beach and their remains displayed in the surrounding area.

The victims' property was 'fought for and torn in pieces by a crowd of greedy informers,' wrote Macaulay.[10]

> 'The brokenhearted widows and destitute orphans of the labouring men whose corpses hung at the cross roads were called upon by the agents of the Treasury to explain what had become of a basket, of a goose, of a flitch of bacon, of a keg of cider, of a sack of beans, of a truss of hay... While the humbler retainers of the government were pillaging the families of the slaughtered peasants, the Chief Justice was fast accumulating a fortune out of the plunder of a higher class of Whigs. He traded largely in pardons. His most lucrative transaction of this kind was with a gentleman named Edmund Prideaux. It is certain that Prideaux had not been in arms against the government; and it is probable that his only crime was the wealth which he had inherited from his father, an eminent lawyer who had been high in office under the Protector.'[11]

Jeffreys did everything he could to prove the complicity of his wealthy captive. He had one witness in Malachi Mallock, but needed more to secure conviction. (The authorities also suspected Edmund of sending Monmouth £500, but could not prove that either.) For weeks on end Prideaux was denied visitors while his country neighbours were threatened with arrest or cajoled with promises of pardon into testifying against him. Charles, the son of George Speke of Whitelackington, was one of them; though under sentence of death, he refused to incriminate his kinsman and was executed. Other prisoners threatened were Joseph Standerwich, a maker of serge, and Samuel Key, a clothier, both of Ilminster; James Butcher of Crewkerne; and William Thompson, a London haberdasher. They all refused, and all survived.

Languishing in jail, Edmund learned of these attempts to suborn witnesses, and of Jeffreys' constant threats to have him hanged. But now the ban on visitors was lifted to allow Prideaux's wife Amy to visit him because he was ill, on condition she too was put under lock and key. Just before Christmas the Earl of Sunderland wrote to the jailer: 'His Majesty's intention is Mrs. Prideaux should for the time to come be confined with her husband, if she desires to see him, and have the liberty of a servant with a physician and apothecary to come and go as there may be occasion.'[12]

Once she was released, Amy enlisted Edmund's sisters Lady Churchill and Mary Lady Tooker to organise a petition through influential friends. They waited a week before learning that there was nothing to be done. King James had 'given' Edmund to Judge Jeffreys as a prize for his energetic pursuit of the Monmouth rebels. This 'gift' meant that the Lord Chancellor, having failed to get Prideaux hanged, was now free to ransom Prideaux and keep the money for himself.

Meanwhile, however, Jeffreys found the second witness he needed, and Edmund's trial was set for the middle of March. Amy was not prepared to take the risk of his being found guilty, even with false witnesses. With great difficulty she managed to see her husband again in the Tower. The couple realized that their only option was to approach Jeffreys directly. This they did, through a Mr. Jennings, who said he could extract a pardon from the Lord Chancellor for £30,000, an enormous sum. He was told to think again. He came back saying £15,000 would be the absolute minimum. It was still a huge sum: at least £2.5m in today's prices.A discount of £240 – 10 per cent – was made for down payment of the first £2,400 instalment of the ransom.

And so Edmund was released on 12th March, nearly nine months after his arrest. The pardon was signed by a courtier of King James on the 20th March 1686.

But things could not be left at that. Edmund and Amy wanted their money back. The problem was Judge Jeffreys had used the ransom to buy himself two estates belonging to the Duke of Albemarle which had cost him £34,000: Dolby in the Wolds, and Nether Boughton in Leicestershire. After the Revolution of 1688, when James II had fled abroad and William and Mary had been put on the throne, they drafted a petition to parliament. It sought leave to bring in a Bill to reclaim the 'extorted' £15,000, plus interest, from the estate of Jeffreys who had died the previous month. The Bill encountered the strenuous opposition of Lord Chief Justice Pollexfen who was trustee of Jeffreys children (and his creditors). Parliament would not pass it.

Edmund died in 1702 at the age of 70 without leaving a will. His wife Amy renounced her interest and passed the abbey to their daughter Margaret, their youngest and only surviving child, born in 1669. Margaret's brother Frraunceis had died at 19. There were three sisters: Amy, who died in infancy, a second Amy who lived to be only 14, and Elizabeth who had married John Speke of Whitelackington, brother of the Charles Speke who had chosen death rather than betray his kinsman Edmund Prideaux.

From Prideaux to Gwyn

The first woman to inherit Forde Abbey brought with her a new name, and Gwyns took over from Prideaux.

Margaret had married Francis Gwyn of Llansannor in County Glamorgan in 1689. He was a first cousin of her mother Amy Frаunceis and possibly, like her, born at Combe Florey. Although a different generation from his wife, their age difference was not so great: he was 41 and she 21. The Gwyns (and later the Fraunceis family under the name Gwyn) were to hold Forde Abbey for the next 144 years.[13] As well as being 20 years older than his wife, Francis Gwyn was already half way through a successful career as politician and minister. Intelligent and resourceful, and 'thoroughly devoted to the Crown', Francis had the reputation of *bon viveur* and chaser of women. But it seems that on his marriage to Margaret he setttled down and took family life seriously. He wrote to his friend the politician Robert Harley (later Earl of Oxford) to congratulate him on the birth of a son, saying: 'if one should write such a letter to Harry Boyle or such rake-hells, they would wonder what the satisfaction a man could take in things of this sort.'[14] Francis had entered Parliament as MP for Chippenham in 1673, and over his long career represented six different seats and held office during four reigns. Under Charles II he was a groom of the royal bedchamber, and under-secretary of state to his cousin Lord Conway. His prize post was as clerk to the Privy Council – a job he 'bought' for £2,500 and sold on. His name appears during this time against an Order in Council dated 1681 telling London magistrates to report on their pursuit of Papist enemies, and provide a list of 'Papists who inhabit and keep Shops, and exercise Trades hereabouts contrary to Law.'

Gwyn lost his plum post at the Privy Council in 1683, inspiring an anonymous wit from Glamorgan to write:

There's Frank, who of late
Knew secrets of state;
Though now he's turned out of employment.
Since that he finds time
To ply women and wine,
Which will prove a more lasting enjoyment.[15]

But 'Frank's' career was far from over. Under James II he became joint secretary to the Treasury under the Earl of Rochester and, like the younger Edmund Prideaux, found himself caught up in the political upheavals of the time. Whereas Prideaux was nearly destroyed by Monmouth's failed bid for the throne, Gwyn witnessed the start of William of Orange's successful one three years later.

William had landed on 5th November, 1688 at Torbay in Devon. King James had joined his army at Salisbury and was attempting, with little success, to rally supporters among the West Country gentry. As a senior member of the government close to the King's circle, Gwyn joined him there with his patron Rochester. He found James looking pale; he was suffering from persistent nose-bleeds and so weak that 'he could hardly put his hand to his head to put on his Spectacles.'

After four days sniffing the political wind, and learning that the King was planning to retreat to London, Gwyn and Rochester decided the game was up. They wasted no time but left for Winchester the next day 'to avoid meeting the King upon that road.'[16] Returning to London, Gwyn wrote to a colleague on Christmas Day:

> 'The poor king...has acted so quite contrary to his interests that one would think his design was to spend the rest of his days in a cloister...But it is now all over. Neither he nor his (if the child be so) are like ever to set foot here again.'

* * *

With James's exile and military defeat, Gwyn lost office but found a post with the interim government. He played a very active part in the so-called Convention Parliament but, perhaps because he was a Royalist with High Tory patrons, he voted against its Bill declaring the throne vacant. James had not abdicated, he argued, therefore the accession of William and Mary was, strictly speaking, illegal. History was repeating itself: Gwyn the Royalist was respecting King James's rights just as Edmund Prideaux the Parliamentarian had respected King Charles I's rights by refusing to sign his death warrant.

In May 1689 Gwyn had found himself reporting on the petition which his future father-in-law Edmund Prideaux had made against Judge Jeffreys' estate. Presumably he was in favour of the motion, because that Christmas recess he and Margaret Prideaux were married. For the first ten years they lived at Francis' house in Scotland Yard beside Westminster Bridge, spending the summers at Forde Abbey.

In 1701 Gwyn followed his patron Rochester to Ireland as secretary when the latter was appointed Lord Lieutenant by King William, and followed him into opposition when Queen Anne took the throne. For his loyalty he was dubbed

'Franck Guin, Ld. Rotchester's guine as they call him' in a letter reporting rumours that might be getting the Post Office.[17]

Gwyn retired to the back benches, as we would say today, but in 1711 after the Tories came to power re-emerged as a commissioner of the Board of Trade. Two years later he reached the summit of his career as Secretary at War. He had done the job for little more than a year when, with the accession of George I and the rise of his political enemies the Whigs, he received a letter from Lord Townsend, the Secretary of State, telling him he was to be replaced.[18]

There was a consolation prize. Queen Anne presented him with the magnificent set of Mortlake tapestries woven from Raphael's designs for the Sistine Chapel in Rome which now cover the walls of Prideaux's Saloon. They were his, and Forde's, crowning glory.

The tapestries arrived securely packed in a metal-covered lead chest more than five metres long. It can be seen, unmarked – and usually unremarked – lying against the north wall of the Undercroft. The five panels hanging in the Saloon are the most valuable possession of the Abbey and one of the finest examples of this set of Raphael tapestries in existence. Yet for more than 200 years the truth about their provenance has been obscured by myth and muddied by contradiction.

Maria Allen, the Abbey's first modern biographer, believed the tapestries were made at Arras in northern France and were intended for the king of Spain but had been captured from a Spanish galleon by an English ship (presumably during the War of the Spanish Succession) in the reign of Queen Anne – who then presented them to Francis Gwyn.

Of this only the last bit is correct; and even that requires qualification. Let us try to unravel the story in reverse.

Why should Queen Anne give her war minister such a lavish present? No doubt Gwyn had served her well. But by the time he was appointed to her War Office in August 1713, the war itself was over (thanks to the military prowess of John Churchill, now Duke of Marlborough) and the Treaty of Utrecht had been signed. Was there another reason for the queen's generosity? There was, and it is revealed by the answer to the next question: why do the tapestries fit the room so exactly?

All but one of the five tapestry panels at Forde (the *Draught of Fishes* is complete) have had reductions made from the original designs, or 'cartoons', painted by Raphael in 1515-16. In three, the omissions are only minor; in a fourth, *The Death of Ananias*, more than two-thirds of the original has been left out.

But the tapestries have not been cut to fit. Not only is there no sign of cutting, but in two cases the weavers have edited out odd arms and legs that would have betrayed their cropping of the original design. This can be seen by comparing the Forde tapestries with the original tapestries made at Brussels in 1517-21 for Pope Leo X. Sections were cropped not only from the sides of the cartoon but sometimes from the middle – an easy thing to do because the cartoons, large sheets of paper (*cartoni*) gummed together for the artist to paint on, were then cut into vertical strips for the weavers to work from, which they did by placing them under the warp of their looms.

So the panels were woven to fit the room.

We know now that the Forde tapestries were made not at Arras but at Mortlake in London, because they bear the shield of the workshop set up there by King James I in 1619. The shield and the rich design of the borders, by Franz Cleyn, tell art historians that they were made in the early 1660s, just after the Restoration if not earlier. Since tapestries of this size take years to complete, that suggests they were commissioned in the late 1650s during the Commonwealth. And it will be recalled that the Saloon itself was built at exactly that time.

All the evidence, then, points to the same conclusion: that the tapestries were made for Edmund Prideaux the Elder, Cromwell's attorney-general. If they were bought, Prideaux was certainly rich enough to afford them; if they were a gift, he was well-qualified to receive them, possibly from the hands of Cromwell himself.

So why did it take fifty or sixty years for them to arrive at their destination? The answer must be 'politics'. The Parliamentarian Edmund the elder died in 1659, Charles II regained the throne the following year, and Edmund's son was about to be thrown into the Tower for treason. Not surprisingly, the delivery from Mortlake was halted, and the tapestries lay – perhaps already in their long chest – somewhere in Whitehall until someone, perhaps even Francis Gwyn, asked for them. Gwyn, of course, was on the opposite side of the political fence, a keen monarchist and Tory, and therefore eligible to receive them.

One more piece of the jigsaw remains to be inserted. The cartoons – or the seven that had survived of the original ten Raphael painted – were bought by Charles I when he was still Prince of Wales. In 1623, encouraged by the painter Reubens, he sent the head of the Mortlake Manufactory to Genoa to buy them. The price was 300 guineas. After his execution in 1649 most of Charles' possessions were put up for sale; but not the cartoons. Either they were of not much value, or Cromwell – who like all gentlemen of his day was keen on tapestries – wanted a set of Raphaels made for himself, or perhaps for a close supporter.[19]

Raphael's scenes from the Gospels and *Acts of the Apostles* were hugely popular. The number of tapestry panels made from them is said to run into four figures. Between 30 and 40 sets were produced, of which about ten survive. What Raphael called his 'woven frescoes' were an attempt – apparently successful – to match Michelangelo's bravura painting on the Sistine Chapel ceiling. The tapestries for the Vatican caused a sensation. Giorgio Vasari said they were 'divine rather than human'; a contemporary called them 'the most beautiful objects in the universe.' An English art critic recently declared the cartoons (now in the Victoria and Albert Museum) to be 'the greatest works of art in this country.'

Yet these days, the Mortlake tapestries are considered better than to those in Rome. Weavers at Brussels under Pieter van Aelst, being trained in Flemish style, could not do justice to Raphael's dynamic figures and expressive faces. According to W. G. Thomson, a leading expert:

> The effect of the tapestry in the Vatican is heavy and dull, notwithstanding the amount of gold and silver thread used in its construction; the noble type of heads and figures is vulgarised – a defect which is [also] observable in the later Brussels versions of the designs. The earlier Mortlake tapestries [i.e pre-Restoration] are infinitely superior; they express that noble dignity in the faces and figures which characterises the cartoons; the colour is full of strength, yet lacking the crudity of the later Brussels series.[20]

To which we can add that, thanks to its long spell in storage and careful treatment since, the Forde Abbey set – with the exception of one panel, *The Healing of the Lame Man*, damaged by light – is one of the best of those earlier Mortlake versions.

* * *

Queen Anne never saw the tapestries in *situ*. She had planned to vist Forde during a tour of the south-west in 1714. She got as far as Hinton St. George but turned back because of a chill, developed mumps and died. Francis Gwyn had prepared for her visit, redecorating the Prideaux suite of state rooms over the cloister, and buying a set of Mortlake tapestry chairs to go with the hangings in the Saloon.

Although he continued as an MP for many more years, Gwyn devoted the rest of his long life to his house, garden and antiquarian research. (His collections were dispersed in the house sale a hundred years later.) He made some alterations, added little to the fabric, but left his name proudly on the rainwater hopper on the south side of the chapel. He seems to have become a pioneer of landscape

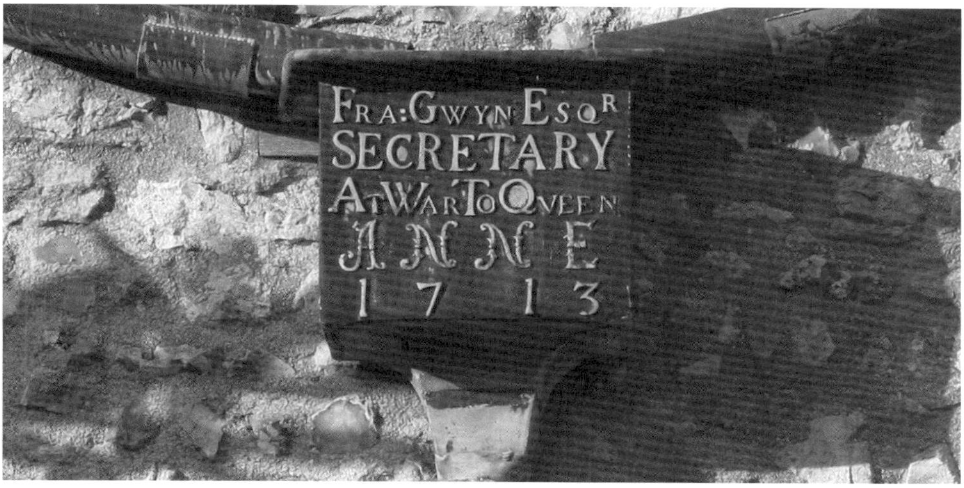

Francis Gwyn commemorated his last job, War Secretary to Queen Anne, on a rainwater hopper on the Chapel.

gardening, though he was a generation older than William Kent its founding father. With help from friends, Gwyn created the lay-out we see today: the avenue of lime trees which approaches the house from the east, and the series of pools descending from the Great Pond.

One of his friends was the Welsh naturalist Edward Lhuyd (now written Llwyd) who as keeper of the Ashmolean Museum in Oxford collected botanic specimens from all over the British Isles, published a catalogue of fossils which was financed by Sir Isaac Newton, and was the first to identify a dinosaur. He also did pioneering work on the Celtic languages of Britain and France before dying young in 1709.

Another of Francis Gwyn's advisers was his 'old friend and fellow collegiate' Colonel James Grahame MP, of Levens Hall in Cumberland, whom he met as an undergraduate at Oxford and worked with under the ill-starred King James. Grahame had employed the French landscape gardener Guillaume Beaumont (thought to have been a pupil of the great Le Nôtre at Versailles) to create the large topiary garden for which Levens is now famous. Beaumont also organized the planting of trees in its deer park. In the summer of 1709 Gwyn wrote to his friend suggesting he pay a visit to Forde and bring with him 'some of the documents about Gardening and Husbandry which take up most of my time. I find this summer is like to passe in Warr and ill weather.' Again in 1712 he asked Grahame to give him 'some of your advice and company at this place where it will be very useful and welcome.'[21]

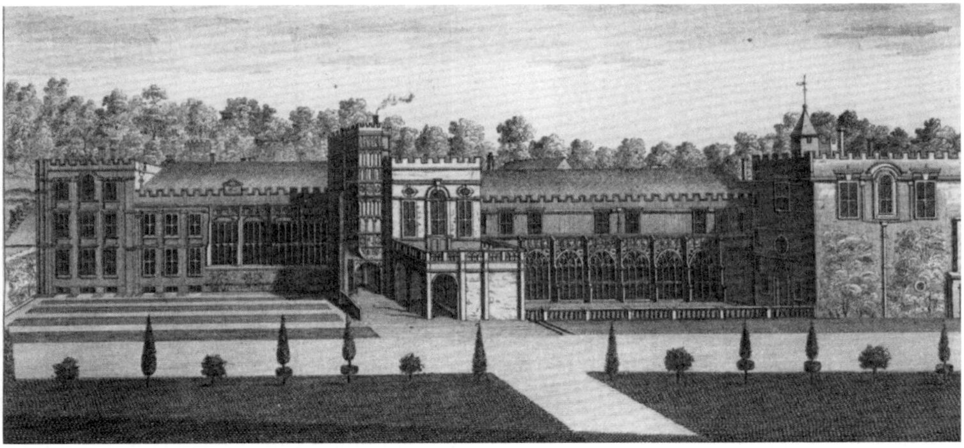

An engraving of the abbey dedicated to Francis Gwyn's heir, Edward Prideaux Gwyn, MP for Wells, who died unmarried in 1736.

Forde and Levens were to be reconnected more closely and permanently in the twentieth century when Mark Roper married Elizabeth (Lisa) Bagot, daughter of the family which inherited the Levens estate.

Margaret Gwyn had died in 1709 aged only 40 after bearing seven surviving children. Francis stood down in favour of his his eldest son in 1727, and died seven years later at the age of 86. But the heir, Edward Prideaux Gwyn, MP for Wells, his father's last seat, died unmarried two years after his father. The family had a record of childless marriages and early deaths: a third son, Edmund, joined the navy and predeceased his father; the fourth, John, became a clergyman and died, also childless, in 1741. Of the three daughters, Amy and Margaret died unmarried, while Catherine married but had no children.

Forde then passed to the second son, another Francis. He, too, became MP for Wells. He ran the estate for 40 years, collected material for a history of Devon, and was an antiquarian like his father. It was during his time that the sash windows with their 'gothik' hexagonal panes were installed on both sides of the house.

But Francis's main claim to fame was that he refused an offer of £30,000 for the Raphael tapestries. The offer is said to have been made by the Russian ambassador, Count Orlov, on behalf of the Empress Catherine the Great. This was presumably Count Grigory Orlov, the handsome army officer, and Catherine's lover, who led the coup against her husband Peter III which put her on the throne. In about 1770 he fell out of favour. Hoping to regain the Empress's affection, he bought for her a 190-carat diamond (known as the 'Orlov'), half

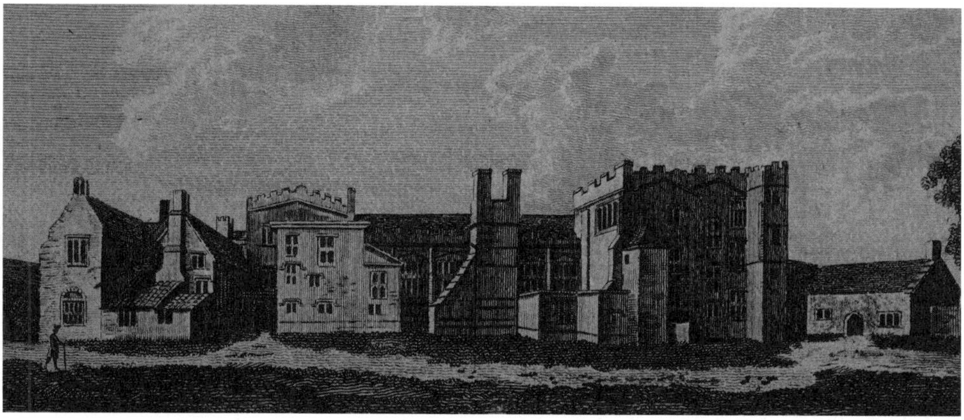

An undated engraving by Samuel Sparrow of the back of the abbey, published in 1783 at the time of John Fraunceis Gwyn. It shows the brewhouse under the kitchen (left), the massive chimney stack of the Great Hall, and the monastic barn (right).

the size of a chicken's egg. It is tempting to suppose that his extravagant offer for the Forde Abbey tapestries was motivated by the same desire. Whatever the truth, Orlov's offer, translated into present values, is by a long way the highest valuation ever put on them.

Francis died in 1777, leaving no children. He left his considerable estates in Devon, Dorset, Somerset and Glamorgan to his second wife Frances Combe of Winchester for her lifetime, and then to his cousin John Fraunceis of Combe Florey and his male heirs, on condition that they took the name Gwyn. This first 'new' Gwyn took possession in 1780 but lived only nine more years, leaving Forde to his eldest son, another John Fraunceis.

Three spellings of the name 'Francis' in one paragraph is bound to cause confusion. Let us summarize the situation: the Francis Gwyn who died in 1777 was related to the Fraunceis family through both his parents. His father, the first Francis Gwyn, was a cousin of his mother Margaret Prideaux and Margaret was the daughter of Amy Fraunceis and the younger Edmund Prideaux. Thus the three families of Prideaux, Fraunceis and Gwyn became closely entwined in the line of succession at Forde Abbey. The confusion is made worse by the habit of fathers giving their sons the same Christian names: we have three Edmund Prideaux, two Francis Gwyns, a female Frances Gwyn and two John Fraunceis Gwyns.

History has left us with much better picture of the second J. F. Gwyn than of the first, thanks to Maria Allen who knew him well, and others who met him. Born in 1761, he was 38 years old when he took over. A well-educated man, ('an elegant classical scholar,' says Mrs. Allen), he was kind-hearted and artistic but also reticent and ineffectual. Unlike his predecessors he had no interest in public affairs, preferring country pursuits. Mrs. Allen remembers him as 'a kind and generous master, a liberal landlord, and a benefactor to the poor. The tale of distress never reached him in vain; for his heart and purse were ever open to relieve the wants of his destitute and less fortunate fellow-creatures: he delighted in doing good.'[22]

Generosity tipped over into lavishness. Although living frugally himself, J.F. Gwyn spent a great deal of money on the house. He married no heiress. Both his wives were local girls: Elizabeth Norman came from Thorncombe, and died in 1807 at the age of only 36; Dinah Good of Winsham, described by Mrs. Allen as possessing 'an elevated mind and enlarged soul', also predeceased her husband, dying in 1831 aged 43. Money worries were probably the cause of Gwyn's decision to let the house in 1814, and to make a three-year tour of Europe (presumably following the defeat of Napoleon at Waterloo). Yet Gwyn's apparent poverty – not to mention his actual appearance – was a puzzle. Gwyn came to meet his tenants in July, 1814, bringing with him Dinah who was then about 26 and about to become his second wife. They stayed for a week. This is the impression he made on one of the new tenants:

> 'Now for the proprietor, who is a curiosity, though of a different sort, as great as his house. The Manor of Ford Abbey is worth to him about £2000 a year, he possesses another estate in this country of about £1500 a year, and another of £1500 a year in Wales. He is notwithstanding very poor, though he has no wife and no child. He has a mistress, however, who came down with him.
>
> 'It is not easy to describe him. What is called the best English education had been bestowed on him. He was at one of the best of the schools and at Oxford...and is said, by the clergyman here who was at school with him, to have been a good scholar at school; but excepting a scrap of Latin which proceeded from him now and then, and of which he seemed to know the meaning, it would be difficult to find a mind more thoroughly vacant, and more wonderfully feeble —to his servants and dependents, full of caprice and unsteadiness—and without real tyranny but rather good nature in his heart, producing the effects of tyranny on those around him.
>
> 'His lady, in whom I expected to find the over-done airs and pretensions of half-breeding, guided by a mixture of jealousy and pride, was a simple country girl whom he had picked up in the neighbourhood, bashful and awkward, but not without beauty.'

If J.F. Gwyn was eccentric, he was hardly more so than the man who in 1814 had taken a lease on the house, and whose identity we shall now reveal.

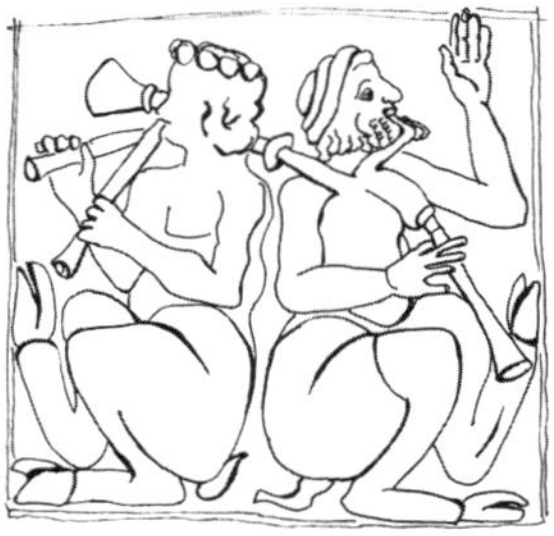

FOUR

The Jogging Philosopher

THE TENANT OF FORDE ABBEY was Jeremy Bentham, radical reformer, Utilitarian philosopher and man of many parts: a prolific writer, avid horticulturist and keen jogger. He arrived in July 1814 to take up a seven-year lease, accompanied by James Mill, his old friend and assistant (whose description of John Frаunceis Gwyn is quoted at the end of the last chapter). Mill brought his eldest child, the eight-year-old prodigy John Stuart Mill. The two friends had hoped to meet their landlord to finalise matters, but found the house empty except for the gardener and an old woman. The proprietor turned up a day later.

Although he had demanded a rent of £800 a year, Gwyn settled for £315. Perhaps the generous discount was a sign of his poor grasp of money matters, hinted at by James Mill in the previous chapter. For Bentham could well have afforded the full rent. He had received a large inheritance from his father, and a year earlier had secured £23,000 in compensation from the government when it dropped his scheme for a model prison to be built on a site at Millbank in London.

The prison project had been one of his obsessions. He had got the idea during a visit to Russia, where his brother Samuel was working for Prince Potemkin. Called the 'Panopticon', it was a circular building with cells arranged round the circumference visible from a central viewing tower, and a chapel below to which the prisoners had access. The idea was that permanent surveillance was a better way of reforming criminals than physical punishment.[1]

Bentham was just as odd as his landlord. This is how a later visitor, Lady

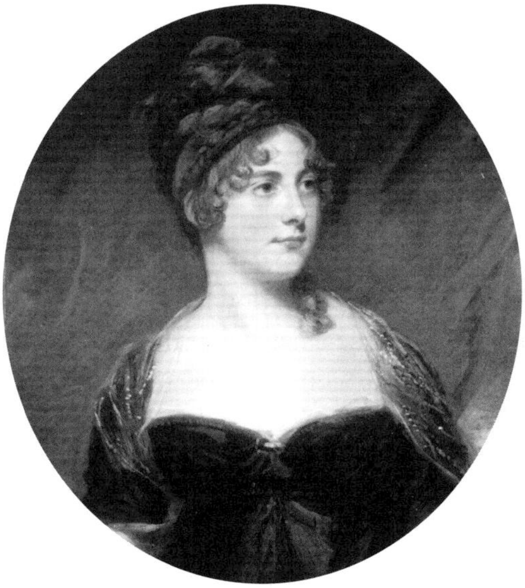

Anne Romilly, wife of the Whig MP Sir Samuel Romilly, left a vivid description of Bentham and his eccentricities. Portrait by Hoppner.

Romilly, describes their first meeting:

'Mr Bentham was in the act of dressing when we arrived, & as we were standing in astonishment he made his appearance in all his singularity in dress; his grey coat & hair of the same colour flying, & bearing evident marks of not having been arranged since a plentiful ablution of soap & water, with which his face was still shining as bright as if it had been polished – The first greetings being over we were hurried from place to place till we were out of breath; he running before us with all the activity of a boy.'

Anne Romilly was the adored wife of Sir Samuel Romilly, a progressive lawyer, Whig MP and friend of Bentham's. At dinner, she found things stranger still:

'If the House & all the accompaniments transported us to other times, so I am sure did the language. A person totally unacquainted with the party would have had difficulty in following the conversation. They have used themselves this sort of language so long, that I really believe it never occurs to them it is not in common use. Can you imagine Mr Mill saying to me when I wanted to find my husband one day 'I fancy Sir Samuel has gone to vibrate with Mr. Bentham'? If you were asked to 'take a post prandial vibration', it would scarcely occur to you it was walking up & down the cloisters after dinner. They vibrate, too, on the Terrace, but when they go round the pleasure grounds it is a 'circumgyration'. I can't tell you half the odd expressions that are in common use. 'Circumbendibus' is a favourite one. What a pity it is that

> Mr. B. carries this oddity of language into his works. It makes them unreadable, & much less use than they would otherwise be.'[2]

A shrewd observation. Modern critics make just the same criticism of Bentham's writing. The philosopher had a mania for Latinate neologisms, of which the most extreme was 'antepostjentacularisation', meaning an extra walk after breakfast.

The country people, however, respected their eccentric neighbour and were amused by his habit of jogging up and down the garden walks with his hands on his hips. Mrs Bonfield, wife of the gardener at nearby Leigh House and hostess of the Knap Inn, became Bentham's housekeeper. She recalled that 'he did nothing, dear old man [Bentham was about 66 at this time] but write, write, write from day's end to week's end.'[3]

Bentham set up what he called his 'scribbling shop' in the Saloon hung with the Raphael tapestries; his many manuscripts were arrayed on music stands set on tables covered with white cloths. The saloon became a sort of monastic scriptorium, with the difference that Bentham, unlike the monks, allowed visitors to come and go freely, peering at him while he worked.

Indeed, Bentham and his acolytes re-created at Forde Abbey the kind of intellectual powerhouse it had been under Abbot Baldwin and John of Forde some 600 years earlier. Not that those early theologians would have agreed with a single word of Bentham's programme, since he strove to put everything – government, the law, the penal code, education, even morality itself – onto a strictly 'scientific' basis.

Bentham's friends were not slow to point out the contrast between his egalitarian philosophy and the magnificence of his country place. Samuel Romilly noted in his memoirs for September 1817: 'The grandeur and stateliness of the buildings form as strange a contrast to his philosophy as the number and spaciousness of the apartments do to the modesty and scantiness of his domestic establishment.'

He wrote to Bentham's French editor:

> I had heard of it [Forde] only as a place that had fallen into decay, and whose gloomy appearance had produced such an effect upon the imagination of the servants that they never ventured into some of the apartments from terror of spirits, with which they supposed them to be haunted. I was much surprised, therefore, by the cheerfulness, and still more by the magnificence, of the house – a palace, I should rather call it, for it is much more princely than many mansions which pass by that name.[4]

It could be said that Bentham was only following precedent: after all, Thomas

Chard was a Cistercian monk, yet lived like a lord of the manor; Edmund Prideaux was a Puritan yet spent lavishly on decoration.

Everyone who stayed at Forde felt bound to describe the house and gardens in letters home. Their compulsive need to put everything down on paper has left us an unrivalled picture of the abbey as it looked two hundred years ago – and a rare glimpse of the daily life of an important group of thinkers.

One of the first, and most charming, descriptions was written by the eight-year-old John Stuart Mill to a friend whom he addressed only as 'My dear Sir'. He writes in a careful hand on faint pencil lines which he has drawn himself, with a scratchy pen and many ink blots.

He starts with a description of one room, which he had been told was formerly the nursery:

> 'though the old farmer Glyde, who lives hard by, called out his sons to hear the [novelty?] of a child crying in the Abbey! which had not happened for the whole time he had lived here, being near 30 years.
> 'The rest of the house is not worth mentioning. If I was to mention the whole, it would tire you exceedingly, as this house is in reality so large, that the rooms on one floor of the wing that we inhabit which make not one quarter of even that floor of the whole house, are as many as all the rooms in your house, and considerably larger.'

The crying baby was presumably the youngest of the five Mill children, little James Bentham, born that same year. (The other children, in ascending order, were Harriet, Clara, Wilhelmina and John). John announces he is keeping a journal which the friend will be the first to see when the family come home, and goes on to complain:

> 'We have not heard once from either my grandmother, aunts or uncles, but have written three letters to them. General Bentham [Jeremy Bentham's brother Samuel] and his family have been here; they did not stay long, and are gone to Paris. I hope to hear from you soon. We have several fish-ponds in the pleasure ground, and get plenty of trout, dace, carp, eels, etc. caught in [there].We have likewise the river Axe running close to the house in which we catch many fish. The grounds about are laid out tastefully. There is a deer park containing a great many fine deer, and we have had much venison and a good quantity of game, considering the time.[5]

Bentham himself rather played down the magnificence of the abbey, perhaps aware of his friends' mockery. He described it in a letter to his brother as an 'odd and venerable place' a mixture of the antique with modern elegance, but rather run down, making an exception for the Raphael tapestries about which he said he had never seen figures more human.

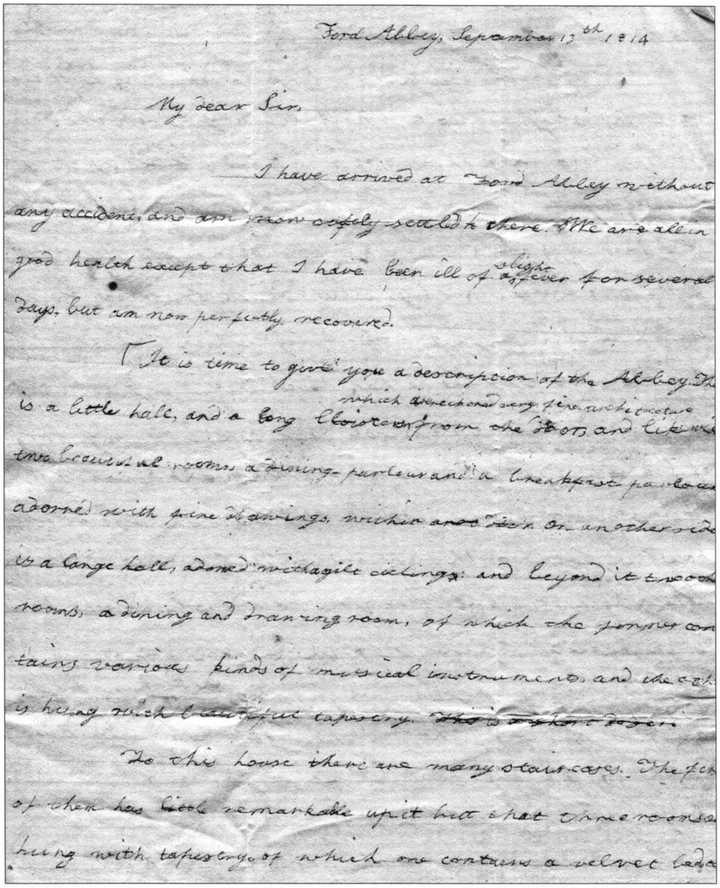

Ford Abbey, September 13th 1814

My dear Sir,

I have arrived at Ford Abbey without any accident, and am now safely settled there. We are all in good health except that I have been ill of a slight fever for several days, but am now perfectly recovered.

It is time to give you a description of the Abbey. There is a little hall, and a long cloister from the [illegible] which are reckoned very fine architecture, and likewise two beautiful rooms, a dining-parlour and a breakfast parlour adorned with fine drawings, neither [illegible]. On another side is a large hall, adorned with a gilt ceiling: and beyond it two other rooms, a dining and drawing room, of which the former contains various kinds of musical instruments, and the other is hung with beautiful tapestry. [illegible]

In this house there are many staircases. The [illegible] of them has little remarkable upon it but that three rooms are hung with tapestry, of which one contains a velvet [illegible]

The first page of a letter from the eight-year-old John Stuart Mill to a friend, describing life at Forde Abbey.

'Statues and pictures – every thing of this kind indifferent or execrable: of the furniture the antique part mostly in tatters, but not the less curious: in several of the rooms, old tapestry. Large trees a moderate sprinkling. In a Park of no more than 50 Acres, 130 head of deer, but the grass still luxuriant. There will, I suppose, be a buck to kill when you come: but at any rate you will not starve.'[6]

His mention of feasting on the park deer is amusing, given that Gwyn had put a clause in the lease to protect them. Bentham had protested about this, saying he was more likely to 'caress' the deer than kill them.

The philosopher followed an almost monastic regime of work, writing for six to eight hours a day. He occupied a desk in the far left-hand corner of the Saloon (as seen from the door), with James Mill in the right-hand corner, and any visiting writer or secretary sitting at a desk in front of his. Mill was working on a history of India. Bentham, as was his custom, was scribbling endless pages on many subjects at once which it was Mill's unenviable job to edit for publication. He was said to cover 15 sheets of paper every day, and to have left at his death some 30 million words of manuscript.

Mill, his wife Harriet and their first five children (they had eight in all) were in residence all the time that Bentham was: that is, six months or more each year. The philosopher rose at seven, took a walk and had breakfast, and started work at eight, writing until twelve, when he played the chamber organ in the Saloon (it is now in the chapel) for an hour before lunch at one. After lunch he and Mill would walk for an hour 'to digest what we have written,' resuming work until six when the grown-ups would have dinner. At eight Bentham would walk for another hour, when there was 'tea', and reading of newspapers and magazines. Bentham might then put in another hour from 10 p.m, until everyone went to bed at 11.

The children's regime was, if anything, more strict. James Mill devised a fearsome schedule for them, especially for young John who was up at five o'clock and spent an hour reading from manuscripts while his father corrected proofs. Then he went to the other end of the Saloon to teach two of his three younger sisters and study geometry himself until breakfast at nine. After breakfast their father heard the lessons of all three in the breakfast room or portico for three hours. After lunch there would be a walk, and perhaps more lessons, until bedtime.

'They have a hard time of it,' said Mill's friend Francis Place, the social reformer known as the 'radical tailor', who spent two months at Forde in 1817. Place wrote to his wife: 'Even little Jim spells words of four syllables well.' Younger sister Clara was 'reading of quadrupeds, and really knows what she reads in a surprising manner.' Mill's method was infinitely precise, but excessively severe. 'No fault, however trivial, escapes his notice; none goes without reprehension or punishment of some sort.' That day, the two girls Wilhelmina ('Willie') and Clara were still 'plodding over their books' at three o'clock, having missed dinner and with no prospect of it until six – all because of '*a mistake in one word.*'[7]

His father boasted that John was already familiar with the first six books of Euclid and proficient in algebra, 'while in Greek he has read since he came here the last half of Thucydides, one play of Euripides and one of Sophocles, two of Aristophanes and the treatise of Plutarch on eduction.' His sister 'Willie' was making rapid progress in Latin and had joined her brother in reading lives by the early Roman biographer Cornelius Nepos.

Years later, Clara recalled those lessons at Forde: 'I was a very little child when we lived there, but I have a very vivid recollection of certain parts of it – the hall, the cloisters, the staircases and the saloon as well as the breakfast room where I with my elder brother John and my elder sister used to learn our lessons.' She remembered a tapestry of Alexander the Great and his horse Bucephalus in her mother's room. 'We used to play at hide & seek behind the tapestries in all parts of the house and get through secret doors of the monks, as we supposed.'[8]

John's recollections were a lot more complicated. He looked back with pleasure on the house, 'so unlike the mean and cramped externals of English middle-class life' and on the grounds, '*riant* and secluded, umbrageous, and full of the sound of falling waters.' Nothing, he archly remarked, 'contributes more to nourish elevation of sentiments in a people than the large and free character of their habitations.'

Yet the indoctrination he got from his father, although it helped him to become perhaps the greatest British philosopher of the nineteenth century, was bound to take its toll – as Francis Place had warned it would.

At the age of 20, Mill suffered a crisis: he fell into a depression, found all pleasures 'insipid' and was shocked to discover that the systematic study of human happiness in which he had been trained did nothing for his own happiness. The 'analytic habits' which his father insisted on were, he said, 'a perpetual worm at the root both of the passions and of the virtues.' Modern psychology would add that there was more to this than loss of faith in the messianic vision of the Benthamite reformers. Mill was having a nervous breakdown, caused by overwork, lack of contact with women and repressed resentment of his controlling parent.[9]

Jeremy Bentham himself seems to have suffered no such setbacks. He, too, had been a precocious child, but weak, small and solemn. His mother died when he was only 11, and of the seven children only he and his brother Samuel survived. The older he got, the more cheerful, playful, healthy and selfconfident he became. Like modern chess masters Bentham was a great believer in vigorous physical exercise as a preparation for intense brainwork. When the weather was too foul for outdoor 'vibrating' or 'gyrating', there was plenty of room indoors for walks and games. While his secretary John Colls was staying, they played shuttlecock and battledore (what we call 'badminton') in the Great Hall every morning. 'Played as we play it, it is hard exercise,' said the philospher. Alternatively there was handball – or 'fives' – played against the wall in the monks' dormitory. Colls remembers the 69-year-old Bentham challenging the

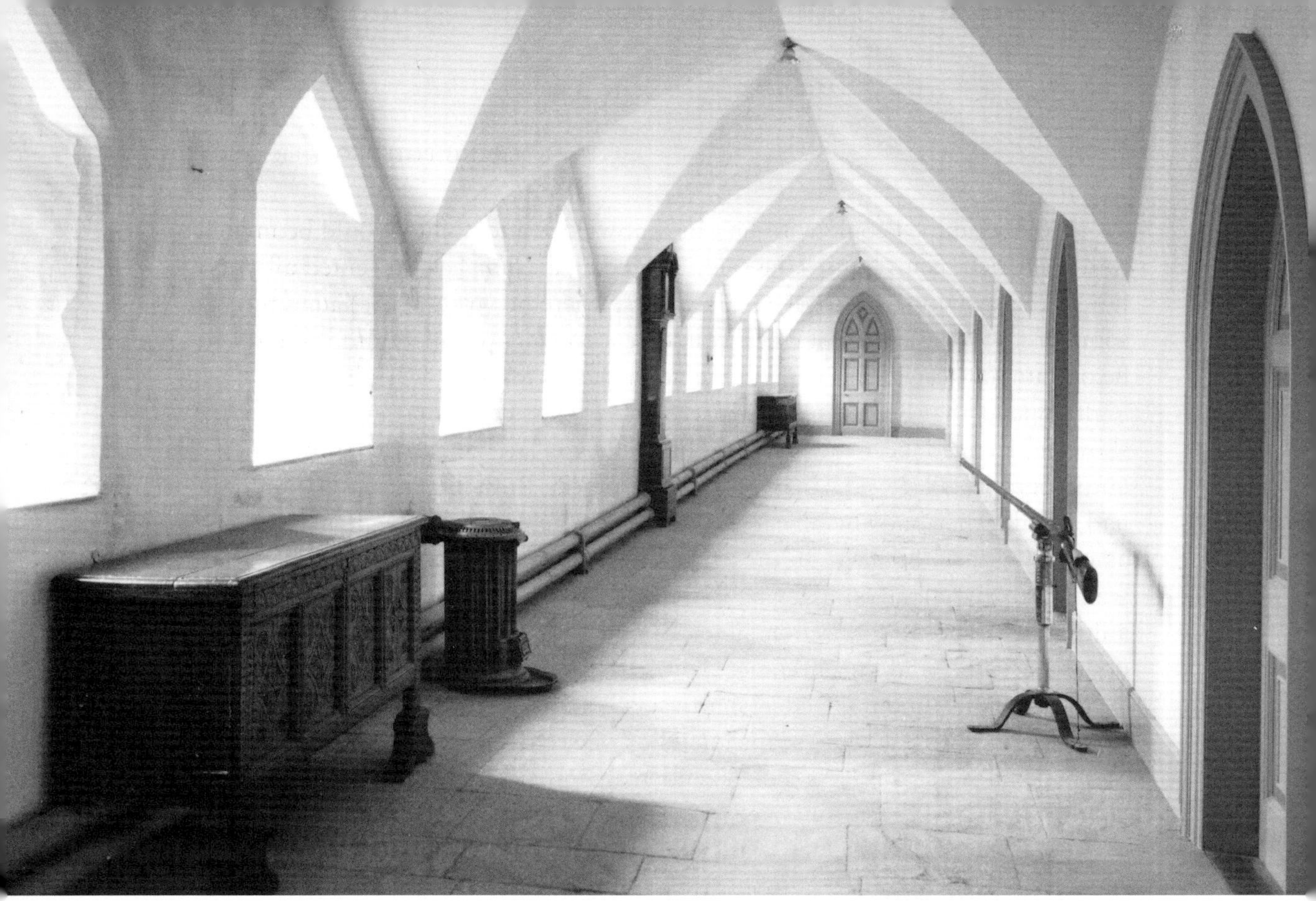

The mediaeval dormitory or 'Monks' Walk', where on rainy days Bentham would play handball. He regularly used the Great Hall as a badminton court.

45-year-old Anne Romilly to a race along the gravel walk. She won.

Among themselves, the resident and visiting Benthamites got on well, though Bentham was middle class – his father Jeremiah was a successful barrister and landlord – while his disciples were mostly working class. This made for some interesting encounters when members of the gentry came to visit.

The upper-class Lady Romilly was intrigued by her first meeting with Francis Place. In the letter to Maria Edgeworth she described how Bentham had seized her husband by the arm, saying: 'Romilly, come here, let me introduce you to Mr. Place, Maker of Small Clothes and Members of Parliament.' She continued: 'To our surprise we saw the famous Tailor of Charing Cross – whom you must certainly have heard of – & whom we found a very pleasant, sensible man who had read a great deal & spoke well without anthing vulgar about him but the tone of his voice.'[10]

By 'the tone of his voice', she clearly meant his London accent.

Place was only too conscious of his low social status: 'My having been a *tailor* and still living at a *tailor's* shop is a mark not easily to be obliterated,' he says in his autobiography. People with half his knowledge and ability would be invited to dine at rich men's houses, he said. 'My being a *tailor* has prevented all but a few of them inviting me to their tables.' Elsewhere he writes: 'The ladies too, of some of my grand acquaintances, condescended when we met in the country to be on familiar terms with me, but we never met in town.'

It appears that Bentham himself was just as class conscious, even if he didn't show it. He had been nervous of introducing Place to the Romillys: in his autobiography Place says that before inviting the Romillys to Forde, Bentham had asked if they had any objections to meeting him because 'Gentlemen cannot associate with tradesmen.' In the event, the encounter went off well. Sir Samuel was unusually talkative, his wife 'quite at her ease, and in all respects amiable, admirable.' The Romillys' daughter Sophie was also there, as was Place's daughter Annie, and they became 'capital friends.'

'Miss Romilly and I played at shuttlecock and battledore in the grat [sic] Hall for exercise, but she had no suspicion who I was; she was much pleased with me and concluded I was no less than a gentleman and a Member of Parliament.' He later told a friend that Sophie 'fell in love' with him.[11]

And indeed Francis Place was a remarkable man who had come a long way. Born in the debtors' jail which his father supervised near Drury Lane, he went to school for only ten years. He was apprenticed to a leather breeches-

Francis Place, the 'Tailor of Charing Cross', social reformer and friend of Bentham.

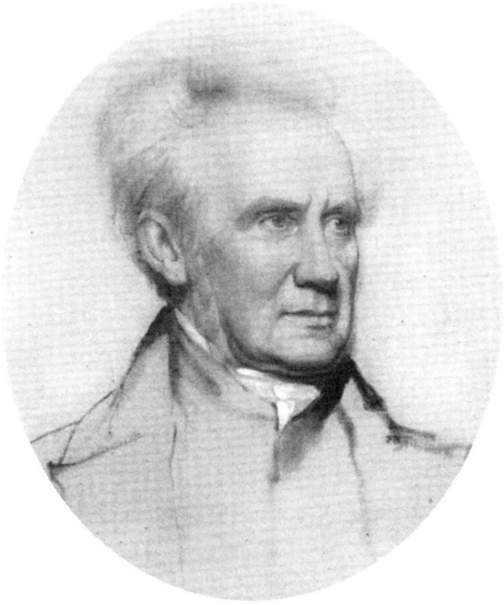

maker, led a strike, was blacklisted, and set up his own business at Number 16, Charing Cross. He read voraciously, campaigned tirelessly for social reform and worker's education, and promoted reformist MPs (hence Bentham's reference to him as their 'Maker'). He became a follower of Malthus, who warned that overpopulation would lead inevitably to famine, and spoke in favour of contraception – yet he and his wife Elizabeth had 15 children. At the time of his encounter with the Romillys he had just left the tailoring business to his son so that he could join Bentham and the Mill family at Forde for several months. He got on well with his new acquaintances yet, as he wrote to his wife, was relieved when the 'great folks' had gone, because 'there will be now no more dressing for dinner in a cold room. Besides, I want to have ourselves to ourselves.'

Samuel Romilly was the son of a middle-class Huguenot refugee, a Soho jeweller and watchmaker. He had worked his way up in the law to become an MP and Solicitor-General in the Whig government of 1806. He was a man of conscience, and a powerful and progressive force in parliament where he was famous for his oratory. He was nearly 40 when he met and fell in love with Anne Garbett, whom he married in 1798.

But their story ended in calamity. The year after they visited Forde Abbey, Anne was taken ill while staying in the Isle of Wight and died. Samuel was at home in London when it happened. He was inconsolable. Five days later, delirious, alone and unguarded in his bedroom, he cut his own throat.

James Mill was the son of a shoemaker from Angus in Scotland. The strictness of the regime he imposed on his children at Forde was the result of his own good education, which he owed to the determination of his mother Isabel and the generosity of Sir John Stuart, a local laird who paid for him to go to Edinburgh University. The *History of British India* which he wrote in the Saloon at Forde was influential in its day, but its severe criticism of Indian culture is now seen as mistaken. He is better known today as a co-founder of classical economics with David Ricardo, who also visited the abbey.

Mill was lucky in his wife Harriet, who managed to keep the children in order without fuss – she had five when they arrived at Forde, one born there, and two later. Her virtues were recognized, though Francis Place and Bentham were both condescending. The Tailor found her good-natured but vain and girlish. Bentham confided to Anne Romilly that she was a 'very worthy excellent woman...but poor thing, she has no mind in her body.'

Among the visitors in Bentham's circle the noisiest was probably the radical Scottish MP Joseph Hume. A schoofriend of James Mill, he was brought up by a widowed mother who supported herself and her children by selling crockery.

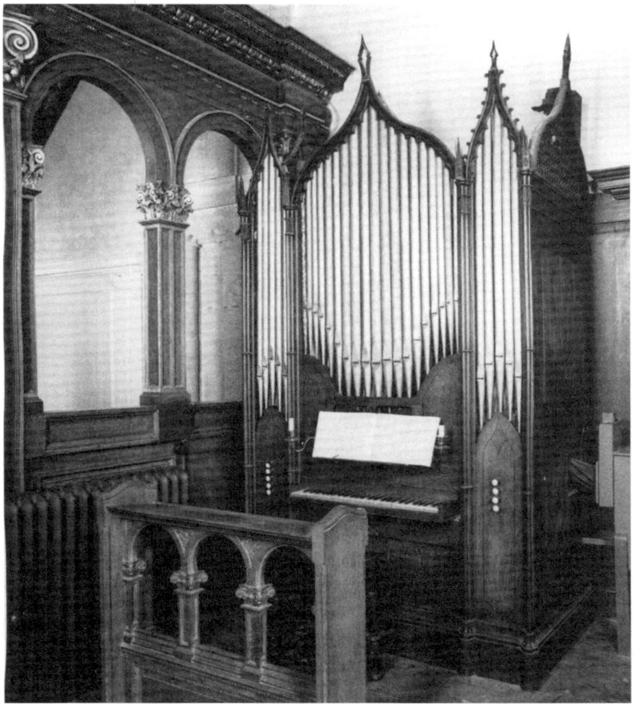

The eighteenth-century chamber organ on which Bentham played in the Saloon. It was later moved to the Chapel.

Hume had made a fortune of some £40,000 – 'probably legally', says his official biographer – while employed by the East India Company as a purser, surgeon, intelligence officer and paymaster. At Mill's behest, and somewhat reluctantly, Place took him on and trained him up for parliament. With his shock of red hair, muddled speech and dogged manner, Hume was a figure of fun to his parliamentary colleagues, who nicknamed him 'the Apothecary'. He seemed impervious to the mockery and became a real force for change.

A few of the locals were invited to dine, especially Mr Festing, vicar of Winsham, and John Bragge, the squire of Sadborow House, whose family came from Burstock on the abbey estate and whose son was rector there and vicar of Thorncombe. Mrs Bragge was described by Bentham as 'the beautiful and virtuous foe' and by Place, less charitably, as 'a singular piece of starched up antiquity.'

Music was one of Jeremy Bentham's many interests. He could play the harpsichord, piano and violin. While at Forde he had the small chamber organ in the Saloon repaired, and asked his secretary in London to send him the sheet music of Handel's Concertos – presumably the organ concertos. He also organized a couple of recitals in the Great Hall, a presage of things to come.[12]

A greater passion was horticulture; and at Forde he had every chance to indulge it. He had hardly settled in before he was drawing up plans to improve the terrace and ordering shrubs. He had the Long Pond cleaned out, and spent a lot of time trying to repair the ice house near the south-east corner of the abbey. He hunted through the newspapers for details of a Devon tree nursery which he had been told was selling up, in the hope of getting a bargain. From London he ordered Periwinkle and Sumach plants, seeds of Bladder senna [Colutea], Laburnum and 'Everlasting Peace'. To stop the 'cursed' geese and peacocks eating the carnations, he had their wings clipped and banished them to the Great Pond. His neighbour, Viscountess Bridport at Cricket St. Thomas, gave him peafowl in exchange for some of the now 'beautiful and virtuous Geese.' He calculated that by the end of his four-year stay he had spent three or four hundred pounds on fruit trees, flowers and shrubs.

Bentham was happy at Forde. His verdict is often quoted: 'Nobody that could stay here would go from hence. Nobody is so well anywhere else as everybody is here.'[13] There were rows, of course. Bentham had a prickly temperament, and on one occasion was so offended by James Mill that Mill felt obliged to write a long letter of apology; he even offered to leave. After many pages of analysis and pacification, he reveals the cause of Bentham's umbrage – he had gone riding in the morning with James Hume instead of going for a walk with Bentham.[14]

Only six months after taking up residence, Bentham wrote to J.F. Gwyn giving notice that he would end the tenancy in June 1815. He then rescinded it. In neither case did he offer an explanation. In the event he stayed for four years. When he terminated the lease it may have been because he was worried about money: he lost £8,000 which he had been persuaded to invest in a marble mine in Devon, run by a man who went 'out of his mind'.

His actual departure, in February 1818, was followed by a torrent of objections to bills he had received from Gwyn's agent Mr. Gould, a lawyer in Honiton. Bentham's grievances – one of his letters to Gwyn ran to 15 pages – were every landlord's nightmare. He quibbled about his responsibility for damage to the stable windows and the greenhouses, complained about the state of the house furniture and of the garden when he arrived, totted up how much he had spent on repairs and improvements, and haggled over the price he should be paid for the firewood he had left behind. Given the elaborately facetious tone of these letters the reader cannot help feeling that Bentham was enjoying himself.

If Gwyn was irritated, he didn't show it. His replies were short and placatory, even ingratiating. He conceded that perhaps Mr Gould had been over-officious. The result was an agreement to let matters be decided by arbitrators: Bentham chose John Bragge. Almost plaintively, Gwyn asked who was going to pay the last instalment of rent due. History does not record an answer.

Among the books Bentham worked on during his sojourn at Forde was *Chrestomathia*, a proposal for a new kind of secondary school based on his theory of education. He also drafted a criticism of the Anglican clergy, *Church of Englandism and its Catechism Examined*, and a treatise called *Not Paul, but Jesus* which accused St. Paul of importing asceticism into the Christian message.

In his time Bentham enjoyed a high reputation. The *Edinburgh Review* ranked him alongside Galileo and Locke, as 'the man who found Jurisprudence a gibberish and left it a science.'[15] He was visited by Talleyrand, courted by Madame de Stael (whom he refused to see), and corresponded with Tsar Alexander I of Russia, James Madison and Aaron Burr, among others.

Today he is known today more for his enthusiastic promotion of the principle of Utilitarianism than for the books he wrote in an attempt to apply it; more for his methods, in other words, than for his conclusions. Although the Utilitarian principle ('the greatest happiness of the greatest number') still appears in ethical debate, it is generally seen as too formulaic, taking no account of custom, culture, human instinct or of human rights – rights which Bentham, characteristically, described as 'nonsense upon stilts'.

* * *

The philosopher of Forde made sure that posterity would remember him. He decreed that after his death his body should be made available for dissection; but his skeleton was to be clothed and a wax effigy made of his head. The resulting 'auto-icon' was supposed to be given a seat at the high table of University College, London, an institution of which Bentham was an early patron. It was kept in a cupboad at the college, where it can still be seen, with his favourite walking stick 'Dapple' on his knee. His head, a gruesome object with wisps of white hair still attached, used to lie at his feet. Following a student prank, it was later moved to a safer place.

There is a footnote to the story. A few years ago an expert employed by Sotheby's was asked by the college to repair the old man's clothes. Since the only place she could do it was her own studio the question arose how Bentham was to get there. Gamely, the expert volunteered to take him home in her car, ignoring the curious glances of the passers-by, no doubt, as she carried him into the house.

A Second Dissolution

J.F. Gwyn went back to live at Forde. It seems he did not live there much of the time. Meanwhile Forde was 'moved' from Devon to Dorset, an overdue recognition of the awkward boundary which had for centuries left Thorncombe and the abbey marooned on a salient of Devon surrounded by neighbouring counties. (To this day the abbey's location remains ambiguous: though now situated in Dorset, its address is Somerset, with a Taunton postcode).

Gwyn died in early 1846. Unlike the rest of his family he lived to the ripe old age of 84, surviving his second wife Dinah by 15 years. He was being cared for by his niece Louisa Griffith when the end came. For much of this time, according to his friend Maria Allen, he was virtually blind: 'But he bore the deprivation with fortitude and resignation – indeed, from his habitual cheerfulness, he endeavoured to make those around him think he did not feel his infirmity.'[16] The picture she paints is at odds with the awkward eccentric described by James Mill, and typical of her good nature.

This is the place in which to say more of the woman whose history of the abbey, dedicated to Gwyn's trustees and modestly signed 'M.A.', has been an important source for antiquarians and amateur historians (like the author) who have followed her. The will of the last Gwyn provides the answer. His most detailed bequest was to one Maria Milverton, a cousin of his late wife Dinah Good of Winsham. This Maria had lived with them *en famille* at Forde until after Dinah's death in 1831,

Etching in one of the state bedroom windows: '(?) F Gwyn 1809-1819'.
It is not clear what these dates refer to.

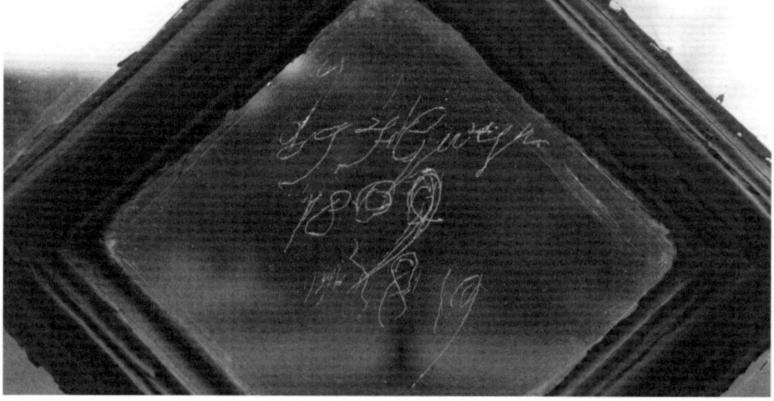

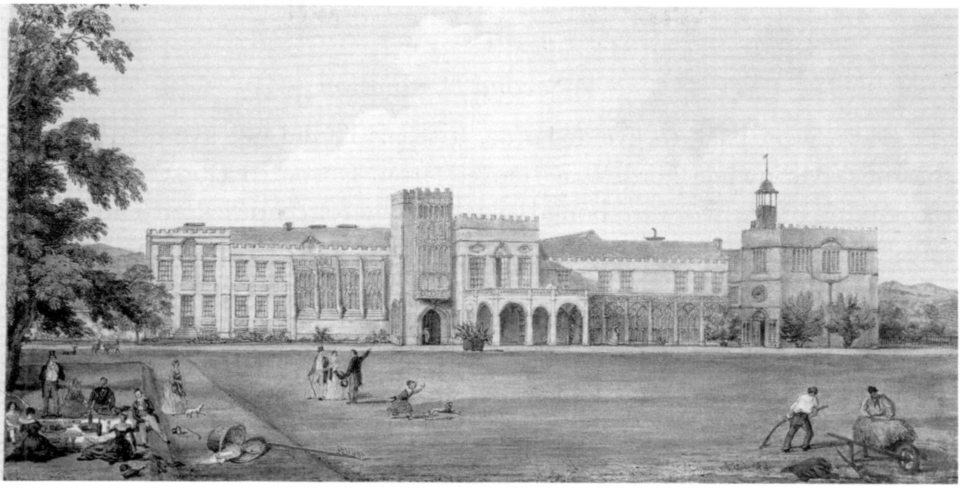

A picnic in the park, painted in 1834.

leaving only to marry William Allen of Winsham in 1836. Gwyn left her £1,000, as well as his piano, harp and sheet music, and a house at Ammerham, the village across the river on the road to Winsham, with some land to go with it. Maria was left a widow when her husband died a year later.

His principal legatee was his great-nephew Francis Griffith of Llansannor in Glamorgan; other nephews and nieces benefitted, as did charitable causes. Louisa Griffith received £1,000. Small legacies were made to his servant Susan, gamekeeper Benjamin Harris at Coppice (now 'Copse') House, and the estate carpenter William Bragg.

There was no heir. Gwyn's only children were two illegitimate daughters, Mary Boult and Joanna Pole, to whom he granted annuities. His will directed that Forde Abbey, along with its park and estates and all his possessions should be sold at auction 'with all convenient speed after my decease', either together or in parcels. The trustees were instructed how to invest the proceeds to pay the various annuities.

Why Gwyn felt obliged to sell is not made clear. It is certain he had been feeling the pinch. Following the Napoleonic wars – boom times for the British economy – there was an agricultural slump and prices had plummeted. Perhaps, as Bentham claimed, the abbey was falling into such disrepair that neither he nor his relatives could afford – or should be asked – to maintain it. Certainly the abbey was in a poor state: it was described at this time as 'a sleeping beauty', its walls almost hidden behind the tangle of creeper that reached up to the roof, and the roof itself constantly leaking.

Mr. Robins feels that some explanation may be expected in respect to the cause of the Re-sale of

THE FORD ABBEY ESTATE.

It is already proclaimed that the Rev. Lawrence Gwynne, of Teignmouth, purchased this Estate on the 9th of July last, and has failed to pay the required Deposit. It may not be out of place here to state, the original cause for this Sale taking place was that the late worthy Proprietor left by his Will directions to the effect that it was to be submitted for peremptory Sale, so soon as it could be accomplished after his demise—and the Trustees have carried out his wishes with great alacrity. The description that follows is mainly Historical, and for the clever addition, Mr. Robins is entirely indebted to a fair and talented Lady, whose name he is not permitted to hand down to posterity; it will be seen she has culled, with much learning and intellect, from all the sources that were open, and added from her own "*brain farm*" much that will instruct and delight the reader. Mr. Robins has only one more observation to make, that FORD ABBEY, as a Monastery, is decidedly in a position to challenge rivalry anywhere and everywhere throughout England—and as a safe Investment, it is quite certain there is nothing to approach it in the Market.

PARTICULARS

OF ONE OF THE MOST

Magnificent Freehold Investments

THROUGHOUT ENGLAND,

And in the description that necessarily must follow, Mr. Robins, without the slightest affectation, proclaims that he approaches the task with fear and trembling. Dugdale is no mean authority, and with this, and a few introductory facts, the herculean task must be approached. The

FORD ABBEY DEMESNES

Are to be traced back to a very distant day, and the Abbey has ever since maintained its proud superiority over

EVERY OTHER MONASTERY IN ENGLAND.

It is a splendidly grand and unique building, altogether realising Lord Byron's glowing description of Norman Abbey:—

An old, old monastery once, and now
Still older mansion, of a rich and rare
Mix'd Gothic, such as artists all allow
Few specimens yet left us can compare.

Its Classic Front extends to near 300 Feet.

The Order of Architecture is in the Tudor style, and may be dated about the time of Henry the Eighth; but to describe it as it deserves is felt to be far beyond the reach of the limited capacity of the composer, and even much wiser heads would be puzzled in the attempt to do it justice—it is indeed

The Great Leviathan of the West

Its fame has been held in the highest veneration from generation to generation, and it is now avowed to have no successful rival amid the vast variety of Monasteries to be found throughout the Country. The first impression on beholding this

ANCIENT AND CLASSIC PILE,

The auctioneer's rhapsodic advertisement for the great sale (actually a re-sale) in 1846.

The Great Sale

Needless to say, no reference to this state of affairs was to be found in the auctioneers' newspaper advertisements and sale brochure. Their rhapsodic description of the abbey and its estate make the rhetoric of modern estate agents sound feeble indeed. 'One of the most magnificent freehold investments throughout England,' declared the auctioneer, George Robins of Covent Garden, in his notice of sale for 3rd September 1846. He approaches 'with fear and trembling' the herculean task of doing justice to the place:

> The Great and Proud Feature of the county, the **Magnificently Fine Abbey** presents by far the most **Classical & Celebrated Monastery** throughout England. And the Field Sports are all that a veteran Sportsman can desire. The Property, which has long been proclaimed **The Great Leviathan of the West,** numbers near 1200 **Acres of rich Land,** With an exceedingly respectable Tenantry. The first impression on beholding this **Ancient and Classic Pile,** the writer feels, can never be obliterated from his memory...

And this is before he has got round to extolling the merits of the gardens with their 'Gravelled Walks between umbrageous Trees interspersed with Ornamental Waters, Cascades and Waterfalls sparkling with foam,' the park 'of great beauty stocked with Deer whose venison has obtained the highest celebrity for its fatness and fine flavour' and the River Axe 'renowned for its piscatory pleasures and delicious Trout, which winds in serpentine beauty through the fair demesne.'

Having elsewhere predicted keen competition for the property, Mr Robins urges his wealthy readers to invest in land, noting the general surplus of capital despite the current mania for investing in railways, the low value of the pound and the new Corn Laws, by which 'we have all been more frightened than hurt.' For the historical summary which followed in his advertisement, Robins paid tribute to a 'fair and talented Lady' whose name, he said, he was not permitted to hand down to posterity. The fair and talented lady can have been none other than Maria Allen, née Milverton.

Mr Robins' eloquence no doubt was fired by the fact – a fact he admits right at the start of his brochure – that this auction was the second attempt to sell Forde Abbey and its estate.

For at auction on the 9th July a certain Rev. Lawrence Gwynne of Teignmouth in Devon had bid 52,000 guineas for it. But he failed to come up with his deposit, and the estate went back on the market. Was this Gwynne (or Gwyn) a relation? It is possible. Yet it seems unlikely that a vicar could afford even to try to buy

Forde Abbey – or that a bachelor vicar should want to. This Revd. Gwynne was, however, the son of a rich man; and it possible that he was acting on behalf of his father, also named Lawrence, who decided not to go through with the purchase.

Gwynne senior had risen rapidly in the world. He was the son of a London candlemaker, had become a prominent figure in the city and a successful property investor. He had moved to Teignmouth where he had married, as his second wife, a girl from the Dorset landowning family of Strangways. The family lived in some style, with as many as eight servants. His son was the eldest of the first marriage and so the heir. Educated at St. Paul's School and Trinity College, Cambridge, he was called to the Bar but became a priest. After a controversial spell as vicar of East Teignmouth he moved to Paris, living just off the Champs-Elysées, and died in a grand Swiss hotel.[17] He left only £20 to his next of kin, his sister. Perhaps the rest of his inheritance had been consumed by high living.

The abbey was forecast to fetch around 70,000 guineas at the second auction. In the event, in spite of Mr Robins' effusive rhetoric and widespread publicity it went for only 50,100 guineas (about £2.3m in today's money), less than the Rev. Gwynne had bid at the first auction.[18]

The buyer was George Miles, a young man of only 25 from Bristol who had made money in the West Indies and returned to become a partner in his father's bank, Miles & Co. His father Philip, a merchant and MP, had shown the way by amassing a fortune as a planter and landowner in Jamaica. He lived in a mansion designed by Sir John Vanbrugh at Kings Weston near the River Avon, now owned by the city of Bristol and visible from the M5 motorway. Philip Miles was very rich: he died the year before the Forde Abbey auction, leaving more than £1m. And although he had 15 children from two marriages, at least some of that fortune must have come to his son George.

The abbey's contents were auctioned separately, at the house, by Messrs. English and Son in a sale spread over eight days in October and November. On the third day George Miles bought the Raphael tapestries for £2,200 (nearly £100,000 in today's money) but a great deal less than the £30,000 (£2m) which Catherine the Great was supposed to have been ready to pay for them.

Miles appears also to have bought, for £50, the set of tapestries which still hang in the drawing room behind the Hall. In the catalogue they are described as Gobelins, depicting Scipio Africanus in triumph, a Roman gladiator, Cyrus of Persia, and the building of the temple in Jerusalem. They have since been identified as scenes from the life of Constantine: entering Rome, fighting a lion on the Danube, his Roman triumphs, and planning the building of Constantinople. They were made in Brussels or Oudenaarde, rather than Paris.

Another survivor was the charming chamber organ played by Jeremy Bentham. 'An excellent and fine-toned finger organ' it went for £28 10 shillings. Apart from the tapestries, the organ and one or two notable pictures the bulk of the abbey's treasures were scattered – Old Master paintings, furniture, ornaments, books and manuscripts, china, silver and plate, even garden tools and watering cans came under the hammer. The family portraits collected by Prideaux and Gwyn came off the walls. So did notable paintings by Peter Lely of Charles I as a youth, of Charles II and his mistresses Nell Gwynn (not a relation) and Lucy Walters; portraits of Monmouth and of the Young Pretender by Godfrey Kneller, of his friend the younger Edmund Prideaux, of Amy his wife, the Earl of Rochester and Sir Edward Seymour. Gone, too, is Cardinal Wolsey by Holbein; portraits by Velazquez and Van Dyck and Zuccaro; paintings by Murillo, Guercino, Salvatore Rosa, Angelica Kauffman, Teniers the Elder, George Stubbs and Snyders. A few pieces survived, and more were bought back by future owners.

With the sales of 1846, the abbey reached the the end of another chapter in its long life. It was a Dissolution of another kind. As with the Dissolution, the new owner did not last long and it was some years before a rescuer appeared. But it was to be another hundred years before the abbey found an heir able to recover – and indeed surpass – its former glory.

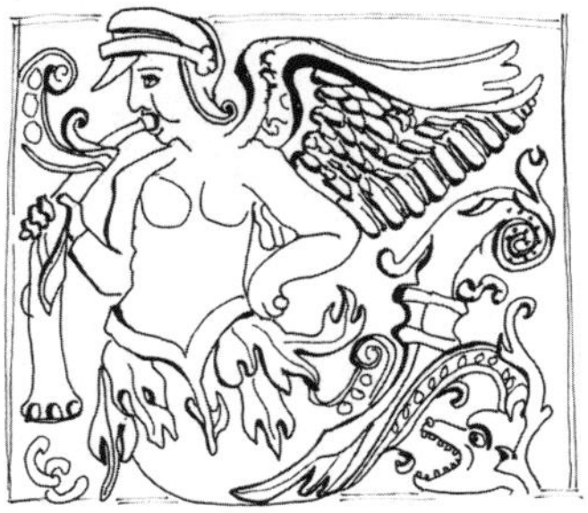

FIVE

A Struggle for Survival

LIKE MANY SONS OF RICH INDUSTRIALISTS in those days, George Miles was in a hurry to become a country gentleman with a sporting estate. Having bought Forde Abbey at a knockdown price he settled there after marrying in 1851. His bride was Augusta Saville from Torquay. Accustomed to describing himself as planter, proprietor or banker, Miles now acquired the trappings of the gentry. He set up a large household of live-in domestic servants: a butler, two footmen, a coachman and a groom; a ladies' maid, a cook-housekeeper, two housemaids and a kitchen maid. There were of course also gardeners and estate workers. His wife's sister Adelaide came to live with them. He was appointed a magistrate.

But the dream was not to last. For whatever reason, George Miles was unable – or unwilling – to repair the abbey fabric and mend the roof. For a dozen years he lived in just five rooms at the eastern end of the house until, in 1863, he sold up and moved to the Brecon Beacons. He did not buy another property but rented Llangattock Park, the Duke of Beaufort's hunting lodge, where he continued to maintain a large retinue of servants.

Forde Abbey was once again in need of a saviour. And a saviour appeared, in the person of Jane Evans, the daughter of a well-to-do Scottish landowner and widow of an MP with a large bank balance and a scandalous past.

Jane Evans 'poured money' into the house, according to one contemporary, spending £10,000 on the roof alone. She did not take up residence herself, however, but installed her son Herbert at Forde while continuing to live with her

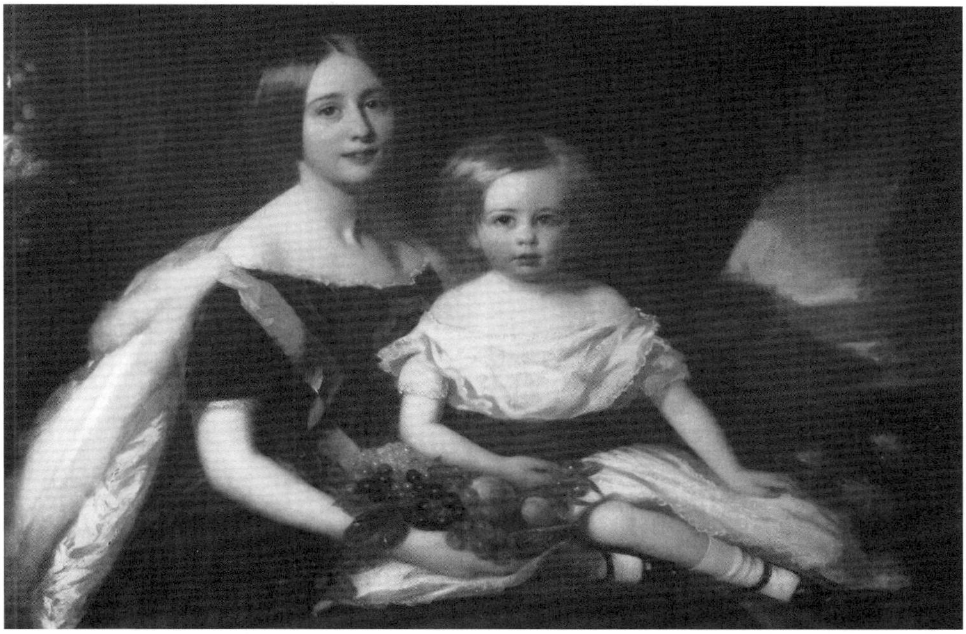

A portrait of Jane Evans with her first child Herbert whom she installed in the house when she bought Forde in 1863. The portrait hangs on the Grand Staircase.

two unmarried daughters at Wimbledon Park House, a grand London residence formerly owned by the Duchess of Marlborough.[1]

It has been assumed that Jane got her money from her father John Boyd whose own father had worked for the East India Company. Boyd had bought an estate called Broadmeadows on the river Yarrow near Selkirk and was sufficiently well off to lend money to his neighbour, the novelist Sir Walter Scott. But when his 20-year-old daughter got engaged to William Bertram Evans in 1833, John Boyd wrote to Bertram's father to say that he could not afford to give her any more than the £46 a year she would get from her mother's estate and the £100 she would get at his death. He had, he pointed out, eleven other children to provide for.

It was not the Boyds but the Evanses who provided the money that Jane lavished on Forde. John, her father-in-law, gave her a dowry of £4,000 on her marriage. Her husband Bertram was not to live long: they had 17 years together before his premature death at the age of 49 in 1850. He left everything to her. She also inherited the bulk of her father-in-law's property in England – he had estates in Ireland, too – and around £140,000 invested when he followed his son to the grave three years later.

Jane's father had not been enthusiastic about the match: breaking the news to a brother that Jane was engaged to Bertram, a friend of his eldest son Archibald, he said it was 'for good or for bad.'[2] His doubts were not surprising. He must have known – as Jane certainly did – that Bertram had a colourful past. Although a thoroughy presentable suitor, a product of Harrow and Cambridge, a qualified barrister and recently elected Member of Parliament for Leominster, he had only just emerged from an illicit affair with another man's wife.

At the age of 26 Bertram had gone to Dublin where his father had business. There he ran off with Catherine Jordan, the wife of an upholsterer. For five years they lived together under the name of 'Estcourt', first at Walworth in London where they were joined by Catherine's eldest daughter, then in France where their own first child Sarah was born. A year later they were in Cheltenham, where a second child was born and died. A third child was born in 1832, and then the liaison ended.

As soon as Bertram married Jane, the wronged husband Henry Jordan began threatening to make a scandal and sue for compensation. Jane seems to have been totally unconcerned, both about her husband's past and the threat of exposure. Nor did Bertram take the threat of legal action seriously: he saw the threat as crude blackmail. It was clear to the couple that Jordan did not want his wife back – he called her a 'strumpet' – while Bertram was sure he had maltreated their children and had given his wife poison to make her miscarry. Jordan tracked his wife down to Margate, where she was living under another assumed name. She wrote in fear to Bertram's father, John Evans, who helped her move to Cork and made her an allowance of £100 a year. Jordan's threats and allegations – he said his daughter had been 'abducted' – continued for 15 years, but nothing came of them.[3]

Jane and Bertram had four children, the last, Harry, being born after Bertram died in 1850. As the eldest, Herbert was made custodian of Forde Abbey. His mother paid not only for major repairs to the Hall roof and plaster ceilings but also a number of alterations: the kitchen was linked to the dining room; a corridor was created extending from the top of the Grand Staircase behind the state rooms; and the upper refectory – which for two centuries had been used as a hayloft for the farm below – was converted into a handsome neo-Gothic library stocked with books of history, travel and reference. She probably also financed the rebuilding of the aisle in Thorncombe parish church dedicated to owners of Forde Abbey.

Herbert had no pressing occupation, and was a keen collector. He found the exotic wooden panels, eighteenth-century bedheads from Brittany, which

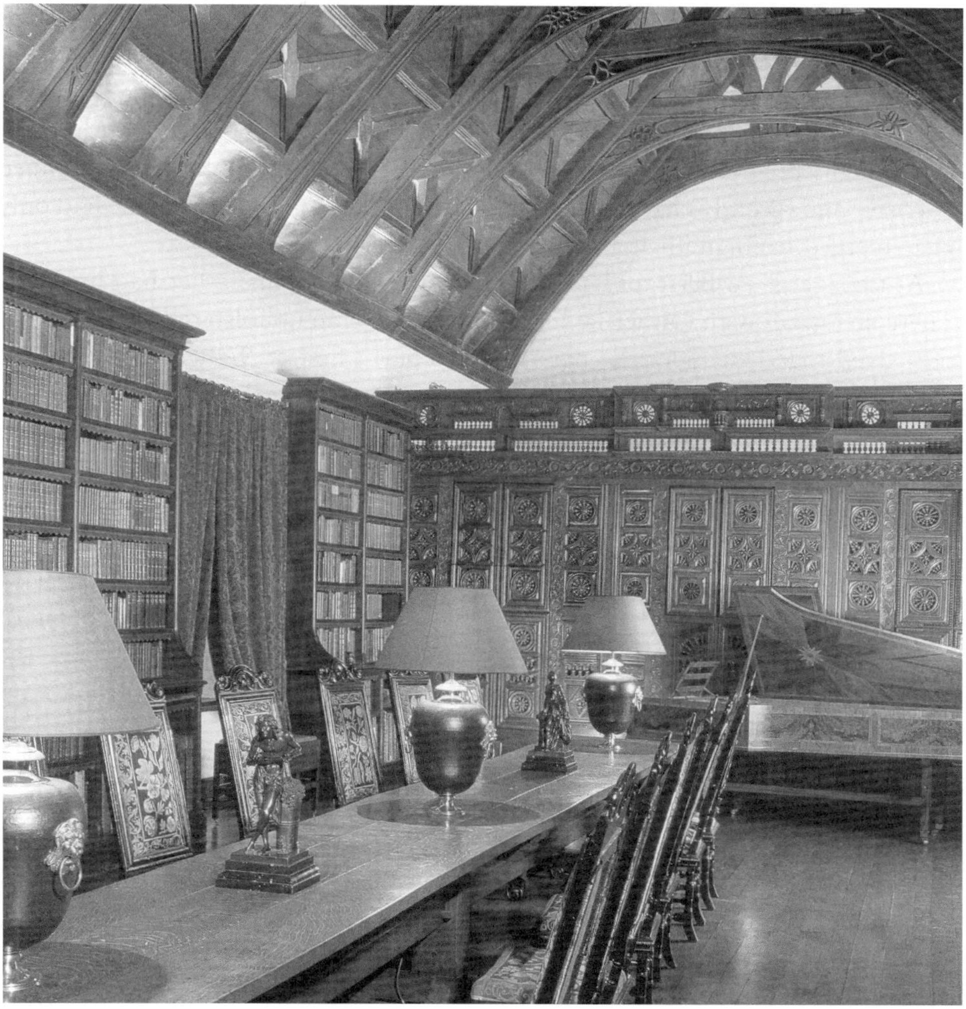

The Upper Refectory, converted into a library by the bibliophile Herbert Evans. It had been added by the monks 400 years before to accommodate meat-eaters, and latterly used as a hay loft.

form the screen put up at the south end of the Library to conceal a new back staircase. He also hunted down and bought back a number of pieces which had been sold in the auction of 1846, including the fine set of tapestry chairs purchased by Francis Gwyn in anticipation of Queen Anne's cancelled visit to the abbey. He acquired the two Florentine *cassoni*, or marriage chests, and the malachite-topped table from St. Petersburg which are now in the Saloon, as well as *cloisonné* from China. He showed to a reporter from *The Bridport News* a

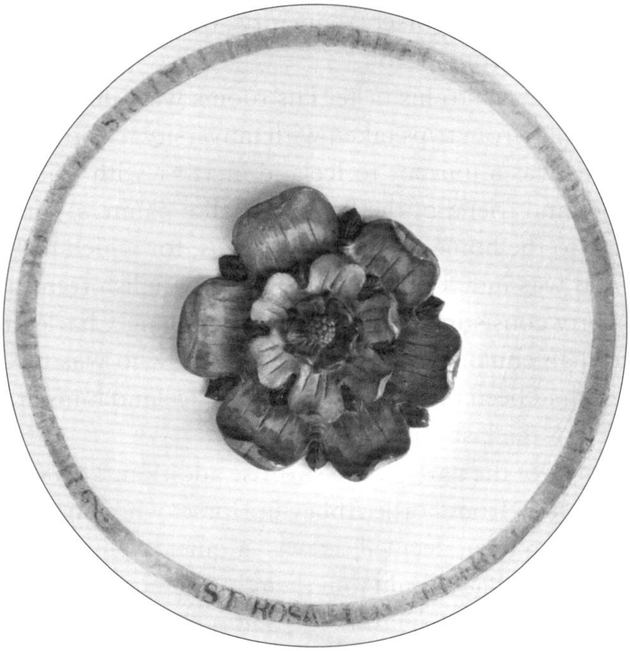

The Tudor rose in the ceiling outside the dining room with its faint Latin inscription, a traditional reminder that dinner-table gossip was *sub rosa* , 'off the record' and should not be repeated.

chest in the window where he kept a large collection of letters and documents which he was planning one day to include in a history of the house. 'He would like not only to carefully preserve from decay every relic of the past,' the *News* reported, 'but to write the annals of Forde as they deserve to be written.'

The reporter was also shown a large wooden rose set into the ceiling outside the drawing room (where it can still be seen). In earlier times it would have been placed above the private dining table to remind people that what they heard and saw was to be *sub rosa*, that is, treated in strict confidence. The rose was surrounded by a Latin motto, now very faint, and much more lapidary than this supposed translation:

'I am Venus's own flower, to silence I'm bound.
Whate'er I may see, I ne'er utter a sound;
'Twas Cupid who bound me, that none should disclose
His mother's gay frolicking under the rose.'[4]

Herbert was only routinely involved in public affairs, as a magistrate, parish councillor and briefly as county councillor. He did stand for Parliament in 1868, as Liberal Unionist for Barnstaple, but failed to win the seat. He engaged in some peaceful soldiering with the Dorset Yeomanry: the county regiment now that Forde had been 'moved' from Devon.

Foreign travel was more to his taste. His rooms were decorated with trophy heads and stags' antlers from trips taken with university friends. One of his more unusual expeditions was a journey to Iceland in 1871 with William Morris the celebrated designer and friend of the Pre-Raphaelite painters. Morris wanted to make a pilgrimage to the home of the Norse Sagas, for which he had developed an infatuation, and was intent on making his own English translation of them. He mobilised a party consisting of his old Oxford chum, Charley Faulkner, and Eiríkr Magnússon, an ebullient Icelandic theologian who was teaching him the language. Herbert had been planning a journey to Iceland himself, and seems to have been included at the last minute.

The fourth member of the party was a surprise addition. This was W.H. Evans, an officer and gentleman from Forde Abbey in Dorset whom none of them knew. Morris had looked him over, decided he was 'a quiet, well conducted chap and not stupid', and suggested he should join them. As he put it to Faulkner: 'He has the advantage of being used to wild travel, and will go where I choose to carry him.' Evans would also, crucially, share the expense.[5]

The party set out in July, sailing from Scotland in a Danish mail boat. They met the president of the Icelandic assembly and travelled on horseback along the south coast, returning to Britain in September. Herbert later got a letter from William Morris translating for him the name of the Icelandic village in which he had bought himself a souvenir – a spoon.

Some years later, in 1880, Herbert was receiving an even more famous tourist. Henry James the novelist was staying with Lady Trevillion at Midelney Place, her new Tudor-Gothic house near Ilminster. She took him round some of the local mansions that had inspired her own. The writer was in raptures: 'I think I have never been more *penetrated*,' he sighed. 'It was the old houses that fetched me – Montacute, the admirable Barrington, that superb Ford Abbey, and several smaller ones. These delicious old houses, in the long August days, in the south of England air, on the soil over which so much has passed and out of which so much has come, rose before me like a series of visions.'[6]

Herbert seems to have enjoyed collecting people as much as he did furniture. He was keen to show off the abbey to the young King Milan I of Serbia, who in 1890 was touring Britain following his precipitate and unexplained abdication. Unfortunately for Herbert, the king was too busy visiting more important people in London. He conveyed his thanks for the 'gracious offer of hospitality' in a letter to an English friend of Herbert's in Belgrade who had organized the trip.

An even greater disappointment that year was the cancellation of a much more important royal visit. Queen Victoria had been due to pay a call, and Herbert had bought new furniture in expectation of it. Likewise, his invitation to Thomas Huxley, the eminent scientist and disciple of Charles Darwin, was also turned down. Huxley replied from the Grand Hotel, Eastbourne, to say that he and his wife were too busy moving their possessions from London to the retirement cottage they had bought on the south coast.[7]

Perhaps Herbert began to feel that something was missing from this otherwise agreeable life of English country gentleman: a wife. He was in his late fifties, and still a bachelor. Some of his younger relations believed the reason for his celibacy was that he was in love with Fanny, his first cousin on his mother's side. Fanny's parents had emigrated to Australia and she had returned, a widow, to England and had settled with her daughter not far away in Devon. Herbert's love for Fanny – if that is what it was – was to have important consequences.

In 1894, his mother Jane died in London, leaving an estate valued at over £60,000. She left to Herbert both Forde Abbey and Wimbledon Park House, along with all her pictures. Her elder daughter Sarah got £12,000 in trust, the younger Eleanor £8,000, and these two unmarried daughters were to divide the jewellery, ornaments, china, plate and London furniture between them. Her companion Ann Pressley received an annuity of £20.

In her will Jane said it was 'not out of want of affection or kindness' that her daughters got so little but because they were already provided for by her father-in-law John Evans, and the marriage settlement for her and Bertram. There was nothing for her faithful gardener George Boreham, one of seven servants and a witness to the will. Nonetheless, somebody – though not the gardener – seems to have challenged her dispositions, because the grant of probate was not straightforward.

Jane's funeral was at Forde. Within months Herbert was married. He was 58 and, as one newspaper announcing the engagement put it, 'mature for a bridegroom'. His chosen bride was no spring chicken either. Rosa Hood was 42, daughter of General Alexander Hood, Viscount Bridport, who lived up the hill at Cricket St. Thomas. The general was descended from the famous admirals Hood, and on his mother's side related to Lord Nelson. He had been a courtier for decades and Rosa, the youngest of his ten children, was a Maid of Honour to Queen Victoria – reputedly her favourite.

Because Jane Evans' death was so recent, the wedding was a small family affair, conducted by the Bishop of Ripon at the little church of St. Thomas on the estate. But the wedding presents were truly splendid. The Queen sent the

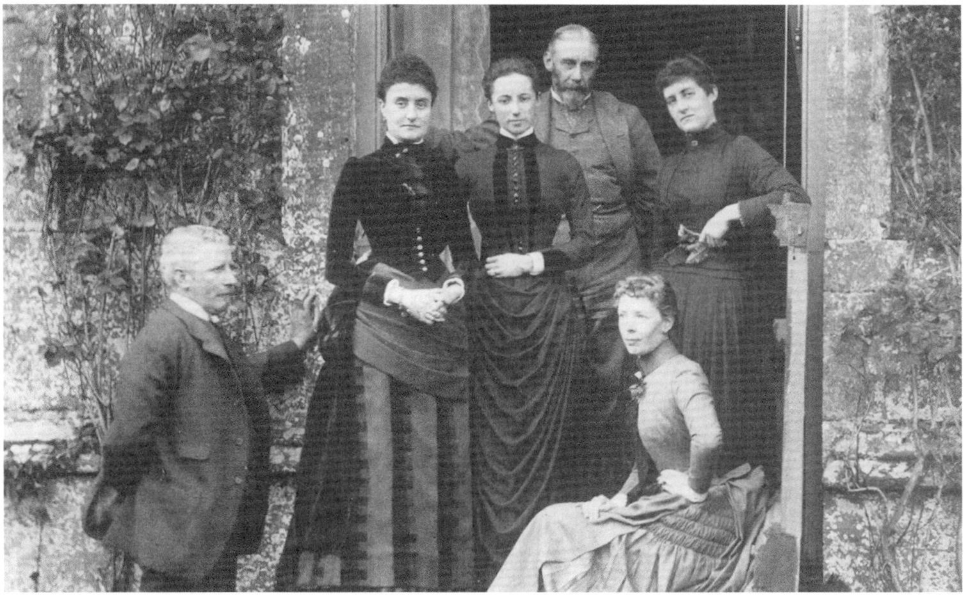

Herbert Evans (*centre*) about the time of his marriage to Rosa Hood, (*standing, second left*). The others are unidentified.

customary Indian shawl, but also a ruby-and-diamond brooch. There were more brooches from the Princess of Wales and the Princess of Battenberg, a sapphire ring from the Princess Henry of Hesse, a gold ring from Princess Alice of Hesse and an inlaid clock from Princess Christian of Schleswig-Holstein. Rosa was showered with jewellery and 'pretty trousseau gowns' from duchesses, marchionesses, friends and relations.

While the couple took their honeymoon (or 'wedding tour') in Scotland, Rosa's father moved into the abbey. The move had been trailed by *Vanity Fair* which said that he wanted to close Cricket St. Thomas now that he was a widower and all his children had flown the nest. (The house was in fact sold two years later).

Lord Bridport was on hand, at any rate, to welcome the couple home to Forde Abbey. A local newspaper described how the carriage arrived through a triumphal arch with flags and banners floating in the breeze on either side of the drive. Tenants, employees and local schoolchildren were mustered to cheer and the Great Hall was opened so that everyone could gaze at the dazzling collection of wedding presents. After lunch for the tenants in the Refectory, Herbert thanked them for their present of a mantel clock and ornaments. They clapped when he promised to spend more time at home now that he was married. Replying on behalf of the tenants, Mr Pinney got up to say they all hoped he and his wife 'would be spared to live among them for many years to come.'

It was not to be. After only six years of marriage, Herbert Evans died. His reign at Forde had lasted nearly four decades. Rosa, with her close connections at court, added social lustre to his final years and may have been partly responsible for his appointment as High Sheriff of Dorset for the year 1895.

But Herbert and Rosa had no children. Neither did the two Evans sisters, the elder of whom, Sarah, had come to live at the abbey. There was no-one to whom Herbert could leave the estate. And this is where his attachment to his first cousin Fanny played an important part in the story.

Fanny's husband had died young, but she had a daughter Elizabeth, always known as 'Elsie'. They lived with Fanny's parents, much of the time at Bovey House, an Elizabethan mansion situated not many miles from Forde inland from Beer in Devon. Fanny's father, Dr. Sprott Boyd, was Herbert's uncle, a brother of his mother Jane. He had emigrated to Australia in 1857 with his family where his daughter Fanny (Frances) married a young Englishman called George Fitzgerald who had been sent out to Australia because of his tuberculosis. When their daughter Elsie was born, George decided to bring wife and baby to England to introduce them to his family. But during the voyage he died of his illness, leaving Fanny and Elsie to complete the journey on their own. When the news got back to Fanny's parents in 1877, they too returned to England to join their daughter.

Of all his Boyd cousins, Fanny was the closest to Herbert – not only geographically but emotionally, too. As one of the Boyd cousins conceded, she was the one that Herbert 'knew and loved the best'. So it was to Fanny's only child Elsie that he left Forde Abbey in his will.[8]

After Herbert's death Rosa retired to her house in Belgrave Square and spent much of her time in Sicily, at Bronte on the western slope of Mount Etna where the Hood family had an estate. Her father Lord Bridport had inherited through his mother the dukedom of Bronte, a title originally conferred on Lord Nelson by King Ferdinand of Naples in gratitude for his support. The estate included the town of Bronte inland and the Castello Maniace on the sea at Syracuse. Rosa was paid an annuity by the Roper family until she died in 1922 at her brother's house in nearby Taormina.

In his will of 1898 Herbert decreed that his sister Sarah should have Forde until her death before it passed to Elsie, who was by now grown up and married to a young Oxford-educated solicitor called Freeman Roper.

* * *

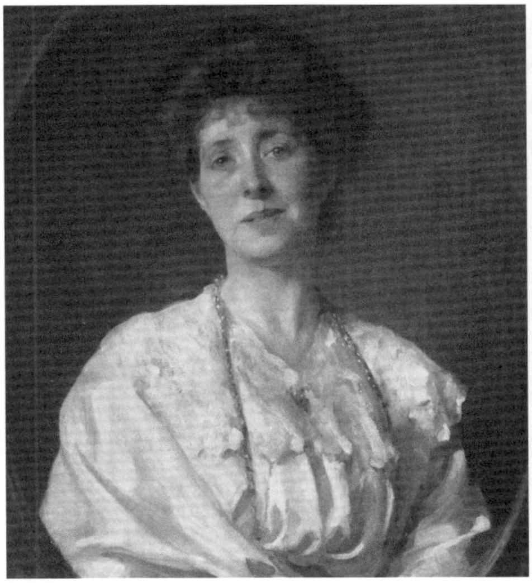

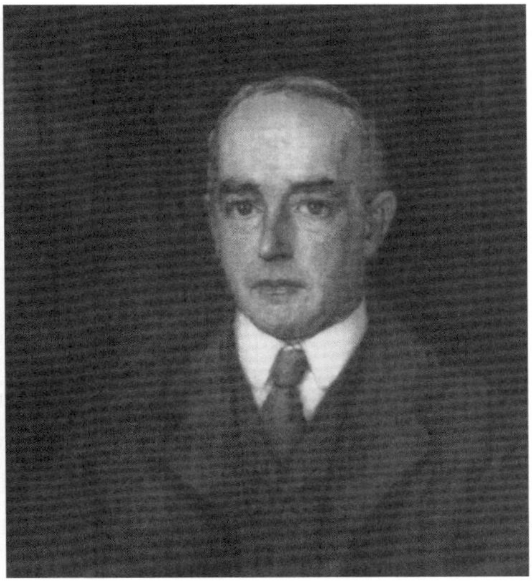

Above left: A portrait of Elizabeth ('Elsie') Roper, who inherited in 1906.

Above right: Her husband Freeman Roper. 'I fear our present modest income will not be at all adequate,' he told Elsie's uncle.

So it was that Forde Abbey, founded by a woman, became for the third time in its long history the property of a woman. Margaret Prideaux had inherited in 1702, Jane Evans had bought it in 1863. Now it came into the hands of Elsie Fitzgerald, Mrs. Freeman Roper.

Her husband clearly felt obliged to explain things to Elsie's disappointed Boyd relations. Although there is no record of any complaint, the Ropers were not allowed to forget that there were many Boyd cousins just as closely related to Herbert as Elsie was. A month after Herbert's death in September 1900, Freeman wrote to Elsie's eldest uncle Archibald setting out the terms of the will. The letter was postmarked Marseilles, where he and his wife were staying on a tour of the south of France taken for the sake of her health.

At the end, Herbert had been in a very bad state both mentally and physically, Freeman wrote. As the person who had been looking after his financial affairs, Freeman could assure him that Herbert's will had been drawn up before his mental deterioration. He acknowledged that in the unlikely event of their son Fitzgerald (known as 'Fitz') dying before he was 21, or of there being no other children, or of Sarah making some other provision, Forde could pass to the Boyds – to Archibald or some other member of the family. Freeman was careful to stress that failing any of these eventualities, the Roper succession would be 'absolute and indefeasible'.

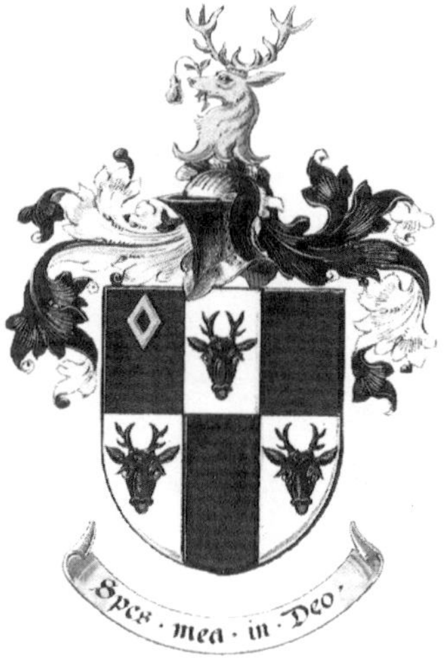

The Roper family's coat of arms.

As if to mollify him further, Freeman pointed out that although the estate was very valuable the income from it was barely sufficient to cover the cost of maintaining it. 'People over there have a very exaggerated idea of Herbert's means,' he added. In fact Herbert's capital was badly invested, money was still owed to Sarah, and death duties would be heavy – around £20,000 – leaving no more than about £30,000 for the new occupants. He even went so far as to suggest that he and Elsie might be too poor to take up her inheritance: 'There does not seem any great prospect our being able to live at Forde, as I fear our present modest income will not be at all adequate.' Here he may have been overstating the case: there was a lot of money in the bank at Chard when the Ropers took over. But his warning that the house was beyond the family's means would one day prove correct.[9]

The Ropers were in the United States when in February 1906 they got the news that Sarah had died. They came back to England in April to Elsie's childhood home, Bovey House, which they had been renting. Elsie was now 36 years old, Freeman 44 and recently retired fom his practice. Their son 'Fitz' was seven, Geoffrey was five and Kate ('Kitty') was a baby of some 12 months.

Freeman noted immediately the poor state of the abbey. 'The house needed considerable alteration and improvement before it could be ready for occupation,' he wrote in the journal which he now began to keep. Electric light was installed, new plumbing, heating and drains. A few structural alterations were made and the place was redecorated throughout.

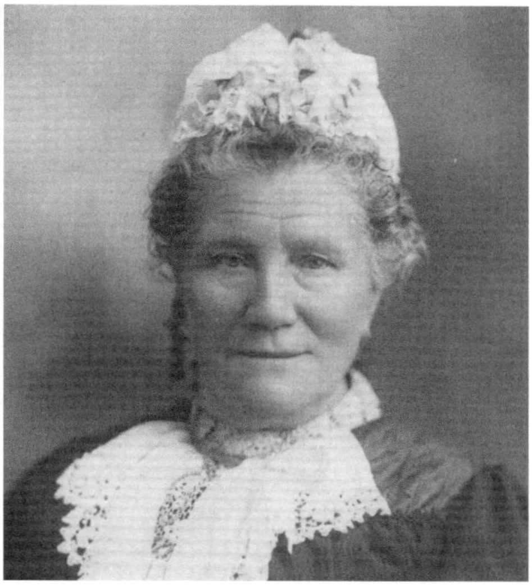

Mrs Hannah Jenkins, the Ropers' housekeeper, in 1914.

The couple moved in during August while the improvements were still in progress. 'Nov 12, first shoot. Bag of 317 over two days with 4 guns,' reads the first entry in the house journal, beneath the high-flown rhetoric of a preamble: 'This book is intended to be a Forde Abbey Common Place Book wherein it is proposed to chronicle all matters great and small affecting the Abbey and its inmates in the hope that it may prove of interest to ourselves and our successors.'

By modern standards, Freeman and Elsie's household was hardly modest. There were eight resident servants: a housekeeper, governess, lady's maid, nurse and nursery-maid; a cook, parlour maid and 'tweeny' maid (who ran between house and kitchen). The coachman-chauffeur and the stable man lived in outbuildings with the motor-car bought in 1911, a carriage and two horses. There was a head gardener with four men to work under him, and a pig man who also looked after the chickens and milked the cow. Laundry and horse-shoeing were done in the village.[10]

Although no countryman, Freeman adapted quickly to his new station. Shooting pheasants, often accompanied only by his gamekeeper, became his chief recreation. But he could be careless. Returning one evening he dropped his shotgun on the floor of the Great Hall having forgotten to unload it. The gun went off, and blasted a hole in the door to the Grand Staircase.

There was plenty to keep the children amused, too. The workmen were still putting in the new water supply, replacing the gutters on the Great Hall, cleaning the plaster ceiling in the Saloon, re-flooring the chancel of the chapel and installing seats. While this was going on Geoffrey, aged about eight, had an unpleasant surprise. Going into the dining room one evening he saw a monk. He rushed out to find one of the servants and described the figure he had seen in great detail. No-one knows whether this was an apparition, or a practical joke.

Outside, the new team was set to work. A bog garden was dug on the west side of the Great Pond. Trees were planted: catalpa, plane, white poplar, pink chestnut and scarlet oak. The house was opened to special interest groups; their ticket money went to charity. There were fêtes, tennis parties and cricket parties in summer, home-grown plays and pantomimes at Christmas.

In 1911, an important acquisition was made. This was the Forde Abbey cartulary, a detailed record of the monastery's lands, rents and services written in Latin on 105 folios in the late fifteenth century. It had disappeared after the Dissolution when it may have fallen into the hands of the abbey's first private owner, Richard Pollard, then passed to the Drake family in Devon. In the early nineteenth century it had been bought back by the last Gwyn, who was trying to reassemble the monastic library. After the big sale of 1846, the cartulary was sold on privately for £100 to Sir Thomas Phillipps, an obsessive collector of books and manuscripts – a 'vello-maniac', he called himself. Phillipps had the cartulary rebound in red Russian leather by a bookbinder in Gloucester. It appeared in the Sotheby's sale of part of Sir Thomas's collection in 1911, when it was bought by a Mr. Hepworth on behalf of the Roper family for £235.[11]

Freeman and Elsie began to take holidays. They sailed to New York on the *SS Mauretania* for a tour of the United States in 1909. Two years later they wintered in Burma, visiting Rangoon, Mandalay and the Chindwin river before returning via Calcutta and Darjeeling. In the summer of 1914 they went to the Dolomites where they witnessed Austrian military manoeuvres along the Dolmitenstrasse, a recently-opened tourist road linking Bolzano to Cortina d'Ampezzo. It was part of the build-up to the First World War.

Freeman became High Sheriff of Dorset. His son 'Fitz', now 17, joined up along with many young men from the villages of Thorncombe and Winsham on either side of the abbey. For the next two years the house became a refuge for army officers, many of them Canadians, who were convalescing or on leave. They were fed on rabbits and chickens from the estate. Elsie recalled that there were 'lots of potatoes, but sugar and butter were always short.' Margarine could be had only in town. The winter was so severe that the family were able to skate on the Big Pond for three weeks, and the snow so heavy it split the shrubs. Elsie noted that the worldwide influenza epidemic in the autumn of 1918 had killed more people in four months than the war had done in four years. Among the staff, Tom White the head gardener had been badly wounded but returned to work briefly before suffering a complete breakdown. Stanley Westlake had survived prison in Aleppo after the infamous siege of Kut in southern Iraq, and another employee had served in Mesopotamia.

But for Elsie and her husband the greatest casualty occurred a year after the war. Their son Fitz was drowned in a sailing accident on the River Orwell in Suffolk. He was 20. Elsie, who was now keeping the house journal, noted that his brother Geoffrey was being groomed to take over the abbey: he had gone up to Magdalene College, Cambridge, to study agriculture and estate management, had hopes of farming in Canada or Argentina but was sent instead to the Lockinge estate in Ardington, near Wantage, to gain his practical experience.

The war had left the Ropers feeling the pinch. The hardship Freeman had warned of in 1900 was now a reality. Two lots of repairs had been made to the roof and gutters, and lead for the roof had become 'desperately expensive'. To pay for indoor repainting and re-papering, Elsie and the two children moved out to the Home Farm for nine months of 'frigid economy.' The number of gardeners was cut from 10 to six. Four farms were sold to tenants: Batehams, Herridge, Broadbridge and Lower Hewood (later bought back).

They were 'too hard up to afford anything but new curtains' Elsie confided to the journal. Wages had kept on rising since the outbreak of war, and now consumed half of their income. They had seven fewer employees than in 1914. 'Everything that can be cut down has been cut, but with the cost of everything double and treble, ends won't meet,' she complained in a letter to her uncle Archie in Australia.

Things were so bad, she added, that she and Freeman had 'ruefully' decided they had no choice but to sell the Mortlake tapestries.

'It will mean a real wrench, but naturally less than leaving Forde altogether. We are certainly not in a position to have our drawing-room walls covered to the value of £2,000 a year!'

Selling the Crown Jewels

The figure of £2,000 a year – presumably the income they could expect from investing the money raised by the sale – seems to have been plucked out of the air. The couple had no real idea how much the tapestries would fetch, but had been assured the art market was at a peak. One snag was that the tapestries were entailed to their son Fitz, and to make their sale possible he was to have signed away his rights had he lived. Because Geoffrey was still under age the courts might need the Boyds' consent to the sale. For if her family were to be 'wiped out in the next two years', as she put it, her uncle Archie would inherit.[12]

There was tragic irony in that remark. Fifteen years later, her third child Kate was to meet the same fate as Fitz. She was killed on a climbing holiday in the Tyrol falling into a crevasse and drowning when an ice-bridge gave way.

It took some time for Freeman and Elsie to work out how the sale of the tapestries was to be done. How do you sell your Crown Jewels without a public fuss? Clearly fearful of creating a storm of gossip and speculation, of being besieged by dealers and the Press, they decided to look, with the help of friends, for 'some wealthy American.' Legally, the tapestries belonged to Elsie. But Elsie was often unwell and for this reason – and no doubt for more conventional reasons, too – it was Freeman the former solicitor, now 60 years old, who took charge.

* * *

The first character to appear in the unfolding drama was Rosalind Wheeler, an American woman who ran a letting agency called the Miss Wheeler Estate Bureau, off Berkeley Square. She had been introduced to the Ropers by friends in Los Angeles; and in September 1923 – three and a half years after Elsie's letter announcing the decision to sell – Freeman invited Miss Wheeler to Forde to look at the goods. Elsie was not well enough, apparently, to meet her.

Miss Wheeler told Freeman that her usual charge for furnished lettings was 5 per cent, but for finding a buyer for the Mortlake tapestries she would want 10 per cent. On the 17th of September she wrote to say she had talked to three art dealers: Duveen, Amor and Partridge, who would offer the lowest sum they could. 'It is well to avoid all dealers,' she concluded (which was just what Freeman wanted to hear), adding that she had 'a very important buyer, a wealthy American in Scotland' who had large estates in the U.S. and was looking for tapestries for her walls.

A few days later Miss Wheeler revealed she had 'a friend with rich friends' who was advising that Freeman name his price and let her (Miss Wheeler) and the friend share the commission. Alternatively, she said, Freeman should name the lowest price he would accept and let them split any surplus. The friend (a man) thought that £75,000 – a sum which Freeman must by then have quoted – was a very high price. Freeman replied crossly that he had been advised to go for £100,000, but would take less from a private buyer.

So began what was to become an increasingly dense and tangled affair lasting until Freeman's early death – which indeed it may have hastened – in February 1925 and even beyond.

In October Miss Wheeler introduced a new character, 'a tapestries expert who buys for all the wealthy people in foreign countries.' This was Mrs. Guy Antrobus 'a well-connected Englishwoman and a lady,' as Freeman later described her. Under her maiden name Mary Symonds she edited the magazine *Needle-Craft*, had co-authored a book *Needlework Through the Ages*, and had lectured at the Museum of Fine Arts in Boston and the Art Institute of Chicago. Mrs Antrobus was off to America in December and would like to see the tapestries before she went. She and Miss Wheeler would share the commission on any sale.

Freeman was pleased to hear about Mrs. Antrobus. As for the commission, he replied, it was up to Miss Wheeler what she did with it. He stressed – as he was to stress repeatedly over the coming months – that he would pay commission to only one person, and to nobody at all if he found a buyer himself.

Hardly had Mrs. Antrobus set sail when Freeman got a letter from an old friend in New York, Irving K. Taylor, who offered to act for him for a straight £1,000. Taylor promised to put him in touch with an antique dealer friend called George Fairchild. Two days later Fairchild wrote asking for photographs and a description of the tapestries. Freeman replied that he wanted £100,000 for them, or nearest offer. But the tapestries were not to be 'hawked round.'

There was silence for several weeks. Then at the end of March 1924 yet another player entered the game. This was Griswold Knox, also an old friend, who wrote from New York to say he had just finished acting as receiver to the Stanley Steam Car Company (a name revered by motoring buffs to this day) and was ready to lend Freeman a hand. He, too, had a friend, a banker who knew lots of rich people and had got one of them interested in the tapestries.

The friend of Griswold's friend turned out to be not the private buyer that the Ropers so badly wanted, but yet another dealer. He was an Austrian called Gustave Herz who had made a fortune as a manufacturer of spark plugs and other automotive components in the U.S. but had retired to become an 'art connoisseur' as well as dealer. Herz believed only a museum would want to buy the tapestries, and he had already hooked one: the Minneapolis Institute of Arts. Herz wanted sole rights as agent for a year, wrote Griswold on 21st March. But Freeman should give him only three months, 10 per cent commission if he got £75,000 and half of any surplus over that. Before this letter arrived, Freeman had received a cable signed 'GrisKnox' outlining the deal. He had cabled back his agreement, with the two provisos 'unless previously negotiated' and 'subject to courts'.

So now there were three sets of 'friends' and agents in the field, of whom

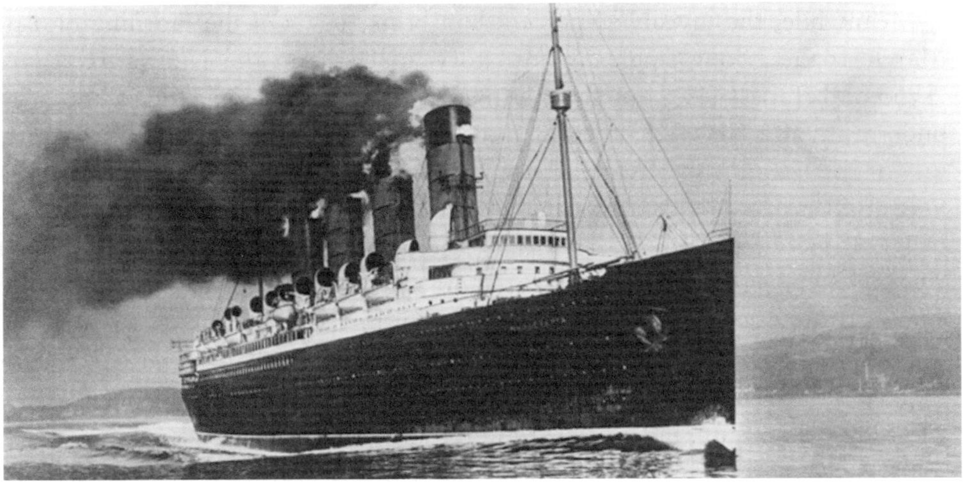

The *Mauretania*, which played a role in the drama of attempts to sell the tapestries to America.

one (unknown to the others) had an exclusive – if qualified – option to sell the tapestries. But there were more actors about to make their entry.

Two days later Griswold received this baffling message from Freeman:

'*Await letter leaving Mauretania Saturday Stop all negotiations entirely until received meanwhile stop previous figures withdrawn Grosvenor Thomas 6 West fifty six St Knows position Stop Cable name your man.*'

The ambiguity and urgency of this cryptic instruction caused no end of confusion. Griswold set about preparing for Freeman's arrival in New York, sending messages to him aboard the *Mauretania*, booking a room for him at his club and telling Herz the dealer to wait on the quayside when the liner docked. But Freeman never apeared. As Griswold explained later, he thought Freeman was coming to New York because he had 'something big in sight' – hence the order to halt negotiations – so was 'quite at a loss when you failed to turn up.' It was, he now realized, the *letter* that was coming on the ship, not the *writer* of the letter. Indeed, as he later discovered, the liner did not even sail that week.

Cables and telegrams were famously liable to misinterpretation. Sometimes it was wilful, as in the case of the newspaper reporter in Peking who in reply to his editor's unanswerable question '*How old Mao Tse-tung?*' replied '*Old Mao fine How you?*' There was nothing deliberate about Freeman's error. But coming as close as courtesy allowed to a rebuke, Griswold wrote that the moral was obvious: it was worth paying for longer cables, putting in the necessary prepositions even at seven cents a word, when the stakes were so high. 'If you had cabled 'await letter *posted by* Mauretania,' he said, 'I would not have made the stupid mistake I did.'

Meanwhile, the invisible Mr Herz had been busy. On the morning of 24th March 1924, a long single-column story appeared in the *New York Times*: '$500,000 Tapestries Coming to America' shouted the headline. The story underneath announced that negotiations were 'understood' to be in train for the sale of the Forde Abbey Mortlake tapestries to the Detroit Institute of Arts. A long and learned description of the tapestries followed.

The Ropers were aghast. They had seen a follow-up version of the story in *The Daily Chronicle* and Freeman fired off a furious letter. Mr. Gabbertas, news editor of the *Chronicle*, apologized for publishing a story which he was now told was untrue, and said he had published a correction. The paper had tried to ring Mr Roper before publication but got no reply; had tried to get their man in Chard to call on him, but had heard nothing.

In fact Freeman was well aware that Detroit was one of the museums approached by the well-connected Englishwoman Mrs. Antrobus during her recent lecture tour of America. He told Griswold this in a letter explaining his strange 'Mauretania' cable. He was now in London talking to Mrs. Antrobus, he said. It was she that was talking to the dealers Grosvenor Thomas at West 56th Street. As far as he was concerned, Miss Wheeler was no longer in the frame. As for the invisible Herz (whom Griswold blamed for talking to the *New York Times*) he should be told to come to some arrangement with Mrs. Antrobus. He owed a lot to her; and she would probably settle for £1,000 of the commission.

This letter crossed one from Griswold, who declared himself disgusted by Herz's behaviour but could not help remarking that it was wonderful publicity for the tapestries: 'Ten thousand pounds could not have bought that notice, so Herz is at least clever.' By now everybody, with the possible exception of Mr. Herz, was unhappy – or about to become so.

Griswold Knox, already upset by the *Mauretania* affair, confessed he was afraid of being sued for damages by Herz if he did not secure at least a three-month contract for him to sell the tapestries. Miss Wheeler, unaware that she was being dropped, wrote to say she had heard the good news of Mrs. Antrobus' success, and was looking forward to her share of the commission. Freeman replied that the news report was wrong, that he was thinking of giving a sole option to 'a gentleman in America' and that their relationship was 'now definitely closed for the time being.'

Mrs Antrobus – the favoured lady – had yet to discover that she, too, was being sidelined.

Ten days went by during which the Ropers seem to have accepted that their attempts to arrange a discreet sale through friends were getting nowhere. There was no alternative but to give Herz a proper contract. Freeman contacted his solicitors, Monro, Saw & Co. On 10th April they sent him drafts of an agreement. In a covering letter Mr. Monro warned that only Mrs. Roper had the authority to sell the tapestries since they were her inheritance, and then only with a court order. Mr. Roper was advised to revoke any authority he had issued. Mrs. Roper would expect £75,000 from a *bona fide* purchaser, pay a ten per cent commission on that, and 25 per cent on any surplus achieved. The option would last six months, expiring at the end of October 1924.

Sitting in his club in New York, Griswold Knox could not know that his advice had borne fruit. Over three successive days he typed three long letters of advice giving Freeman the benefit of his experience as a businessman. He was motivated, he said, purely by friendship: he had no commercial interest to serve.

The first question was whether to keep or ditch Herz. There was no way Herz was going to share the commission with Mrs. Antrobus, and it was tempting to punish him for his indiscretion by switching the rights to her. But that would be a mistake. Mrs Antrobus was a poor woman to whom ten per cent of £100,000 was a fortune, but she had had six months in which to earn it, without success.

So the second question was the asking price. The tapestries were only worth what someone would pay for them. Duveen Brothers (who had known about them all this time) would be happy to earn £5,000 with them. 'After all these years of waiting, and with the Abbey itself at stake, I, were the tapestries mine, would take £55,000 this week [even] if someone else were morally sure he could get me £100,000 next week.'

He gave an example from his own experience – a curious one, since it was about steam-powered tugs on the Pacific coast. He told Freeman that he owned two tugs, worth around $10,000 each when he decided to sell them. He had tried to get more, but when called away on business instructed his agent to get whatever he could. The agent ignored this instruction and held on hoping to do better. He held on, in fact, until the market for steam tugs on the Pacific collapsed. Diesel powered tugs had arrived, and Griswold's steam tugs were not worth even $1,000.

Herz was sailing to Plymouth on the *SS Nieuw Amsterdam* and would arrive on the 19th April, Griswold concluded. Freeman should meet him and let him see the tapestries at Forde. 'He is even less prepossessing than his name and nationality suggest, but I think he is to be taken seriously and, after all, the thing is to sell the tapestries and save the Abbey.'

While Griswold was going to great lengths to justify his advice to his friends in Dorset, Freeman was busy clearing the decks with the help of his solicitor. He told Monro's to deal with Gustave Herz directly when he arrived in England. He broke the news to Mrs. Antrobus that his arrangement with Miss Wheeler was over and that he was engaging Herz. She replied in her graceful looping handwriting that she quite understood, but would hope to get three-quarters of the commission if one of her leads came good.

Miss Wheeler was not so emollient. She reacted badly to the news, and was incensed by Freeman's casual observation that Mrs. Antrobus had, in any case, originally been introduced to Elsie not by her but by someone else. She got the famously litigious firm of Charles Russell to threaten a suit for damages if she didn't get commission from a sale by Mrs. Antrobus.

Mr Herz arrived in England and put up at the Hotel Russell in London where he told Freeman's solicitors that he thought it would be very difficult to get the £75,000 for the tapestries that the Ropers wanted. He also said he'd been advised the commission was 20 per cent, not 10 per cent. There was no further discussion and he left for Vienna, where he had a dealership on the Ringstrasse.

On the first of May, Monro's drafted Herz's contract for sole agency until the end of October. It was written in Elsie's name, and took the story back to the beginning: a price of £75,000 – less if Mrs. Roper agreed – with a commission of 10 per cent and half of any sum achieved above that. Price and commission would have to be approved by the court, and Herz was to indemnify the Ropers against any other claims.

And there the correspondence halted. A long silence fell. And eight months later, Freeman Roper died. He was not yet 63.

Because he had taken charge of the negotiations, Freeman appeared to be the architect of the whole plan and therefore responsible for its failure. But events after his death suggest Elsie had been just as keen to sacrifice the tapestries for the abbey, even if she was less inclined than her husband to hold out for the highest price.

In November, 1925, Elsie made one last spin of the wheel. Another New York art dealer was invited to see the tapestries while on a business trip to England. He was Frank E. Washburn Freund, whose sister-in-law was a good friend of Elsie's and godmother to her daughter Kate. On his way home Freund wrote from London proposing an arrangement. The dealer he knew (and seems to have worked for) in New York, P. Jackson Higgs, would price the tapestries at £62,500 to yield £50,000 for Elsie and a commission of 25 per cent for Higgs. Any surplus would be divided in the same ratio. Higgs's option would last for 'a season'. It might be useful to ship one of the tapestries to New York for people to look at: Higgs would have it insured.

In January Freund told Elsie that Higgs thought the price 'stiff.' He wanted a year's option from April and would try to get interested parties to view the tapestries *in situ* – provided, of course, they didn't try to do a private deal with her. He wanted a lot more information about the history of the hangings. This Elsie was not able to provide: her earlier researches had turned up nothing new. The moment she got this missive, Elsie sent both Freund's letters to Monro asking whether he could find – as she quaintly put it – 'any nigger in the fence.'[13]

More importantly, from that day on Elsie seemed to be going off the whole idea of selling the tapestries. It was beginning to look as if they were just not going to fetch enough to be worth selling.

Elsie had told Griswold the previous April that a sale price of £55,000 would, after tax, increase the estate's income by only £1,000 a year. Now she conferred with Monro about disposing of the tapestries in England where, she agreed, '£25,000 would be nearer the mark than £50,000.' She turned down his suggestion of going to the London auctioneers Puttick and Simpson: she just did not want the publicity that would ensue.

At the end of February, Elsie virtually admitted defeat. She wrote to Higgs to say Monro would be sending him ('just in case') a form of agreement for his contract due to begin on 11th April. But she could not meet his other demands. It would be difficult to dig up more historical information, and she was not willing to send one of the tapestries to New York for viewing.

'Under the circumstances,' she concluded, 'you may not care to attempt the sale – and from our point of view, unless fairly certain of success, we should much prefer no move being made in the matter.'

Geoffrey takes over

After the death of his father it was natural that Geoffrey should take on more responsibility for the running of the estate. He was in his mid-twenties, had a degree from Cambridge in estate management and a spell of practical experience on the Lockinge estate in in Berkshire. Not that his mother was ailing, in spite of her chronic poor health. A writer from the *Daily Mail* who visited Forde in 1929 was clearly somewhat overawed:

> 'Dressed in a pale grey coat and skirt, she stood erect in the huge fireplace of the hall, where in the dim past had dined many a hungry pilgrim on the way to Glastonbury. Her white hair gleamed in the light from the lantern windows 'neath the carved roof. She would close her alert blue eyes, as though to shut out the present, and as she talked I seemed to see the old Abbot at the high table on the raised dais.'

Geoffrey was a countryman, not a businessman. He ran Forde as if he were a smallholder or peasant farmer, living the sort of rustic life eulogized by the Roman poets – but working much harder than they had to. He always felt poorer than he was. The area between the house and the kitchen garden became a mass of hutches where chickens and geese were reared. Geoffrey organized a weekly delivery of eggs, poultry, butter and flowers to London, taking his turn to drive the van every third week. He had hives of bees foraging busily in the orchard. But his money lay idle, on deposit in the bank at Chard.

Under the ironic title 'The Working Day of the Idle Country Gentleman' , Geoffrey described a typical day in 1930:

6 a.m. Wake up – roll over and go to sleep
6.30. Get up
7. 00. Feed and water chicken brooder house
7.20. *ditto* goslings
7.40. Pick Flowers
8. 00. Breakfast
8.30. Dewax chicken
9.45. Open post and give orders
Telephone
Ledger etc. to Secretary (Auntea) [Miss Marsh, a former governess and friend of Elsie]
10. Finish picking flowers
11. Return to plucking shed
Sew up torn chicken
11.15. Mc Phail arrives to see bees
Arrive in kitchen garden to find a swarm just settling on the strawberry net.
Go through hives, take swarm and leave Shennan [the head gardener] to take my place
12. Find Americans wanting to view House and Garden
Motor to station to fetch 240 day old chicks
Put chicks in Brooder House
Return to Mc Phail in the orchard
1. Lunch
1.50. Pack butter and honey
Write letters aned a/cs [accounts]
4. Tea
5.30. Pack the Van
6. Feed the swarms of bees
7.30. Dinner
8.15. Drive swarm
9.30. BED

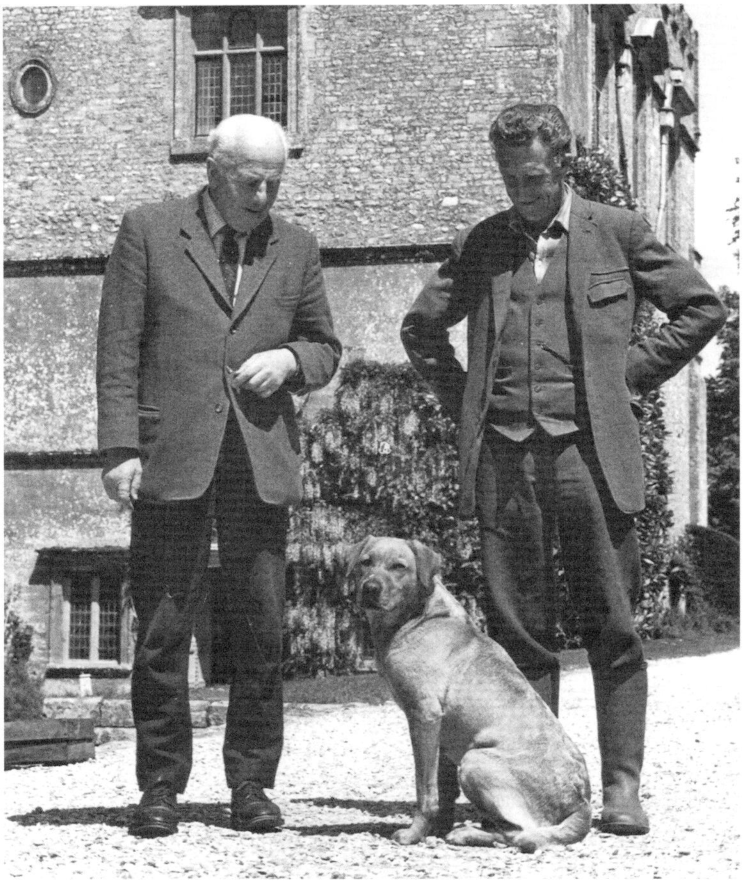

Geoffrey Roper, *left*, with his gamekeeper Mike Smith and dog Sarah:
'a countryman, but no businessman'.

* * *

The economic crisis of the Thirties, years of low agricultural prices, forced many 'gentlemen farmers' off the land. The Ropers did what the monks had done during times of hardship in the Middle Ages: they converted rents into leases to meet financial emergencies and fund essential projects.

The family enjoyed a good reputation as employers, according to the son of a young woman taken on as lady's maid to Mrs. Roper in 1932. Elsie Collins had been working at the local lace factory replacing shuttles. In her new job she ranked just below the housekeeper and was paid £20 a month. Her day started at 7 a.m. The job involved setting out her mistress's clothes, dressing her, doing

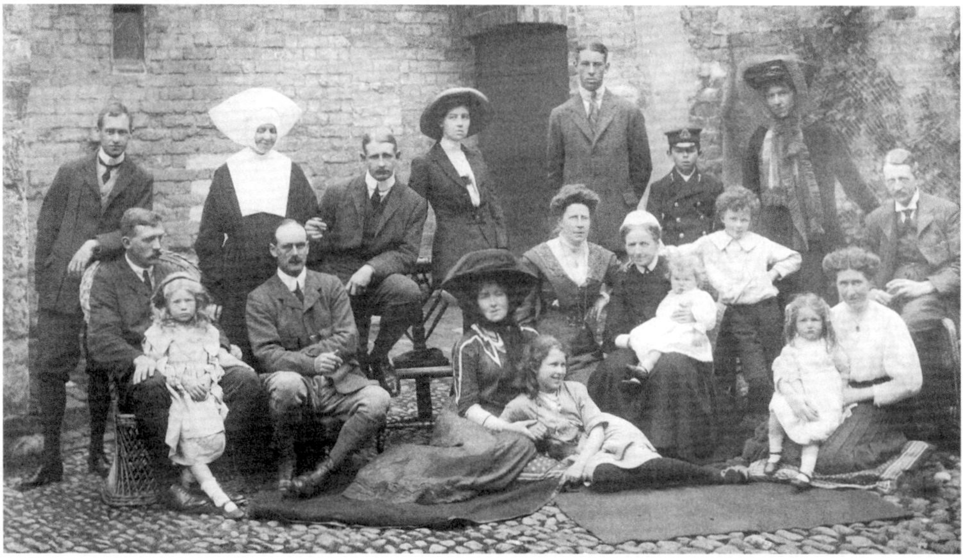

The Congreve family at West Felton in 1909: *centre, front,* Diana with her mother Dorothy King. *Back row, right to left:* Diana's uncle Walter Congreve, his wife Celia, their sons Geoffrey (in naval uniform) and Billy. All four won medals: Walter and and Billy the VC, Geoffrey a DSO and Celia the Croix de Guerre.

her hair – and even designing outfits for her. In the afternoons she would put out clothes for walking or riding in the dog-cart. She helped her if she went shopping, and dressed her again for dinner. Her day ended at 10 p.m, and she slept in a room next to her mistress. Elsie stayed a year and left to get married. [14]

If the highest rank of servant included the lady's maid and the governess, the lowest was the boot boy. One of his jobs, after the railway was laid along the north bank of the Axe, was to wait by the tracks each morning and catch the newspapers as they were thrown from the train by the guard.

Life for Geoffrey was not entirely taken up with chickens and bees. In 1930 he and his mother went to California and Arizona for several months, probably to visit Boyd relations. Meanwhile his sister Kate went to Palestine with her friend Diana King and Diana's mother Dorothy. The connection was to prove fruitful, for within a few years Diana and Geoffrey were engaged.

Their marriage united the Ropers with the Congreves, an old Staffordshire family with a fine military record. Diana's mother was the youngest sister of General Sir Walter Congreve, who won a V.C. during the Boer War, had been a Corps Commander during the First World War, G.O.C. Egypt and Palestine after the war and Governor of Malta. Her father Arthur King was an officer in Sir

Walter's regiment, the Rifle Brigade, in which Walter's son Billy Congreve also served. Both Billy and Arthur were killed in the trenches.

Major King went missing on 15th March 1915 at St. Eloi on the Ypres salient. Billy set out to find him. It was not until 3rd May that he discovered his uncle's body, riddled with machine gun bullets and lying about 30 yards from the German trenches. Unable to retrieve the body because of enemy fire, Billy took the few possessions he could find in his pockets and sent them to his aunt Dorothy.[15] Billy was killed on the Somme in July 1916. At the age of only 25 he had become one of the most decorated officers of the war, awarded the VC, DSO, MC and Legion d'Honneur.

At her wedding in 1934, Diana was led up the aisle of Chelsea Old Church by Billy's brother, Sir Geoffrey Congreve, a naval commander who was to win a DSO in the Second World War and was killed on 'Operation Chess', a commando raid on the Pas-de-Calais in 1941. Among the bridesmaids were Geoffrey's two younger daughters, Marygold and Carola. The eldest, Henrietta, later became godmother to the couple's daughter Charlotte. Diana's Congreve aunts and uncles were to become regular visitors to Forde Abbey, and have a big influence on the children.

To mark his marriage, Geoffrey planted the avenue of lime trees which runs up the park to the top road. About the same time he and Diana were offered the handsome pair of iron gates and urns which now stand at the entrance to the abbey's main drive. They came from Brooklands, the first purpose-built motor-racing circuit in the world which was built by Diana's cousin Hugh Locke King and was now closing down.

Almost exactly nine months after the wedding, in June 1935, Diana gave birth to her first child, Mark. All this was recorded by Elsie in the abbey journal. She did not, however, refer to the tragedy that befell the family in the same week that Mark was born, when her daughter Kate met her death in the Tyrol. The birth of an heir was marked by Geoffrey in the way he liked best: he planted a beech house by the Big Pond with a window from which the little boy could watch the ducks and swans. More trees were planted in 1937 when King George VI was crowned following the abdication of his brother.

Meanwhile the abbey had been adapted so that the young Ropers could move in. They and the children occupied the east wing, Elsie and Miss Marsh ('Auntea') lived at the west end, while the Great Hall was awkwardly divided by a screen to make a shared sitting room.

Geoffrey may have had no feel for business but – as can be seen from his love of living monuments – he was a passionate plantsman. The garden, the orchards,

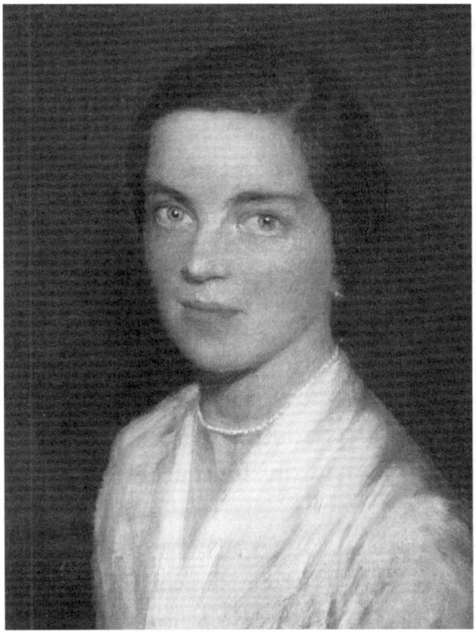

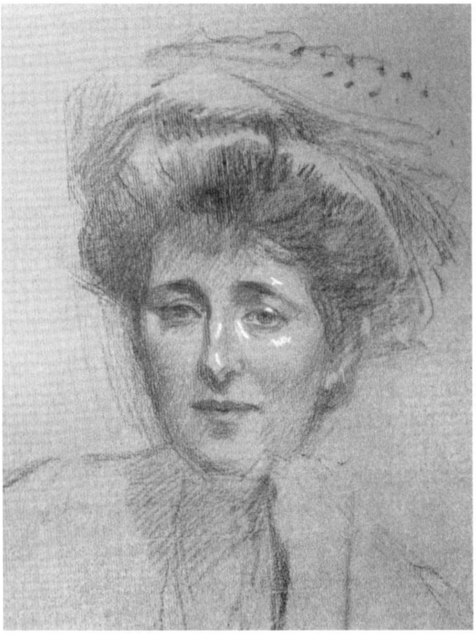

Above left: Kate Roper, Geoffrey's sister, who died in a holiday accident in 1935.

Above right: Dorothy King ('Dorchy'), who spent her last days at the abbey.

the park and the estate woodlands were his domain. In this he was aided by the new head gardener, James Shennan, a strong-minded Scot who was chosen from 60 people who applied for the job in 1934. His predecessor had given notice in protest at Geoffrey's scheme for reinstating the Long Pond: the pond, he declared, would never again hold water and the herbaceous border planned along it would never work at a distance from the wall. Of all the planting, the forestry nursery which Geoffrey created was to prove the most profitable in the long run.

* * *

But now the routine of the Abbey was thrown into disarray by Britain's declaration of war against Germany on 3rd September, 1939.

The first casualty was the weekly van delivery to London. The van was sold, and the chicken flock reduced. Building schemes and painting work were cancelled for lack of labour as the men joined up. There had been 11 staff and a houseboy before the war. Now they were depleted, while the family was growing.

John had been born at the end of 1936, Christopher at the end of 1939; their sister Charlotte was to be born in 1941. The staff shortage meant that soon the family were making their own beds, tidying their rooms and taking turns to do the washing up. The Great Hall was closed and its furniture stored in the Saloon under dust-sheets. Diana brought her widowed mother Dorothy (always known as 'Dorchy') from London to live with them at the abbey. Elsie stopped writing the house journal.

The house consisted mainly of the very old and the very young, a Canadian soldier stationed in England reported after a weekend visit to Forde. He found Geoffrey 'very shy and very nice' and accompanied him on his daily rounds. He was particularly impressed by Geoffrey's diligence, rising at 6.30 to milk the three cows and still serving the meal and polishing the silver and a glass at the end of the day. He described how the butter was rationed out. 'Geoffrey goes and solemnly weighs out and shapes one two-ounce pat for each member of the household. These are put in separate butter dishes – individual dishes – and that is what that individual makes do for the week. The surplus goes to neighbours.'

It was remarkable, he concluded 'that people could live such ordinary lives so well in surroundings as beautiful and rather unreal as theirs.'[16]

* * *

Geoffrey, who was in the Dorset Yeomanry, was called up in 1940 but at 38 was considered too old to serve abroad. After a year in the officer reserve he was able to spend the rest of the war at Forde, and set to work with his customary energy to make ends meet. The garden was kept going by Shennan, with the help of an old labourer, a boy and an apprentice girl. But tomatoes replaced flowers in the border under the front of the house and the lower front lawn was converted into a giant rabbit farm, with moveable pens and hutches. The top lawn was put to the plough to grow oats, and later potatoes, while the cricket ground to the east of the monks' dormitory became a wheatfield. In a further patriotic gesture, crops were sown between the trees in the apple orchards, which did them no good. Milk for the children was in short supply, so the three cows were bought. Two pigs were employed to eat the scraps and milk leftovers; hams and bacon were cured 'with great success.' Chickens ran free in the orchards.

Fifty acres of woods were felled for their timber and replanted. Christmas trees provided a good income, as did the wild rabbits which had multiplied during Geoffrey's time away and now were harvested as vigorously as the farmed ones: using ferrets and gas he killed 3,000 of them in one year and sold them for one shillling and fivepence each.

The winter of 1940, the longest and coldest in memory, killed many of the best garden specimens and forced the closure of many of the greenhouses for lack of oil to heat them. All through the war – and after it – the house was freezing cold because the central heating was considered too expensive to run except at Christmas. The children's nursery in the Oak Room was warmed with a coal fire. At night the children would find the kitchen floor alive with cockroaches and beetles, and would occasionally be allowed to watch the servants while they pursued the rats with sticks.

Evidence of the bigger battle going on outside came mainly from the air. A barrage balloon crashed into one of the orchards, and four lots of German bombs were dropped on the estate. The first cluster fell at Shedrick, killing two heifers. A second was dropped near Leigh, on the other side of the railway line, but failed to explode. The third was at Holditch to the south, which did no damage.

The most dangerous was the fourth. A single aeroplane came up the valley one foggy day seemingly intent on bombing the milk processing factory at Yonder Hill and the railway station at Chard Junction. The pilot first mistook his target and came in so low over the stables that he nearly hit the chimneys of the gardener's cottage. Mark, a small boy, saw it all. He was feeding the rabbits at the time, looked up and not realizing it was a German bomber, gave the pilot a wave. The pilot, fortunately, discovered his mistake and went on to the factory, dropping four bombs. They did little damage but killed one person. The blast was felt at the abbey, where it blew out one window in the porch and another in the alcove over the back door, and cracked a few more panes of glass.

Elsie Roper died in 1943, at the age of 76, as preparations for the Allied invasion of Europe began with a big build-up of troops and support workers in the area. Some of these were billeted at the abbey, making even more work for the family. In order to pay the death duties Geoffrey had to sell Westford Park farm, where the first monks of Forde were thought to have lodged while building the monastery.

When peace broke out, Geoffrey recorded his gratitude to his wife 'for the wonderful way she has tackled the running of this vast place and the large numbers she has catered for...She is one in a thousand.' To celebrate the Allied victory he began, naturally, to plant an arboretum.

Some improvements were made also at the house. The old Ruston Hornsby engine that generated electricity in the Undercroft was sold with all its appendages, and the abbey was connected to the national grid. The first electric washing machine was installed. The first grey squirrel was spotted sitting in a tree 'so unaware of the dangers of life, having lived only in city parks' that it waited while Geoffrey fetched his gun, returned and shot it.

Life after the war was, if anything, more difficult than during it. Wages had doubled, from 36 shillings a week to 70 shillings. Money was short. Staff numbers had shrunk to an all-time low. The house was bitterly cold, with only log fires and the kitchen range to compensate. It was clear that the future of the abbey was hanging by a thread.

For many country houses the Second World War was the final straw. Some owners did a deal with the National Trust, making over their houses and seeing them opened to the public in exchange for being allowed to go on living in a wing at a peppercorn rent. Others simply packed up and went, having the roof taken off and leaving the house to die. Of all the country house owners in the area, the Ropers at Forde seemed the least likely to survive. But survive they did – and prospered, too.

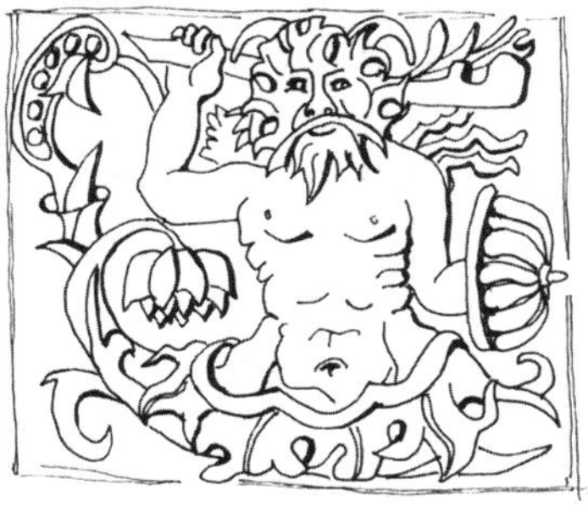

SIX

Glory Regained

One late summer day in 1959, Mark Roper came home from his final year at Cambridge University to find the desk in his father's office cleared and the chair vacant. Nothing was said, but the message was clear. From now on, the responsibility for running Forde Abbey was his. He was just 24, having spent two years doing his National Service with the Rifle Brigade in Kenya before going to Magdalene College to study land management.

The situation confronting him was less than ideal. The house was cold and the roof leaked. There were elderly dependants living in the abbey which gave it, so his brother liked to say, an atmosphere of Boot Magna, the ancestral pile in Evelyn Waugh's novel *Scoop*. There were 13 outside staff employed on the farm, in the sawmill, in the garden and the woods – most of them unprofitably. There were two 'house cows', 200 hens, the odd sow with piglets and six hives of bees.

Father and son could hardly have been more different. Geoffrey was like a smallholder who had found himself in a palace. He was cautious rather than conservative, felt himself to be poorer than he was, and reacted to poverty by pinching pennies. He hated spending money: investing for the future was for him a gamble and running up an overdraft was a sin. His son, on the other hand, had a good business brain, a nose for opportunity and a quick – if not always infallible – judgement.

Yet without his father's perserverance, Mark was sure, the house and estate would have been lost. Few estate owners were ready to endure the shortages or live on 'short commons' as Geoffrey Roper had done; few would have set such an

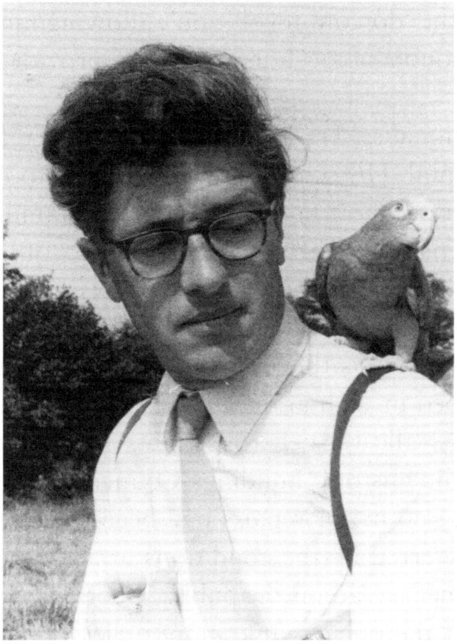

Mark Roper as a young man, with his pet parrot Jason.

example to their staff by getting to work at 7.00 in the morning.

Having put his son in the driving seat, Geoffrey let him get on with it. 'Many fathers and sons find great difficulty working out ways of operating together,' Mark recalled. 'I was extremely lucky and had a father who did not interfere with what I wished to do and was happy to continue with the jobs that he enjoyed. I fear that at times he was slightly alarmed by developments.'

It was clear, however, that a passive approach would lead inexorably to collapse. Unlike the conservative landowners around him Mark was, in the words of a one friend, 'completely unsentimental' about cutting his losses when something wasn't working. He made sure everyone employed was earning their keep. Though tough-minded and sceptical, he was at heart an optimist, facing setbacks with a stoical shrug. 'We struggle on' and 'no doubt we shall survive' were typical comments.

Mark brought financial discipline to the abbey, taking advice from people he respected but shunning expensive 'experts'. He was not ashamed to borrow other people's ideas, and would always give others the credit they were due. He had a close adviser in his younger brother Christopher, a man of similar outlook. Christopher had started life as a Reuters journalist in South America (where he broke the news of Che Guevara's death), had gone into business and had made a small fortune during the 'dotcom revolution', allowing him to buy a large boat, a bigger house and a couple of racehorses – which provided much entertainment for the brothers.

Mark was a traditionalist. He accepted the necessity for change, but liked change to be incremental. His schemes were designed to make sure that things continued as they were – above all, that the Roper family continued at Forde Abbey. His favourite maxim was the famous paradox of the writer Giuseppe di Lampedusa, whose Prince in *The Leopard* remarks: 'If we want everything to remain as it is, it will be necessary for everything to change.'

Things were not as bleak as they might have been. Before the handover, the government had stepped in with grant aid. The Historic Buildings and Ancient Monuments Act of 1953 allowed generous grants of up to 90 per cent on essential work, supervised by the Historic Buildings Council. Forde was high on the list as a 'building at risk': no major repairs had been done for 100 years. If other house-owners were deterred by the conditions attached to government grants, especially the requirement to admit the public, Geoffrey did not hesitate. He put himself at the head of the queue while more or less ignoring the conditions – even though more visitors would have meant more income.

Two of the big roofs were re-leaded, and the west face of the dormitory range – whose masonry was largely held together by ivy – was repointed. The bigwigs of the Council were generous and they moved quickly. In the winter of 1963 snow drifts over a metre deep collected above the ceiling of the monks' dormitory. 'Tradition decreed that this was scooped out with shovels, dropped through a trap door at the north end and finally carried to a bath to be melted,' Mark recalled. He remembers going to London to negotiate a grant for the snowbound roof: it was agreed in under a month, with few questions asked.

His father had given Mark a free hand, but there were restraints. The 1953 Act allowed country house owners to avoid death duties by setting up trusts. Donald Burgess, the Ropers' family solicitor, advised Geoffrey and Mark to transfer ownership of the estate to a discretionary trust and become tenants of the trustees. This allowed capital taxes to be managed during the lifetime of Mark and his successors, rather than the estate having to pay large death duties when they died. The house and park were included in one trust, the estate in another.

Trustees were appointed, old friends of Mark who proved more conscientious than Mark thought sometimes they needed to be. In practice Mark felt he had been given 'power without ownership, a good combination.' On the other hand, as friends, the trustees were able to advise on important matters outside their remit. There was never any great dispute over the day-to-day management of the estate, and all agreed that Donald Burgess had created a good structure, flexible yet durable.

The trust was designed also to ensure the succession. If an heir died young, as had Geoffrey Roper's elder brother, the trustees could choose another. (Mark himself had come close to death while serving with his platoon in Kenya, when a Bren gun went off accidentally and a corporal sitting two feet away from him was killed.) If, on the other hand, an heir fell on hard times, he or she could be prevented from selling up.

An early crisis for the new boss occurred a few weeks after he had taken over and while his parents were on holiday. Henry Record, one of the woodsmen, was hit from behind by a bicyclist and killed instantly. It was the first, and only, staff fatality during a 50-year reign.

* * *

The abbey had been open for six Sundays a year in summer, with ocasional coach parties admitted by appointment. Visitors paid a shilling (5p) to see the house and a shilling to walk round the garden. That brought in about £600 a year, with the sale of plants another £1,000. Additional revenue came from the sale of apples, eggs and honey, Christmas trees, fencing stakes and other kinds of timber and seedlings from a small tree nursery. The four farms were let to tenants, at an average of £5 an acre.

From this assortment Mark set out to create three businesses that could be built up over the years, the paying visitors, the tree nursery, and a pick-your-own fruit farm.

Opening the house two days a week between May and October he watched the visitors multiply during the long period of economic growth which began in the early Sixties. The eight acres of apple trees were dug up and blackcurrants planted instead. The house cows, chickens and pigs were despatched. Sales of firewood and fenceposts were halted and the plantations closed to let them regenerate – but willow trees for cricket bats were planted along the river in place of the alder.

The large cash balances amassed at the bank were reduced. A contract made by his father to sell gravel at the meagre price of £600 an acre was torn up when Mark discovered that the contractor was not even keeping up with the payments. At the same time he bought back gravel-rich land beside the river which Geoffrey had sold. The Great Pond was dredged to deal with the weed, dumping 20,000 tons of mud onto the park – which took two years to recover –

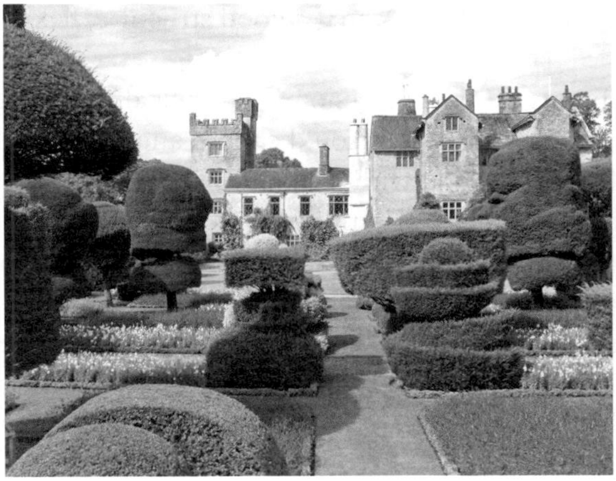

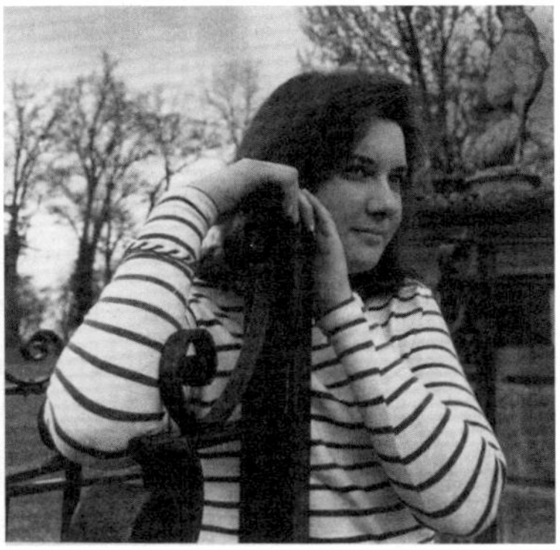

The young Lisa Bagot at the gate of her family home, Levens Hall.

Above: The topiary at Levens Hall. Its former owner, James Grahame, was a friend of Francis Gwyn's and influenced his garden designs for Forde in the early eighteenth century.

and a pump was installed to irrigate the 25 acres of blackcurrants. The tree nursery was moved from the arboretum to a 25-acre field at Forde Grange.

Employees' demarcation lines – a legacy of the pre-war country house hierarchy – were erased. Instead of a whiling away the day in relative peace in the sawmill or garage, or pruning unprofitable apple trees, staff might find themselves selling tickets to visitors or driving a tree planter in the nursery. Gerald Singleton who joined in 1946 as assistant estate carpenter was still pouring drinks for paying dinner guests a few months before his death in 2005. For some like James Shennan, the proprietorial head gardener and a fierce traditionalist, it was a step too far. After he retired in 1974 visitors would ask: 'How many gardeners do you have here?' 'None,' was Mark's not strictly truthful answer. But what he meant was that no-one was just a gardener.

By the end of the 1970s, Mark was able to declare that all the estate operations were in profit.

* * *

In the meantime the abbey had acquired its greatest new asset, Mark's wife Lisa, the second of three daughters of Robin and Annette Bagot of Levens Hall in Cumbria. They met in 1964 when he was invited to a party near Penrith and was offered a bed for the night at Levens, the house with the famous topiary garden. This was the place which Francis Gwyn had known in the eighteenth century as the home of his fellow MP and gardening enthusiast James Grahame.

Mark recorded the meeting: 'I vividly remember being greeted at the door by a stunning girl, and this was when I first met Lisa. She was 17, and it took me three years to persuade her to marry me. But here we are, 50 years later, happily together.'[1] After their wedding the couple moved into Berechapel Farm while Copse House was altered for them. Three daughters were born: first Alice, followed 18 months later by Victoria and 30 months after that by Lucinda.

Even for a young wife brought up in a large country house, Forde Abbey presented an intimidating challenge. When in 1975 the old Ropers and the young Ropers swapped places, Lisa found a great deal of urgent repair work awaiting them. The house was cold, dark and inconvenient. Lisa rose to the occasion. 'She was young, attractive and brought a sense of light and warmth to the abbey,' said a friend. 'The abbey became a comfortable, warm and welcoming place,' recalled another. 'There was a sense of them wanting to share their beautiful surroundings as much as they could.' Mark was hospitable by nature – the little wine glasses that his parents had used were quickly replaced – and his wife was not only a good cook but proved adept at organising dinner parties and celebratory events. Realising how competent she was, Mark gave her a free hand in making the house as habitable as it was hospitable.

Geoffrey and Diana had consulted an architect but had balked at the amount of work involved. He was Richard Tyler, who specialised in adapting large country houses for modern families without domestic servants; he had worked on some of the best-known houses in the country. It helped, no doubt, that his wife Henrietta was a Congreve, a cousin of Diana's.

Richard and Lisa set to work. Many of the ornate plaster ceilings were found to be in danger of falling to the floor, especially in the Saloon where the Mortlake tapestries were hanging and where the cornice was in an even worse state. This entailed a nerve-racking operation in which the plaster ceiling, as fragile as the icing on a wedding cake, was supported with Acrow props while the rotten timbers were peeled away from behind it and replaced.

The house had not been rewired since 1906, and all the meals had to be cooked in the monks' kitchen then carried on trays to the dining room beyond the Great Hall. A new kitchen and breakfast room were installed in the west end, a bathroom upstairs and a local heating system for the family. At the east end three more bathrooms were added for the guest bedrooms.

For six months the Ropers lived like nomads, moving from one end of the abbey to the other as the work progressed: new wiring, new plumbing, modern central heating and a complete re-decoration. When the panelling of the Great Hall was repaired the hole in the door to the Grand Staircase made

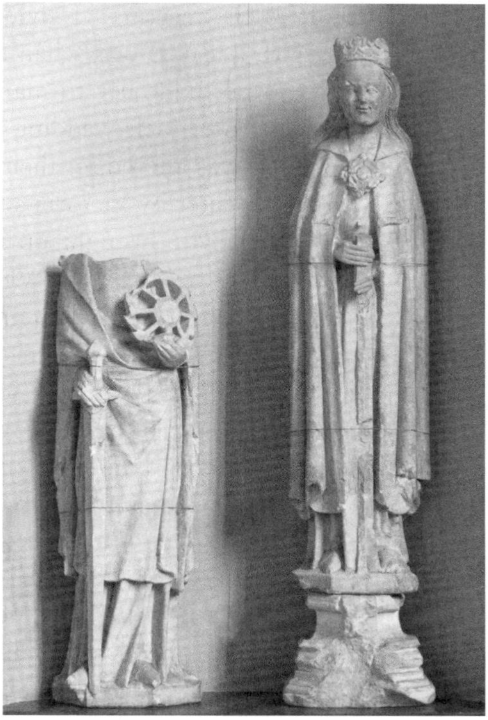

Mediaeval statues unearthed during alterations in the 1970s: a headless Saint Catherine of Alexandria, with the wheel of her martyrdom, and a figure identified as Saint Margaret, the eleventh-century Queen of Scotland.

by Freeman Roper's shotgun was discovered, and papered over. After much deliberation the panelling was painted rust red with gold edgings, a colour scheme which has not been changed.

Lisa later added more bathrooms and opened out the monastic kitchen, uncovering numerous fireplaces. An interesting find was the monks' 'dishwasher', an open water channel in the floor. The water would have come from the Big Pond or from a spring by Copse House, flowed under the abbey church and across to a *lavabo* in the cloister where the monks washed their hands before meals. From there it was carried underground to an open conduit in the kitchen, and finally through the north wall to empty in the drain outside.

Outside, the appearance of the abbey was greatly improved by removing the broad gravel drive that divided the house from the lawns. The drive had created a harsh horizontal line which elongated an already long façade, was in a bad state and was used for parking cars. It was one of Richard Tyler's rules that all traffic be sent round the back. It wasn't popular with everyone, but it greatly enhanced the look of the house.

The digging unearthed two mediaeval statues which must have stood in the old abbey church. One was a headless Saint Catherine, recognisable from the wheel she carries in her left hand. The other, with a shy smile and a huge brooch, has been identified as St. Margaret. The discovery was a reminder not only of what was lost with the destruction of the abbey church but of what might still remain underground where the abbots and patrons of the monastery lie buried.

* * *

Having cleared the decks, made the house liveable and the estate viable, the Ropers had to think about the future. The farming was marginal and most of the farms were leased out. The woods were exhausted, and only the tree nursery was making money. In short, the estate was too small and the land insufficiently productive to guarantee the future of the house. And there was no family fortune to bail them out.

Government grants were a lifeline, but not a solution. Ministers recognized a duty to preserve country houses but could not afford to be seen subsidising a grand lifestyle for their owners. At times they could be positively hostile. Nicholas Ridley, Mrs. Thatcher's Minister of the Environment in the 1980s, flatly declared that impoverished country house owners should not expect to be kept afloat: they should sell to people who could afford it.

Of course, to live in a country house like Forde Abbey was a privilege. But it was not an easy life. It had proved almost too much for Freeman and Elsie Roper. Geoffrey and Diana had managed by living frugally. What none of them realized – or if they did were unable to act on the realization – was that a country house was no longer a way of life. It was a job. You were in charge of a business, and you worked from home because your work *was* your home.

One part of the answer was visitors – as many as possible. Entrepreneurial aristocrats like the Duke of Bedford at Woburn, Lord Montagu at Beaulieu and Lord Bath at Longleat installed train rides and funfairs, zoos and safari parks in order to draw the crowds. For the Ropers this was not an option. Even if there had been space for such entertainments, they would have destroyed the ambience of the abbey.

Yet visitors had to be wooed with an enthusiasm that no previous occupant of Forde could muster. Fortunately, the abbey had always attracted the curious. In the early nineteenth century its tenant Jeremy Bentham had allowed people to wander freely through the rooms, even while he and his amanuensis were scribbling at their desks. During the Evans's time, fashionable persons staying in the neighbourhood would ask permission to drop in.

In the Fifties, the abbey opened for a minimal six days a year and bus parties came by arrangement. But Diana Roper, like many of her generation, could not bear the idea of strangers walking through her house and garden. Her son, however, saw visitors as a vital source of income. He thought it foolish to expend effort on a garden that was not going to be admired and enjoyed: 'It's like putting on a theatre production – what was the point if no-one came to see it?' He had only two rules: charge not too little, and keep the overheads down.

Having opened the house two days a week he was rewarded with queues of cars extending back to Chard Junction. The age of the Sunday excursion in the family motor car had arrived, and the house and garden raised enough money to cover the wages of all the staff. By the 1970s the abbey was seeing 25,000 people a year. As car ownership boomed, visitors might make 100-mile round trips and holidaymakers poured down to the South-West, swelling the numbers.

There was competition, of course, not least from the National Trust which had two million members by the mid-80s. Forde had some bad years in the 1980s – due to the weather rather than competition – but Mark steadfastly refused to compensate with attractions such as 'animal arks, bird gardens, adventure playgrounds, butterflies, sheep and heavy horses.' One concession to modernity was to install a first-class ladies' lavatory, following a pronouncement by the Duke of Bedford: ' If you have a really good car park, a first class restaurant close at hand, and top quality lavatories, no-one will notice if you do not have a house at all.' Another good investment was the tea room, and later the souvenir shop, an idea urged on him by his daughter Alice, while the sale of plants also multiplied over the years.

There was local competition from Cricket St. Thomas, former home of the Hood family, where a small zoo proved popular for a number of years. When that failed and the house was turned into a hotel with a large annexe in the grounds, Forde gained more sightseers. Opening days at the house were increased to five a week. Tourism became the biggest business, with numbers settling at around 40,000 a year but sometimes reaching over 50,000 (this did not include the 5,000 who attended the one-day summer fairs that began in the mid-70s). Mark confided to his journal: 'We are happy, our accountants are happy.'

* * *

As the garden's importance to the financial equation increased, it became clear that more had to be done. With the house alterations completed, the estate more or less under control (even if the tenants were not), and finances stabilised, Mark turned his attention to the 15 acres (six hectares) of gardens that separated the house from its 65 acres of park.

The basic shape of the gardens had been dictated by the hydraulic ingenuity of the monks: the Great Pond fed by two leats (one of which was now defunct), the water issuing in a millrace which ran down to the outbuildings in the monastic farmyard at the west end. The three intervening ponds and their cascades had been created by Francis Gwyn in the early eighteenth century when the millrace was sent underground.

A rapturous description of the gardens as they appeared in 1846 has been left to us by Maria Allen:

> 'They abound in delightful walks between rows of lofty and umbrageous chestnut, beech, lime and fir trees: there also a magnificent cedar of Libanus, of great size and beauty, around whose trunk a curiously formed seat invites the lover of woodland scenery to repose from the heat of the noon-tide sun; whilst through a vista, formed by Nature's hand, a peep at the ornamental water below is obtained, the murmuring sound of the distant waterfall wrapping the mind in an elysium of delight.'

She went on to describe 'rich meadows teeming with flocks of the purest breed, the gently sloping hills, covered with waving corn, the extensive woods and plantations, with their every-varying tints of light and shade.' Deer were to be seen 'reposing in luxurious ease and security' in the shade of the chestnut trees and wildfowl gliding over the glassy surface of the well-stocked lake.

In the early 1980s, however, the gardens were looking distinctly unkempt. One reason was that every winter and spring the gardeners were diverted to work in the tree nursery, then the mainstay of the abbey's economy.

Mark started in 1983 by reviving the Bog Garden on the west side of the Great Pond. It was to become his particular pride and joy: he was often to be seen there armed with spray gun and protective boiler suit. Needing further advice and a broader perspective – and anxious not to spend too much money in the process – he spoke to his brother Christopher, who suggested they consult Allen Paterson, recently curator of the Chelsea Physic Garden. Paterson was pleased to be asked, and came for a couple of weekends. 'It was as if Allen had turned a switch,' Christopher recalled. 'No plans were drawn, but he talked to Mark in the right way and opened his eyes to some lost vistas. He gave him confidence.'

In much the same way the rock garden on the east side of the front lawns, where the monastery's ice-house had been located, was given a facelift. The project was engineered by Mark's sister Charlotte. One day in 1990 she met by chance, walking round the garden, Jack Drake. Former owner of Inshriach, a famous alpine nursery near Inverness, he was now in his eighties and living in Crewkerne. Bored in retirement, he became her willing and expert helper until his death. Their efforts helped the abbey set a new record for visitors. Two years later came a further prize: the Garden of the Year award sponsored by the Historic Houses Association and Christie's auction house. That resulted in a half-page feature in the *Daily Telegraph*, a lot of local Press attention – and 17,000 more visitors. Soon afterwards Charlotte was invited to appear on the

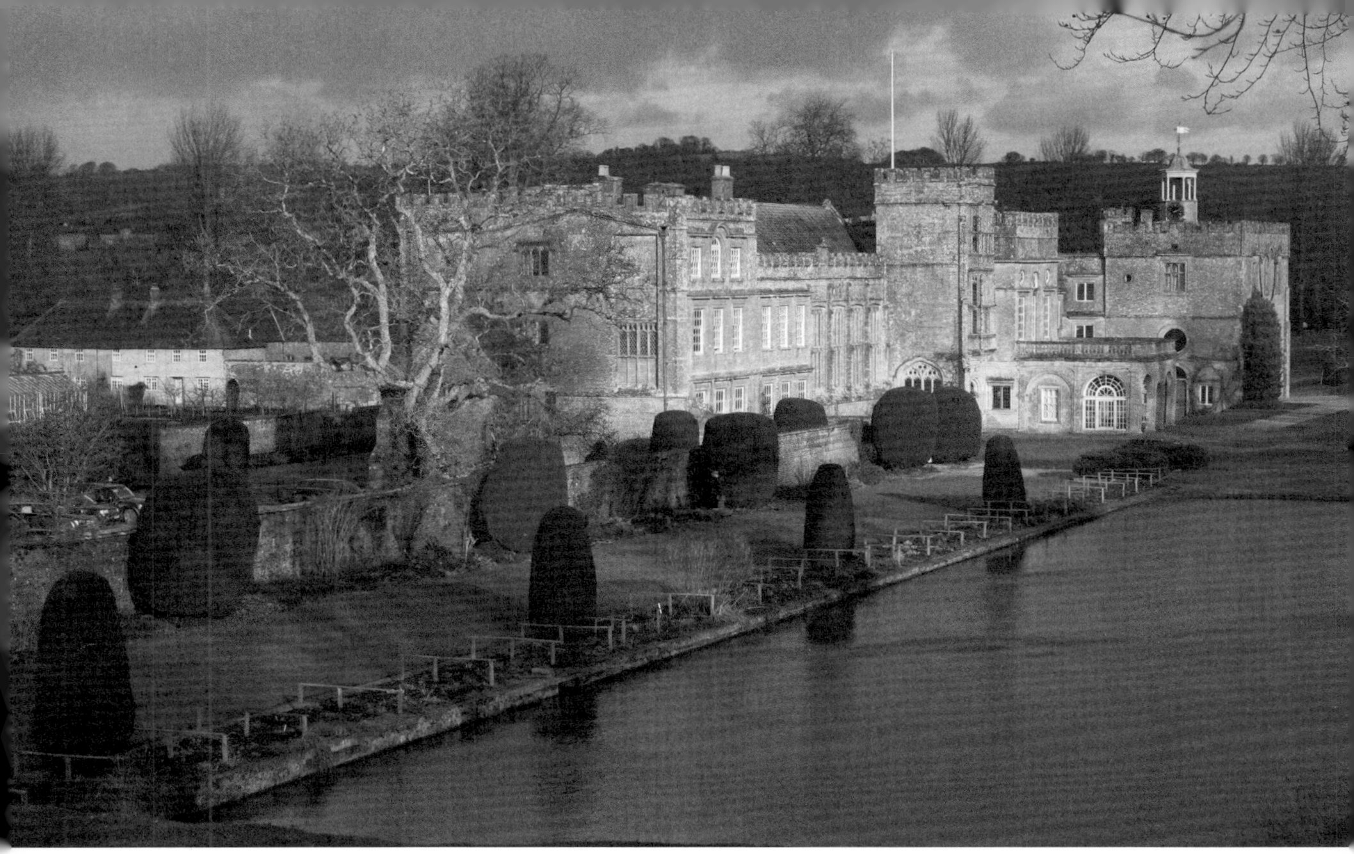

The Long Pond, created by Francis Gwyn, restored in the 1930s and dredged in the 1980s.

TV programme 'Gardener's World'.

The policy of spurning artificial attractions and making the best of what was already in place seemed to be paying off.

Later improvements included dredging the Long Pond, the lowest of the three created by Francis Gwyn. It had been filled in at the end of the nineteenth century. By 1930 it had become an octagonal pool, and was restored to its full length by Geoffrey Roper in 1934. The Great Pond, last cleared in the 1960s, was dredged again; this time a large bulldozer and three dumper trucks were enlisted and the job was done in under a week compared with the ten weeks it had taken 40 years before, and at a fraction of the cost.

Meanwhile Lisa designed a Chinese roof for the stone columns found at the home farm and presumed to have come from the abbey church, and had them set up as a 'pagoda' beside the Mermaid Pond. A Japanese bridge was built in the Bog Garden, a Ham stone circular *tempietto* was erected at the west end of the Long Pond, and new gates installed at the exit to the back drive to commemorate the birth of the latest grandchild, Marcia.

Meanwhile the kitchen garden had been restored to its former splendour, as befitted its role as the first thing – the opening fanfare, as it were – to greet every visitor to the abbey. Bordered by small box hedges, vegetables were planted

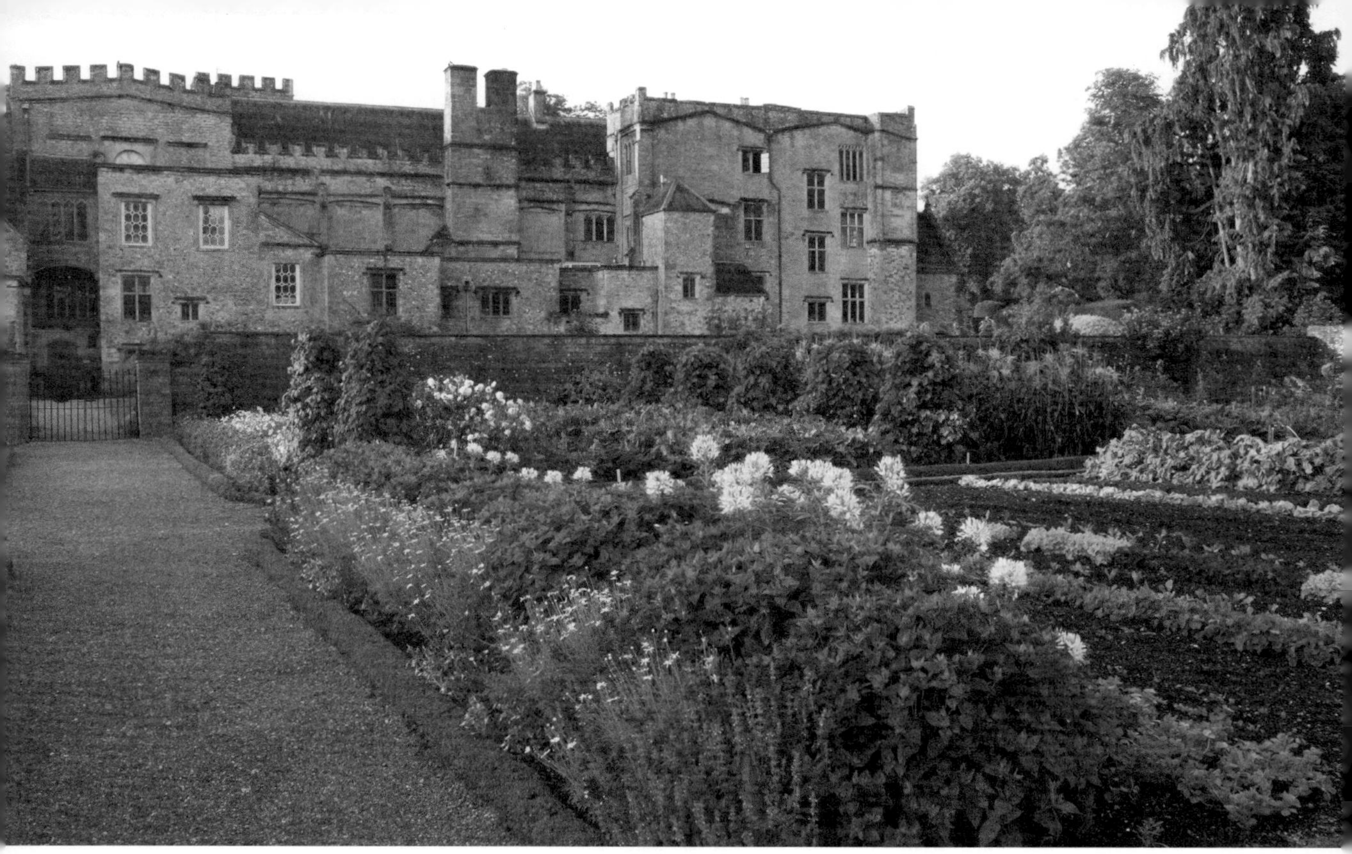

The kitchen garden: 'the opening fanfare to greet every visitor'.

in regimental ranks to supply the restaurant in the Undercroft and flowers cultivated to decorate the house. Giant pumpkins swelled on the earth for the amusement of the children at Hallowe'en. In the Victorian glasshouses built by George Miles during his brief tenure, Charlotte Roper was often to be found, tending the peaches and nectarines or poring over trays of seedlings.

* * *

Over the centuries the estate had dwindled to something closer to its size in the twelfth century. At 1,600 acres, mostly tenanted, it was not enough to support the house, family and staff. Farming became ever more unpredictable, even though the price of agricultural land rose inexorably over the half century that Mark and Lisa Roper were in charge of Forde, and there were generous subsidies to be had from Europe.

The farms were tenanted on long leases which in the early years Mark extended or renewed. He later realized this had been a strategic mistake. He was seriously short of land – the fruit and tree nurseries alone needed about 150 acres of the best land. Besides, long-term tenancies could sometimes be problematic.

Over the following decades, as the leases expired, land was taken back or let out for

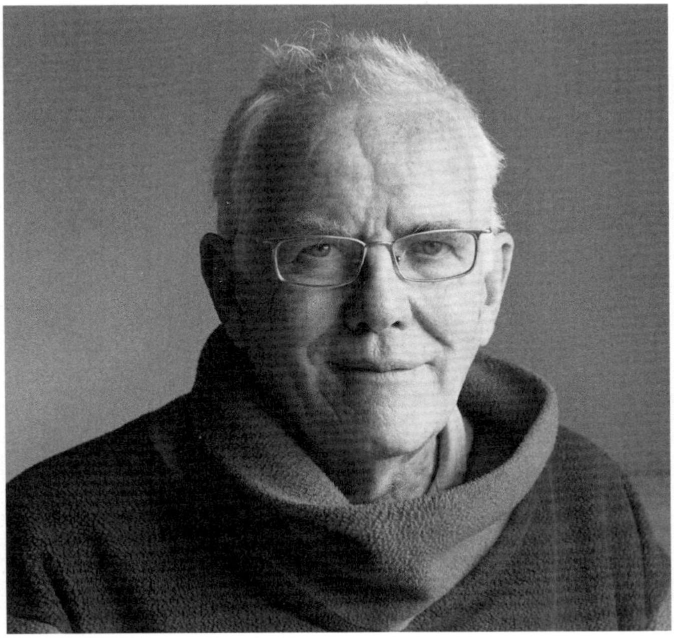

Christopher Roper, Mark's younger brother. A journalist-turned businessman, he became a close adviser.

short-term grazing. One of the farmhouses was sold, one re-let, while the tenant of a third was bought out for £50,000. By the turn of the century the 20 or so cottages on the estate had become some of its most profitable assets. Seeing the way the property market was going, Mark invested in two small houses in Chard and eventually set up a small property company with a friend to buy and restore houses. They called it 'Squashed Frog.'

The mainstay of the estate for more than 20 years was the tree nursery. This was a legacy from his father which Mark expanded to become one of the biggest in the south of England. It produced mainly sitka spruce seedlings – three or four million a year – which were sold for planting in Scotland, Wales and the West country. Extending over more than 50 acres, it employed a dozen hardworking local women under the direction of its foreman Derek Upham, and was more profitable even than the visitors. The key to its success was that in the warm south-west the seedlings were ready for transplanting a year sooner than in the north.

In the early days there was tax relief for forestry plantation and many City magnates took advantage of it. In 1970, at Christopher's suggestion, Mark decided to follow the money and bought 750 acres of land at Craigengillan in Dumfriesshire for £18 an acre. Most of the cash came from Lisa's dowry, which caused some nervousness. But the purchase was to prove one of the best investments they made. In the first ten years the plantation's value rose to £300 an acre. Shortly afterwards another 165 acres were bought near Helmsdale in Sutherland and Mark invested in a cold store at home to hold two million tree seedlings.

The nursery was bringing in almost £300,000 a year when in 1988 the whistle blew. Mark heard the news while fishing in Scotland: the chancellor, Nigel Lawson, was announcing the end of tax relief for planting. Forestry would be taken out of tax altogether, so there would be no tax relief, but no duty either on sales of timber. There was nothing to be done. Mark wrote: 'We had no choice but to carry on until we hit a brick wall and people stopped buying trees.'

By 1989 the nursery business was clearly dying: turnover had halved and two million plants had to be burned. But there was a bonus payout from Scotland when 15 acres of the Helmsdale plantation were sold for a road widening scheme at twenty times what they had cost. Insurers paid out £50,000 after a fire and the plantation was then sold for over £100,000. Mark had been under pressure to cut his losses at Craigengillan too, but decided to hold on – a decision that was to be rewarded in spades.

Mainstream farming was not attractive. The Ropers had no desire to milk cows. But there was a way of making money from milk without carrying a pail. Dairy farmers operated under a system of quotas, and the estate was able to lease out the quotas it inherited from tenant farmers. From 1986 till 2000 this form of 'sofa farming' brought in serious amounts of money. Even as quota prices fell in response to national milk surpluses, putting real dairy farmers out of business, the amount of quota claimed by the estate rose, eventually reaching nearly a million litres. Even after the EU Commission put a brake on the merry-go-round in 2003, it was still legal to 'park' a quota with a farmer who actually milked cows, and so continue to make money.

Another erratic but durable enterprise was the pick-your-own fruit. Started in 1970 in place of the blackcurrants, it proved very popular with car-borne visitors as a cheaper – and more entertaining – excursion than a trip to the shops. For ten years it did well, slowing in the Eighties, and again after 1990 when the family traffic fell away and seasonal workers were recruited from Bulgaria and the Ukraine to pick for the supermarkets. Strawberries remained popular, particularly after they were lifted onto raised beds.

The fruit, like almost everything at Forde, was vulnerable to the weather. South-west England had what Mark Twain famously claimed for New England, 'a

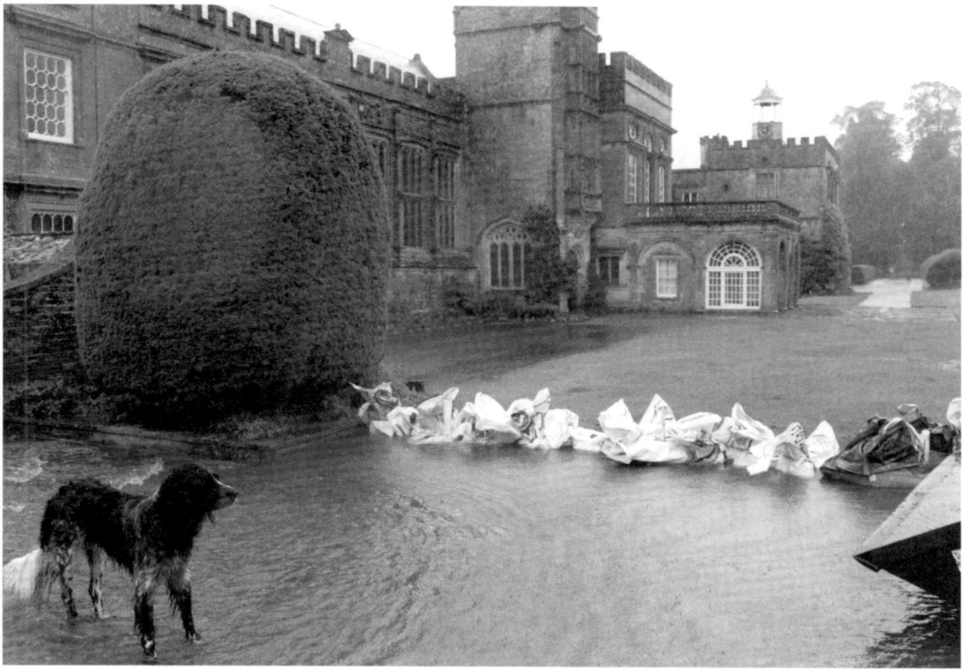

Flooding in 2012: 'The weather seems to rule our lives,' Mark Roper noted in the estate diary.

sumptuous variety of weather.' The only thing certain about it was that there was going to be a lot of it.[2] As far back as the 1930s, the house journal was bewailing the destructiveness of Nature: storms of 'Biblical intensity', hurricanes of wind and snow, torrential rain, gales which uprooted the big old trees in the garden or rampaged through the conifer plantations. 'The weather seems to rule our lives,' says one rueful entry. For the owners of Forde, meteorology was not just a hobby.

Floods were a greater hazard. Because of its situation the abbey was particularly vulnerable. One night in 1993 Lisa woke to the sound of water pouring into the cellar and the Great Hall. She and Mark ran around with sandbags until they got the flood under control. Another year brought storm water into the crypt of the Chapel where it swirled about the coffins of the Prideaux and Gwyns buried there. On a third occasion it penetrated a room behind the Chapel where the archive was kept, destroying many important documents.

But the greatest danger was fire. The couple were first alerted to the risk when they hosted the Cattistock Hunt Ball in 1985 and nearly a thousand people came. Many of the guests got very drunk, suggesting greater precautions were needed. The worst incident was a fire in the linen cupboard upstairs in the family

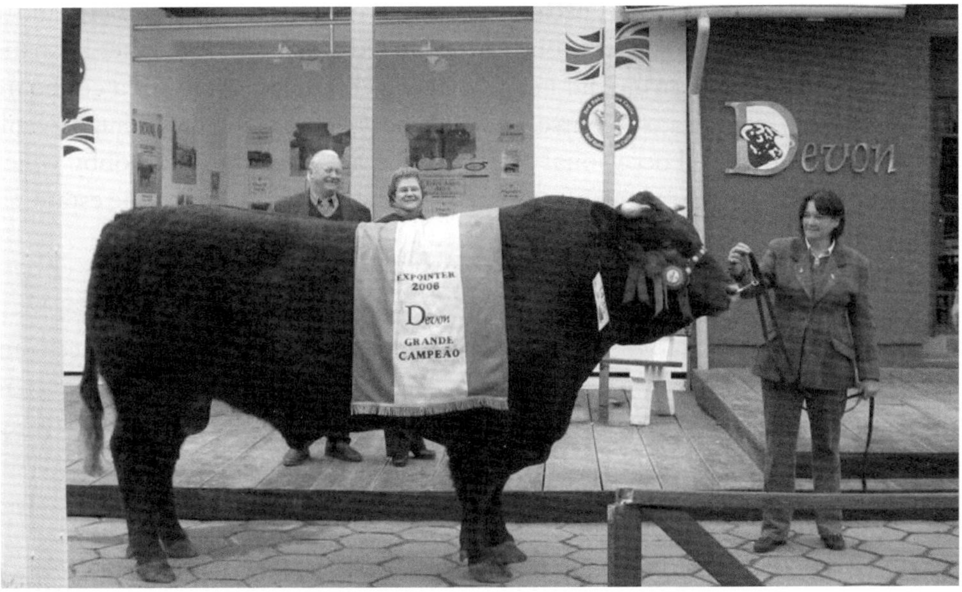

Lisa Roper, honorary vice-president for life of the Devon Cattle Breeders Society, as judge with a champion bull in Brazil.

quarters two days before Christmas 1991. Again it was Lisa who discovered it and raised the alarm. Men from the estate rushed in to drag the linen out and the fire brigade arrived to pile everything into an enormous tarpaulin and drag it down the stairs. Everything was burned except for an Aubusson carpet that Lisa had been storing for her sister Priscilla. For the family – and the abbey – it was a narrow escape.

In 1981 Lisa began her own enterprise, rearing Devon cattle; a demanding business but a decorative addition to the abbey landscape. She had become tired of the unkempt appearance of the Friesians put on the park when the grazing was let to a local farmer. Her first experiments were not a success. Animals chosen for their good looks were bought at local markets, singly or in lots, and kept in byres until the spring. But market animals can be difficult, vulnerable to disease and easily frightened. When the doors were opened, several of them disappeared over the horizon. 'One of them went miles,' Lisa recalled. 'Another refused to get into the lorry, so we left it behind and came back for it. Stupidly, we didn't make sure that the rest of the herd were in sight, so when it emerged and saw no friends it, too, just took off. We didn't find it for three weeks.'

Devons were more docile. Starting with stock from the Leighway and Kingston Lacy herds, Lisa was breeding prizewinners after only five years, at first in local shows, then nationally. She became president of the breeders' society and a show judge, visiting Brazil and touring the United States. Although her husband reckoned that cattle rearing did not pay, he was happy to admit to 'a cupboard full of silver'. For Lisa, of course, it was a hobby – worth the midnight vigils with calving cows and occasional bruising from a careless bull – a hobby which continued to absorb her long after she and Mark gave up running the estate.

'Musick has Charms...'[3]

It was thanks to Lisa that the abbey found itself running one of its most successful enterprises: recording early music in the Great Hall. Other monastic spaces had already been put to work. Miles Maskell, the owner of Greens, the City wine merchants, was a friend of Mark's from Cambridge and a trustee: he used the abbey to store up to 2,000 cases of fine wine for his customers. But the music was an altogether bigger operation.

From the start Lisa had wanted to give concerts, as her father Robin Bagot had done at Levens. She found a willing helper in John Simpson, a local Anglican vicar and organist who in an earlier life had been a submariner and had come to know the Bagot family while working at Barrow-in-Furness.[4] The concerts were more for pleasure than money: they just about broke even. But they led to a far more lucrative sort of music-making: recording.

The venture began with a recital given by the soprano Emma Kirkby and the lutenist Anthony Rooley, founder of 'The Consort of Musicke'. The recital was sponsored by BMW, the West German motor company, which in return was allowed to display some of its high-powered motorcyles on the front lawn. In spite of the further distraction of having to help round up Lisa's wandering cattle, the musicians felt the show had gone well – so well, indeed, that when they were asked by Klaus Neumann of West German Radio to make a recording in some suitable English venue, they suggested the Great Hall of Forde Abbey. Its acoustic, they said, was ideal. Mark gave his assent, on condition that the two visitor days each summer week were respected, and a new industry was born.

The Hall owes its good acoustic to its shape (an approximate double cube), to its height and the materials used in its construction: stone on the floor and wooden panelling on walls and vault. Though too small for orchestral works, it was ideal for chamber groups, soloists and singers. It was cheaper than a recording studio; and the digital revolution of the 1980s meant that high-quality records could now be made without one.

Its situation made it reliably quieter than the London churches which were

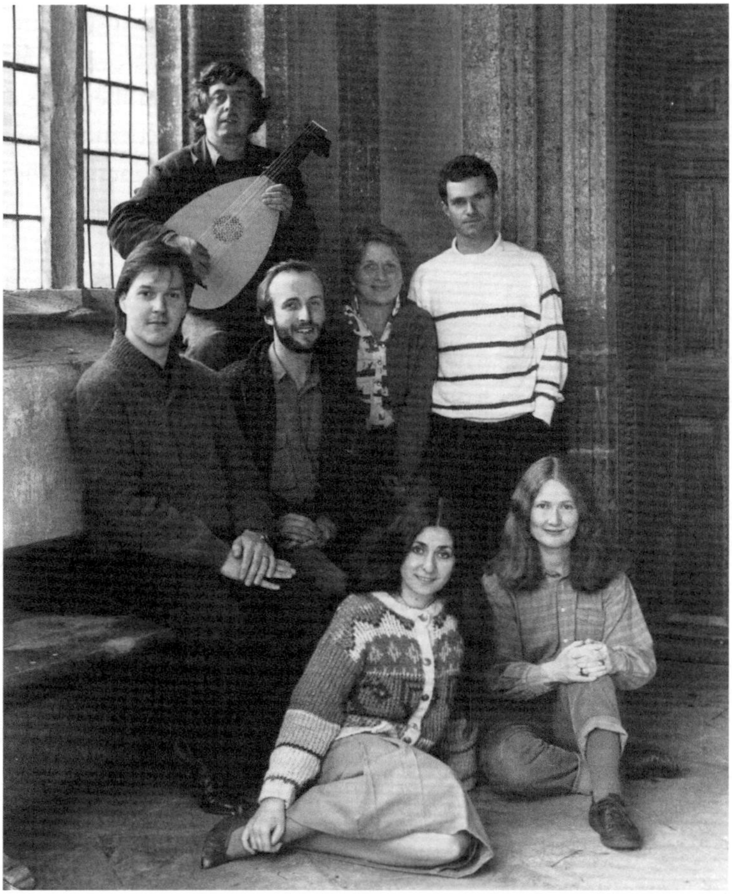

The 'Consort of Musicke' at Forde. *Top*, Anthony Rooley; *l-r middle row,* Alan Ewing (bass), Rufus Müller (tenor), Mary Nichols (alto), Andrew King (tenor); *on floor*, Evelyn Tubb (soprano) and Emma Kirkby (soprano).

often used for this kind of recording. Although the London to Exeter railway line ran past not far away, the Hall windows on that north side had long ago been blocked up. The trains came by twice an hour but were hardly noticed if the wind was in its prevailing direction. Helicopters from the Fleet Air Arm base at Yeovilton were a nuisance when they used the railway as a marker for training flights. A telephone call to the base was usually sufficient to intercept them. Jet aircraft were more disruptive. The military air traffic controller in Lincolnshire, Sergeant Snowball, was bribed to re-direct them – melted by a gift of the latest abbey recording of The King's Singers.

Forde became a popular venue. For the musicians, working in a country house was like being on holiday – there was tennis and croquet in the summer – and living on site was a luxury. Besides, it felt right to be performing music of the era in which the Hall was built. Within a few years the abbey was letting over 100 days a year to parties of eight or nine people and the income looked as if it would match that from tourists. Mark noted with satisfaction that recording was 'a relaxed enterprise, and we make many new friends.' Music provided as much enjoyment as it did money.

Much of the work fell to Fiona Laidlaw Smith who was living in the east end of the abbey at the time. She looked after the players, engineers and producers, tidied their rooms, cooked their meals and collected the bed-and-breakfast money. Responsible for allocating rooms for the wives, husbands or lovers that accompanied the musicians, she had to know who was sleeping with whom.

Fiona soon discovered that musicians can be unpredictable. A star booking was the Borodin Quartet from Moscow, one of the best known in the world. They came twice, both times to record Beethoven string quartets for Virgin Classics. On the first visit, in 1987, they wanted to fish in the Great Pond. Fifteen-year-old Lucinda escorted them up there but was helpless when the biggest of the four men fell into the water trying to get into the boat. The bedraggled Russian made his way back to the Great Hall where he began to strip off his clothes. There was no KGB 'minder' to intervene, only a woman translator, and it fell to Fiona to bundle the half-naked, dripping player out of sight. 'At dinner on the last night one of them toasted us in broken English,' she recalled. 'And another chased me round the sofa...'

The Borodin Quartet's second visit to Forde the following summer rated a mention on the BBC news. A few months later the Berlin Wall fell, and in November the harpsichordist Mitzi Meyerson presented Mark and Fiona with pieces of masonry from that grim symbol of the Cold War. Among others who came to record were Andras Schiff the pianist with Heinz Holliger the oboist; they liked to play cards after supper and dance Scottish reels. Jakob Lindberg, the Swedish lutenist, sat on the lawn and played for the visitors.

Melvyn Tan brought with him Beethoven's Broadwood piano, so valuable it had to be guarded day and night; when the guard tried to join the party for supper, he was ordered back to his station. The South Korean violinist Kyung Wha Chung brought her little dogs. Nigel Kennedy, who came several times, brought his bulldog. He was popular; the dog was not. Nikolai Demidenko brought his mother, who sat knitting in an adjoining room while he thundered through the Bach-Busoni transcriptions on a Fazioli grand with his teddy bear watching from the music rest.

More than 150 classical albums were made. Other performers included the ensembles Musica Antiqua, Florilegium, the Rasumovsky Quartet, Beaux Arts Trio and Kings Singers; the soloists Julian Bream, the Labeque sisters, Dmitri Alexeev and Viktoria Mullova; and the singers Catherine Bott, Michael Chance and Thomas Allen.

* * *

Recordings began to fall away in 1994. The digital revolution which had allowed the Great Hall to flourish as a studio now began to undermine the entire recording industry. Although some of the recording artists had also given concerts, there was no formal link and the concerts – four a year – were not affected. Indeed, they were benefiting from the expert advice and high-level musical connections of Lisa's brother-in-law, Erik Smith.

The musically-gifted son of the German conductor Hans Schmidt-Isserstedt, Erik had been a producer for Decca and Philips. With his wife Priscilla, Lisa's

Erik Smith, Lisa Roper's brother-in-law, a gifted musician and record producer who helped organize concerts at the abbey.

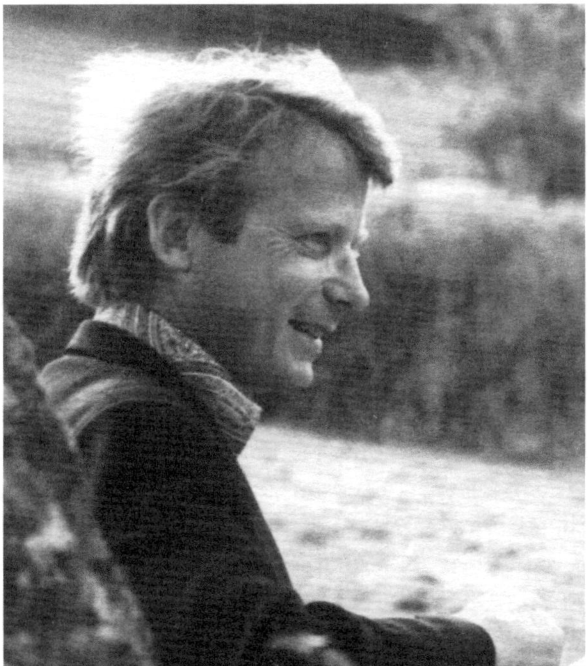

elder sister, he had bought a house across the river from Forde in the 1960s. Priscilla soon persuaded their friends Neville and Molly Marriner to buy a country retreat which she found for them a few miles away. Erik had worked closely for decades with Sir Neville Marriner and his orchestra, the Academy of St. Martin in the Fields. Although not involved with the music at Forde – he was busy conducting round the world – Neville took every opportunity to come down, playing tennis in a foursome with Lisa, Charlotte Roper and their neighbour Andrew Bullivant. The Marriners became part of the extended Roper family.

Erik took over the job of organizing the concerts in the mid-eighties – sometimes performing on the keyboard himself – and continued until his untimely death in 2004.[5] The role passed to his son-in-law Douglas Paterson, a viola player from a musical family whose day job was running the family farm near Winchester. Douglas and his wife Miranda were able to offer musicians a double deal: a concert in the 200-seater Hall at Forde, followed by a concert in their barn at Cranbourne Farm.

Relying largely on word of mouth, the abbey built up such a following that concerts were often sold out – at least when the programmes were not too innovative. The further you were from London, it became clear, the more conservative the audience became and the harder it was to attract young listeners. But if the Forde Concert Society on the whole preferred 'the music of dead Germans', it could tell the difference between good playing and bad. This was the advice of John Simpson to a young string quartet which came to give a concert including a piece by Shostakovitch. They were badly under-rehearsed and, unfortunately for them, learned too late that Neville Marriner was in the audience that night.

Every concert promoter knows the problem of a sudden cancellation. An ensemble Douglas Paterson had signed up for a concert one September had to pull out at the last minute. It was harvest time and Douglas was in the fields, sitting in the cab of his tractor enjoying a broadcast on Radio Three given by a piano trio. When the presenter announced the players' names, Douglas immediately reached for his phone. He knew the two string players personally, and recognized the pianist as a Leeds prize-winner. The group 'Les Apaches' was duly booked. Their performance a few days later brought the house down.

Among concert performers at Forde were the pianists Arthur Pizarro, Paul Lewis and Christian Blackshaw; the baritone Jonathan Lemalu; violinists Rachel Podger and Anthony Marwood (with the Raphael Ensemble and Florestan Trio). Other ensembles included the Endellion Quartet, the Janacek Quartet, the Haffner Wind Ensemble, the London Chamber Orchestra, and the Academy of St Martin in the Fields string quintet. Most years featured a concert given by the Forde Ensemble, a band of family and friends including Douglas, one of his two violinst sisters, Erik Smith on the harpsichord, or Andrew Marriner on the clarinet.

Concerts cost up to £3,000 to put on, made no profit and had to pay for themselves. Douglas started giving the abbey a fee for the Hall; and although audiences fluctuated, there was always enough cash in the bank. The concerts continue to the present day.

* * *

The house began to earn money from wedding receptions and use as a film location. But something else was needed to fill the hole left by the evaporation of the recording business. One answer was to dig more holes. For 50 years gravel had been quarried from a seam 100 feet deep along the bend of the River Axe. The first site was by West Ford farm, the supposed first home of the monks, which had been let by Geoffrey in 1929 because he could not afford the £2,000 it would cost to install machinery.

Mark had a new quarry opened at West Lears in the 1990s which was to produce about 120,000 tons. When this was exhausted the site was returned to nature, the sides re-seeded with grass and a lake created for ducks and swans at the bottom. If Mark felt any scruple about making money this way, he did not show it. He pronounced the restoration 'top class', adding rhetorically, 'the gravel has to come from somewhere. Why not here?' The contractors now moved eastwards, to Hodgeditch where eight acres were excavated (along with two Stone Age axe-heads) and 6,000 fir trees planted; then on again to Carter's Close, a very large site which was a longbow's distance – though invisible – from the garden gates.

Gravel produced a predictable income stream, though it could be embarrassing for the trustees who, in order to get planning permission for its extension, had to argue that whatever it might do to the environment, it was essential to the abbey's economy. By 2012 it looked as if the gravel bonanza might, in its turn, be coming to an end. It was not the real answer: more than £2m had been raised on the new site but a third of that had gone in tax – and there was another huge hole left in the ground. The proceeds were, however, put to good use. They helped fund the the last and biggest investment of Mark Roper's fifty-year tenure – the goat farm.

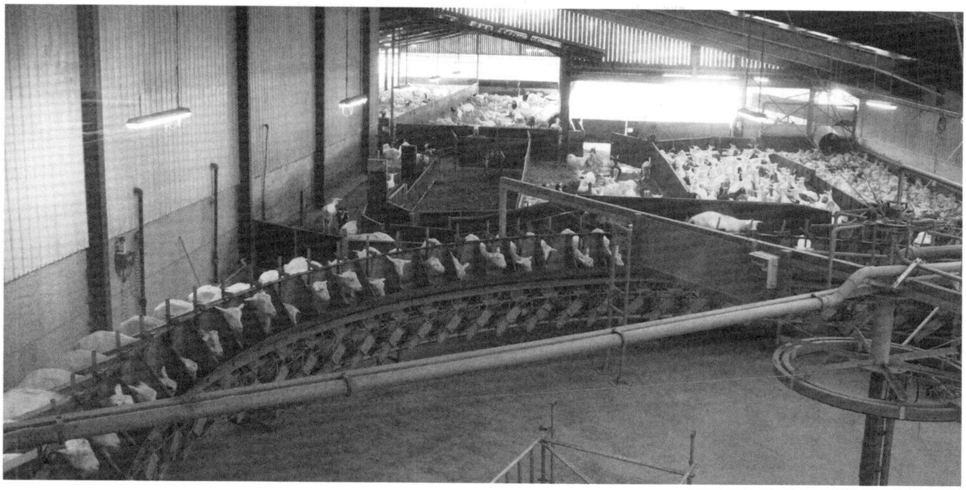

The 80-berth milking carousel at Forde Grange, which became the second largest goat farm in England.

This had been started by Tim Frost, an entrepreneurial local farmer, in 1996. The abbey provided the buildings at Forde Grange, the land and capital; the animals were managed by Tim Frost with his son Will. In 2006, a much more ambitious scheme was launched: an investment of over half a million pounds and a target of 1,000 milking goats, which the Frosts later pushed up to more than 2,000. A big new shed was built for them at Forde Grange farm with photo-voltaic panels on the roof. The panels were Christopher Roper's idea. Although solar panels would cost nearly £1m to install, the government was offering absurdly generous subsidies for the surplus electricity sold to the national grid. It was a chance too good to miss, Christopher argued, and he was prepared to become a co-investor.

The goats had to be milked three times a day. The answer was a spectacular machine like an outsized merry-go-round. The animals queued up a long ramp leading onto a slowly-rotating carousel of 80 stalls into which they were lured by mangers full of hay or grain. The giant milking machine required only two men to operate it: they clamped the suckers onto the goats' udders, which were automatically released when they'd completed their circuit.

To achieve the optimum size of flock took longer than expected due to deaths, miscarriages and culling in the first years. It was profitable at last, however, and with 4000 animals, including 2,500 milkers, Forde became the second largest goat farm in England selling wholesale to producers of milk for babies, cheese, yoghurt and ice cream.

* * *

The mid-1990s marked a watershed for the prosperity of the estate. Mark Roper's confidence in his own management was apparent from the optimistic tone of his annual entries in the house journal. His comments on powerful institutions – the National Trust, English Heritage, the EEC, the Government – became more lighthearted. He was amused rather than affronted by people's behaviour. His satisfaction was only enhanced in 1996 when Alice, their eldest daughter and heir, announced her engagement to Julian Kennard. Recording it in the diary, Mark added in almost the same breath: 'Clouds of butterflies from Africa on the strawberry fields. Also humming bird hawk moths.'

Alice and Julian had met while students at Cirencester agricultural college. Their union contained uncanny echoes of the past: Julian had been brought up on his family's *estancia* in Argentina, with a system of land management which the historian David Knowles had cited as the nearest modern equivalent to the early Cistercian regime. By coincidence, too, Alice bore the same name as the daughter of the abbey's founder, Adelicia. The couple married the following April, under a deluge of rain.

The millennium approached and with it Mark's 65th birthday, the official age of retirement. His father Geoffrey had been 60 years old when he vacated the chair, dying in 1982 at the good age of 81 with a splendid funeral service in the Chapel. His mother Diana had followed six years later. In 1992 there was a family tragedy when his younger brother John, a doctor, and wife Mahony died together in New Zealand.

But Mark had no thought of retirement. His schemes were paying off. Although the millennium year confirmed his fears that farming in Britain was doomed, the abbey entreprises seemed to be all in good health. Within two years he was able to declare: 'It is now as good as I think we can make it. All we now need to do is be better known and be renowned for quality.' There was no reason, he added, why his infant grandson Ben should not be running the place job 40 or 50 years hence – '*deo volente,* weather permitting'.

Financial pressures lifted, he and Lisa began to take long-distance holidays, to New Zealand, round South America, to the Pantanal region of Brazil. At home they hosted the *Antiques Road Show* for television. Lisa bought a bronze horse from Marcia Astor, their sculptor friend, to put in the rock garden.[6]

To celebrate the approaching 100th anniversary of the Ropers' occupation of Forde Abbey, a spectacular fountain was commissioned for the Mermaid Pond.

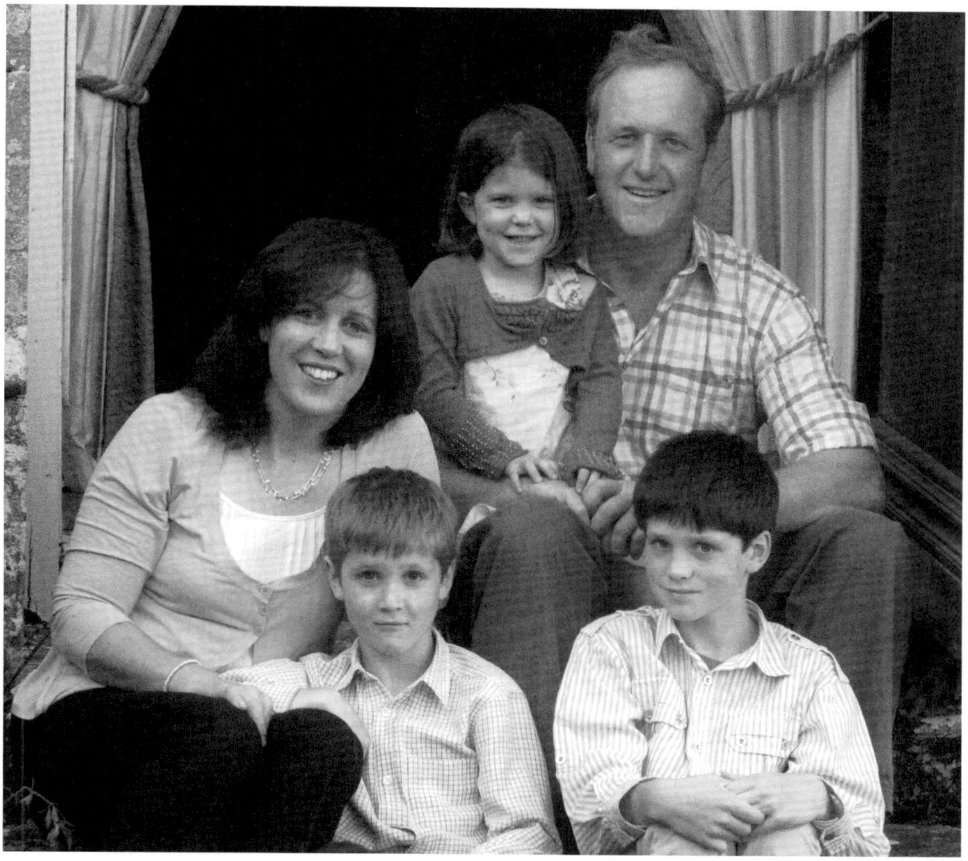

Alice and Julian Kennard, with their children Marcia, Sam and Ben.

Powered by the old pump installed in 1964 for irrigation, it could send a jet 160ft into the air which made it – so Mark claimed – the highest in Britain. The centenary year, 2006, which was also Mark's 70th birthday, was marked by lunch in a big marquee on the front lawn for family, friends and the larger Forde community. In between, Mark amused himself by playing the stock market, buying watercolours, keeping an eye on the garden and going to the races – a diversion which became even more diverting, and even occasionally profitable, after Christopher bought his racehorses.

* * *

Although it had certainly been discussed in the family for a while, the first admission that Mark might be ready to hand over appears in his diary for

2007. Whereas his own succession fifty years before had been sudden – if not unexpected – his hand-over to Alice and Julian was to be gradual. As head of the family business, Mark found it difficult to let go of the reins. Deeply attached to the house and garden that he and Lisa had recreated, he was fearful of what the future might bring. Like many fathers he found it hard to believe the next generation could cope. Fortunately, his daughter and son-in-law recognized this, and were prepared to let Mark dictate the speed of change.

The hardest part for him was moving out. On all sides he had been urged to consider that unless Alice and Julian's children were allowed to grow up in the abbey itself they would not think of it as home and would feel no commitment to it. They might none of them wish to take it on. Since Mark's overriding aim was to keep Forde in the family, he agreed.

Lisa wanted to move to the Home Farm, which Mark felt was too far from the centre of things. He suggested the gardener's cottage, but she thought it too exposed to inquisitive visitors. Eventually he relented and in May 2009 the Ropers moved out of the abbey and the Kennards moved in. The large Home Farm house proved more adaptable and comfortable than Mark had feared.

Lisa found herself for the first time in a house which didn't have the public walking round. She missed the abbey, but was pleased to have her herd of Devons living next door. Once settled in, Mark was ready to make one more important step. Although he began to delegate to Alice and Julian, he continued to keep a close eye on the finances, especially when it came to the goat farm and the Craigengillan forest in distant Dumfriesshire – the investment which he liked to call his pension fund.

Some of the forest was felled in 2011, for a decent profit. But it was clear that replanting without tax relief was a non-starter. So that autumn Mark put Craigengillan up for sale. He heard that a neighbouring landowner had offered £1.7m, but might be ready to go to £2m. A silence ensued. After Christmas he contacted agents, who put it on the market with a guide price of £2.1m. It seemed that City advisers had begun stocking their rich clients' portfolios with trees in order to avoid estate duty, for the following April the forest was sold – and for a million pounds over the guide price.

Mark was jubilant. 'Clear blue financial water appeared before me for the first time in my life,' he said. He and Lisa were able to help with the granchildren's education and to set up a trust for them. He was able to buy 120 acres of land at Chaffeigh Farm on the eastern side of the estate, badly needed to feed the growing flock of goats.

It was a fitting finale to a long and successful stewardship. 'We wouldn't

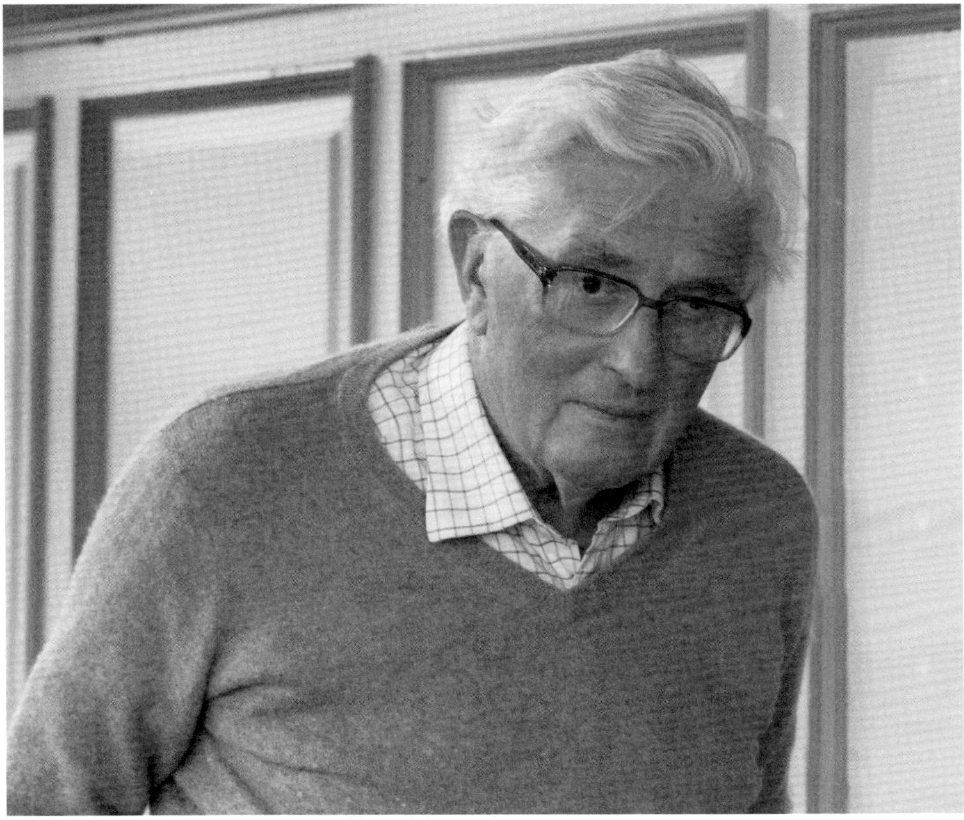

Mark Roper in his eighties: 'a long and successful stewardship'.

be here now if Mark hadn't been clever at making money,' was Christopher's verdict. For his part, Mark claimed that he and Lisa had been lucky. The only courage required was 'the sort of courage you need to jump in the river when the fire's behind you.' But there was satisfaction, too, that the estate had been made more or less fireproof.

Mark and Lisa had shown what could be done, and their daughter and son-in-law know they have a hard act to follow. As Julian said: 'He has set the bar very, very high.' But Alice and Julian are developing their own strategy for the abbey – a story which will no doubt be told in its turn – and they are enjoying it. Julian recalls a day when he and Mark were driving together in the Land Rover. 'He turned to me and said: 'Its enormous fun, you know.' And he's right.'

Conclusion

IN SOME RESPECTS Forde Abbey has come full circle. The estate is back to the sort of size the monks knew nearly 900 years ago. The land is again under central management as it was at the start of Cistercian rule. Lay brothers and farmhands have given way to heavy tractors, monastic sheep replaced by secular goats as the main agricultural enterprise. But the abbey is again a place of refuge as it was in the Middle Ages, even if it its hospitality now takes the form of public recreation and entertainment rather than public welfare: the hungry no longer queue for alms at the western gate, they buy lunch or tea in the Undercroft restaurant.

Since the Dissolution, Forde has been a trophy asset for political climbers, a pleasure ground for the rich, a summer retreat for philosophers. Today it is more like a business. Its occupants are, as the monks were, entirely committed to looking after the place, living not merely on the estate, but from it. Over time they have gradually distanced themselves from national affairs, first from the Court, then from Parliament.

Self-sufficiency is once more the rule. For its first 400 years, Forde Abbey depended on its estates and its benefactors. For most of the 500 years it has been in private ownership it has lived off the wealth of outsiders – Edmund Prideaux in the seventeenth century, Jane Evans in the nineteenth. In both cases their successors eventually ran out of money. The failure of the Prideaux-Gwyn dynasty resulted in the Great Sale of 1846; the financial struggles of the Evans-Roper dynasty were overcome, as we have seen, by the business acumen of the last heir, with the help of government grants.

Women have played a large part in the abbey's history, from Adelicia de Brionne, the founder, to Alice Kennard, the latest to inherit. Amy Prideaux saved her husband from the gallows; her daughter Margaret brought the house into the Gwyn family. Jane Evans saved the house and her great-niece Elsie inherited, bringing it to the Ropers.

A recurrent motif of the Forde story has been an odd combination of austerity with affluence. The early rigour of the Cistercians gave way to a more worldly outlook, with the last abbot Thomas Chard inadvertently saving the house – though he lost his monastery – by means of his magnificent additions. The Prideaux were Puritans, but lived in the grandest style. Jeremy Bentham preached equality, but rented a mansion for his workplace. Geoffrey Roper lived in that mansion with almost Cistercian frugality.

Forde Abbey is today enjoying a renaissance, perhaps one of the best periods of its long history. Nothing can be said for certain, of course, but there is every reason to hope it will survive another 900 years.

Endnotes and Sources

CHAPTER ONE

1. Forde is included in *The Best Buildings of England*, Viking 1986, a selection by Bridget Cherry and John Newman from Pevsner.
2. A boundary change in 1842 put it in Dorset.
3. The monks would soon have put up temporary shelters on the main site.
4. Knowles, *Monastic Orders,* p.216.
5. *ibid.,* p.220.
6. Gerald of Wales, *Journey*, p.205.
7. Fuller, *Worthies of England,* vol.2, in 'Devonshire writers'.
8. The Mss. that survive include: *De Sacramento Altaris*; *De dilectione Dei; De diligendo Deo; De promissis Dei; De resurrectione Domini; Quomodo Christus in nos spiritualem requiem quaerit; De utilitate sermonis Dei vivi; Sermones varii;* and *Epistolae.*
9. The stanza is:

   Ecce doces quia sobrietas virtus specialis
   Dum puerum modici fonte liquoris alis
   Cur igitur monachis Montani venter adheres?
   Quid monachis sacies, crapula, forma teres?

10. St. Bernard had died in 1153. Gilbert of Hoyland had tackled the job unsuccessfully before his own death in 1172 and Geoffrey of Auxerre had done a complete rewrite which was 'scrappy and derivative', says Holdsworth.
11. Holdsworth *et al. Gathering*, p.37.
12. Rotha Mary Clay, *Hermits and Anchorites of England*, 'Antiquary's Books' series, 1914.
13. Fr. Jerome Porter, *The Flower of the Lives of the most renowned Saincts of the three Kingdoms of England, Scotland and Ireland*, vol 1, Douai 1632.
14. John of Forde, *De Vita Beati Wulfrici Anachoretae Haselbergiae* ch 30; author's translation.
15. *ibid.* ch 14.
16. Balliol College MS 24, quoted in Holdsworth, 'John of Ford and English Cistercian Writing, 1167-1214'.
17. Knowles, *Monastic Orders.*
18. The cartulary, the abbey's most important mediaeval document, was bought back by the Roper family in 1911. It was edited and translated by Steven Hobbs for the Somerset

Record Society in 1998.
19. Its first article read: 'That the church of England [then of course the Roman Catholic Church] shall be free, and enjoy her rights intire, and her liberties inviolable.'
20 The story is told by the anonymous 15th-century Forde chronicler in Dugdale's *Monasticon Anglicanum,* pp.787-8.
21. *ibid.*
22. Knowles, *Religious Orders* vol.1.
23. Interview with Professor James Clark, University of Exeter.
24. Gasquet, *The Great Pestilence*, p.149.
25. Knowles, *Religious Orders* vol.2.
26. Adam Hamilton, *Buckfast Abbey*,1884 (Kessinger Publishing reprint).
27. Knowles, *Religious Orders,* vol.1, pp.281-3.
28. *ibid.* vol.2.
29. *ibid.*
30. 'Sepultus vero sine magna pompa in suo coenobio; quod nunc sumptibus plane non credendis abbas magnificentissime restaurat.' Leland, *De Scriptoribus Brittanicis*, cap. CCVI.
31. Gordon M. Hills, 'Ford Abbey' in *Collectanea Archaeologica* of the British Architectural Association, vol.2, part ii, 1864.

CHAPTER TWO

1. Knowles, *Religious Orders,* vol.3.
2. Pulman, pp.413-4.
3. Revenues consisted of 'temporal' income from rents and leases of land and buildings, and 'spiritual' income from parish churches and tithes paid by parishioners.
4. Allen, p 48.
5. It was probably after July 1537, because at that time the king himself was refounding an abbey at Chertsey. Knowles, *Religious Orders*, vol 3.
6. *ibid.* pp.270 ff.
7. Landowners had been avoiding royal fees on their land ('feudal incidents') by putting their estates in the name of another person for the benefit of a third party, usually themselves. The practice was outlawed by the Statute of Uses, 1536.
8. *The Lisle Letters,* vol. 5, no. 1217, dated 8th September 1538 from the abridged version, ed. Muriel St. Clare Byrne (Penguin Books, 1985).
9. From a photocopy and translation of the document no.34823 in the Devon Record Office.
10. It is not clear whether this list accounts for all the monks of Forde. The number 13 allowed by the court is suspiciously close to the number traditionally required to found a Cistercian monastery.
11. Letters and Papers xiv i, 468-9 quoted in Youings, *Dissolution,* 12.
12. Knowles, vol 3, p.387 n.

13. The stone from Waverley was used by its new owner, Sir William Fitzherbert, to build a mansion at nearby Loseley for Sir William More, an MP in the time of Elizabeth I.
14. Youings, *Devon Monastic Lands*, vol. 1, Devon & Cornwall Record Society, 1955.
15. William Blackstone, the eighteenth century legal commentator, recognized the charitable work of the monasteries but blamed them for 'encouraging the poor in habits of indolence and beggary'. Quote taken from M. Tugendhat, *Liberty Intact,* p.154 (OUP, 2017).
16. Hamilton, *Buckfast Abbey,* 1884. See also Duffy, *Voices of Morebath.*
17. Colin G Winn, *The Pouletts of Hinton St. George* (1976, 1995).
18. The buyer was Walter Congreve, great uncle of Mark Roper and great-grandfather of the present writer whose mother grew up at Chartley. She claimed to have seen Mary's ghost there, and often swam in the moat.
19. Most of what follows is from the only account of the Rosewell family I have found: Frances B. James,'Sir Henry Rosewell: A Devon Worthy' in *Transactions of the Devonshire Association*, 1888, pp.113-122. A reprint is in the Forde archive.

CHAPTER THREE

Proceeding of House of Commons 1680-95 pp 309-355 Convention Parl (William) 1/5/1689. *British History Online.* For the text of Prideaux's petition see M. Allen *History of Ford Abbey,* pp. 60ff.
to check] Keeler, Long Parl. 315-16; CJ, x. 116; CSP Dom. 1682, p. 26; July-Sept. 1683, pp. 216-18, 369; 1683-4, p. 362; D. R. Lacey, Dissent and Parl. Pols. 433-4.

1. 'Prideaux, Edmond' by John Andrew Hamilton, DNB 1885-1900 vol 46.
2. I am grateful to John Allen for this information.
3. *Book of the Axe,* p. 427.
4. R. Tyler, *Forde Abbey guidebook*, 1987.
5. The book is now in the Dorset History Centre, Dorchester.
6. Letter from Capt. Gregory Alford of Lyme Regis to a cousin at HM chapel, Whitehall, dated 14th January 1682.
7. By this marriage, incidentally, the Prideaux family and its Gwyn descendants became distantly related to the family of Thomas Chard. The Fraunceis and Chard families were both descended from the Ivedon or de Ivedons.]
8. 'The History of England' in *Macaulay: Prose and Poetry,* selected by G.M.Young (Rupert Hart-Davis, 1952).
9. Wigfield, *The Monmouth Rebellion,* p.118. Hs very readable account notes that among those deported was Azariah Pinney of Bettiscombe whose money enabled him to buy the status of a "free emigrant". He made his fortune in the West Indies.
10. Macaulay 'History'.
11. *Ibid.*
12. *Calendar of State Papers*: James II vol 1. Dec 1685.

13. Francis Gwyn's father was Edward Gwyn, whose sister Catherine married John Frаunceis of Combe Florey, father of Amy Fraunceis, Margaret Prideaux's mother. The Gwyns claimed descent from the Herberts, Earls of Pembroke.
14. Boyle was an Irish peer, Lord Carleton, nephew of Lord Rochester.
15. Quoted by Basil Duke Henning in 'Francis Gwyn', *History of Parliament Online.*
16. Quotations from Francis Gwyn's journal, *The Fortnightly Review Sept.*1886.
17. Letter from Peter Wentworth to his brother, *Wentworth Papers* 1705-1739, ed James J. Cartwright, p.163 (London, 1883).
18. Allen, p.67.
19. *Raphael's Cartoons*, by J. Shearman (London, 1972, quoted in *The Raphael Tapestry Cartoons* by Sharon Fermor, Scala/Victoria & Albert Museum 1996.
20. W.G.Thomson, *A History of Tapestry* (London, 1906), quoted in a letter from Sotheby's to Mr. and Mrs. Roper, 27th January, 2009.
21. Letters of 29th June 1709 and 4th September 1712, from the private collection at Levens Hall.
22. Allen, pp. 72-3.

CHAPTER FOUR

1. Prisons of the same sort were later built in the U.S. and Cuba.
2. Both extracts from a copy of a letter to Maria Edgeworth, 6th October 1817, at Forde Abbey.
3. Pulman, p. 423.
4. Autobiography of Sir Samuel Romilly, n. p. 474, quoting his letter to Pierre-Etienne-Louis Dumont, 2nd Oct 1817.
5. This and the previous extract are from the original letter from J.S. Mill dated September 13th, 1814, given to W.H.Evans, owner of Forde Abbey, by J.S. Mill's younger sister Clara Digweed in 1878.
6. *Correspondence of Jeremy Bentham*: Bentham to his brother Samuel.
7. Francis Place, letter of August 17, 1817.
8. Letter from Mrs.Clara Digweed (*née* Mill) to W.H.Evans, dated London 2 Sept 1878, at Forde Abbey.
9. This and the earlier quotation are from Mill's *Autobiography.* See also Jose Harris's discussion in the DNB.
10. Anne Romilly to Maria Edgeworth.
11. Quotations from *The Autobiography of Francis Place*, ed.Mary Thale (Cambridge University Press, 1972).
12. The organ, with its case of Cuban mahogany inlaid with parquetry, was made by Samuel Gillespie in the late eighteenth century and is a rare (perhaps unique) surviving example. It was removed to the chapel in 1909 and overhauled in 2006. (Information from sleeve notes of a recorded recital by John Mingay in 2007).
13. *Correspondence:* letter 2299 to an unknown correspondent, 13th Dec. 1814.

14. *Ibid.* Letter 2291 from James Mill, 19th Sept.1814.
15. *Edinburgh Review*, vol iv, p.552 ER.
16. Allen p.74.
17. I am grateful to John Allen for this information.
18. One newspaper suggested that 'a Catholic institution' was interested in buying the abbey. This may have been one of the exiled Benedictine communities which, thanks to the various Catholic Emancipation Acts, wanted to return to England. From the early 1800s several did so. Forde Abbey might have become, like Milton Abbey, a public school – at a cost to the fabric and grounds which can only be imagined.

CHAPTER FIVE

1. The former manor house, later an Elizabethan palace, rebuilt in 1802 by Henry Holland for the second Earl Spencer and sold by the family in 1846. In 1860 its land was turned over to housing; after a succession of owners the house was demolished around 1949. The manorial title was sold by the ninth Earl Spencer, brother of Princess Diana, Princess of Wales, to a Brazilian buyer for £171,000. (Wikipedia).
2. Letters from John Boyd 23rd October and 24th December 1832, in *The Boyd Family Story*, pp. 52-3, by Eleanor Sprott Boyd Boushey (privately printed).
3. Catalogue of Evans papers at Hereford County Record Office, ref. E42/.
4. *The Bridport News*, Friday 7th June, 1895. The story is that Cupid gave a rose to Harpocrates, the god of silence, as a bribe to stop him divulging the love affairs of his mother Venus.
5. Fiona MacCarthy, *William Morris, A Life for Our Time* (Faber and Faber, 1994).
6. Richard Gill, *Happy Rural Seat*, p. 37 (Yale University Press, 1972).
7. From orginal letters in the Forde Abbey archive.
8. *The Boyd Family Story*, p.59.
9. Freeman's letter dated 23rd October 1900 is in the Forde archive.
10. Terence Keary, *Generations Apart*, Wise Owl Publications.
11. *The Cartulary of Forde Abbey*, introduction by Steven Hobbs. 'Thomas Phillipps' in Wikipedia.
12. Elsie Roper to Archibald Boyd, 22nd February, 1920.
13. Not, apparently, a racist term: the OED gives one meaning of *nigger* as 'a strong spiked timber by which logs are canted in a saw-mill', which would ruin a fence if it got mixed up with the posts.
14. Keary, *Generations Apart.*
15. *The Congreves, Father and Son,* pp. 268-80, by Lt.-Col. L.H.Thornton and Pamela Fraser (John Murray, 1930). Walter's wife Celia, who became a nurse with the Red Cross, also won medals for bravery under fire, including the Croix de Guerre.
16. J.W.Walker, letter to his mother-in-law, 21st June, 1942.

CHAPTER SIX

1. Mark Roper, autobiographical notes, 2014.
2. Samuel Clemens ('Mark Twain') speaking to the New England Society, *The New York Times*, 23rd December, 1876.
3. 'Musick has Charms to soothe a savage Breast', the first line of *The Mourning Bride* by William Congreve (1670-1729).
4. John Simpson had with him a harpsichord that needed attention; he consulted Robin Bagot, who built them.
5. Erik Smith's funeral was held in the Chapel, with Neville Marriner making the address. His ashes were buried on the slope at the end of the Long Pond under the beech and lime trees. Neville lived on, still conducting and playing tennis, right up to his death in 2016 at the age of 92.
6. A smaller version of her 18ft. sculpture which dominates a roundabout on the main road by the Rowley Mile course, Newmarket.

Bibliography

WORKS OF REFERENCE

Oxford Dictionary of National Biography.

The History Today Companion to British History, ed. Gardiner & Wenborn (Collins & Brown, 1995).

Hutchins, John, *The History and Antiquities of the County of Dorset*, vol. 4.

Calendar of State Papers, *British History Online*: www.british-history.ac.uk.

Wikipedia.

History of Parliament online: www.historyofparliamentonline.org/research.

London Library online.

PRINCIPAL WORKS CONSULTED

(Other sources are given in the notes)

Allen, M, *A History of Forde Abbey, Dorsetshire* (Hamilton Adams, London, 1846).

Clery, Peter, *The Monastic Estate* (Phillimore Book Publishing, 2015).

Clifton, Robin, *The Last Popular Rebellion: the western rising of* 1685 (MauriceTemple Smith, 1984).

Cobbett, William, *A History of the Protestant 'Reformation' in England and Ireland* (London, 1824).

Conway, Stephen, ed. *The Correspondence of Jeremy Bentham*, vols. 8 and 9 (Clarendon Press, Oxford, 1989).

Dugdale, Sir William, *Monasticon Anglicanum* (Latin edition) pp.785-92 (London, 1655).

Duffy, Eamon, *Voices of Morebath: Reformation and rebellion in an English village* (Yale University Press, 2001).

Fuller, Catherine, 'Bentham at Ford Abbey', *Journal of Bentham Studies*, vol.7, No. 1 (University College London, 2004).

Fuller, Thomas, *Worthies of England* (London, 1662).

Gasquet, Francis Aidan, *The Great Pestilence, AD* 1348-49 (London, 1893).
Henry VIII and the English monasteries (London, 1899).

Gerald of Wales, *Journey.*

Hobbs, Steven, ed., *The Cartulary of Forde Abbey*, Somerset Record Society vol. 85, 1998

Holdsworth, Christopher, 'The Cistercians in Devon', *Studies in Mediaeval History presented to R. Allen Brown,* 1989;

'John of Ford and English Cistercian Writing 1167-1214', *Transactions of the Royal Historical Society,* 5th series, 11 (1961).

'Baldwin of Forde, Cistercian and Archbishop of Canterbury', Friends of Lambeth Palace Library annual report.

'John of Forde', *A Gathering of Friends: The learning and spirituality of John of Forde,* ed.with Hilary Costello, Cistercian Studies Series No. 161, (Cistercian Publications, 1996).

John of Forde, *Life of Wulfric of Haselbury*, ed. Dom Maurice Bell, Somerset Record Society 47, 1983.

Knowles David, *Monastic Orders in England,* 943-1216 (Cambridge University Press, 1963); *Religious Orders in England,* vol. 1, 1216-1340, (CUP, 1948); vol 2 *The End of the Middle Ages,* (CUP, 1955); vol 3, *The Tudor Age* (CUP, 1959).

Leland, John, *Commentarii de Scriptoribus Britannicis,* ed. A. Hall (Oxford,1709).

Matarasso, Pauline, ed., *The Cistercian World: monastic writings of the twelfth century* (Penguin, 1993)

Oliver, G., *Monasticon Diocesis Exoniensis* (Hannaford, Longman, 1846).

Prince, J., *The History of the Worthies of England,* (London, 1662) .

Pulman, George P.R., *The Book of the Axe,* 1875 (Kingsmead Reprints, Bath, 1975).

Pring, James Hurley, *Memoir of Thomas Chard D.D,* (T. Richards, London and Taunton,1864).

Roper, John, *An Illustrated Survey of Forde Abbey* (1968).

Wallas, Graham, *The Life of Francis Place* 1771-1854 (Longmans, London,1898).

Wigfield, W. MacDonald, *The Monmouth Rebellion, a social history* (Moonraker Press, Bradford-on-Avon, 1980).

Youings, Joyce, *The Dissolution of the Monasteries* (Allen and Unwin, 1971).

The Illustrations

I am grateful to the following for allowing the inclusion of illustrations in their possession or for which they hold the copyright.

Colour plates: De Brionne family tree, The Powderham Estate and Exeter Digital Humanities; the Prideaux portraits ascribed to Kneller, courtesy of the Prideaux-Brune family, Padstow Place; Jeremy Bentham by Henry William Pickersgill, c. 1829, © UCL Art Museum, University College London; the photographs of the stone friezes, Tony Parker of Picturebox Productions.

Black and white: Dean and Chapter of Canterbury Cathedral page 21; Levens Hall, Kendal, Cumbria, p.139; Robin Mills for Marshwood Vale Magazine, p. 147; Porcellini Publications, p.154; Lucy Sclater, p. 152; Richard Tyler, p.67. Tyne & Wear Archives and Museums, p.122; Jeremy Whitaker, p.97; Sandra Wood, p.117

Other illustrations are from the Forde Abbey Archive, the Dovecote Press, or were photographs taken by Maisie Hill or the author.

Index